John the Baptist

INTERFACES

Series Editor: Barbara Green, O.P.

John the Baptist

Prophet of Purity for a New Age

Catherine M. Murphy

A Michael Glazier Book

LITURGICAL PRESS

Collegeville, Minnesota

www.litpress.org

A Michael Glazier Book published by the Liturgical Press

Cover design by Ann Blattner. Watercolor by Ethel Boyle.

1	2	3	4	5	6	7	8	9

Library of Congress Cataloging-in-Publication Data

Murphy, Catherine M., 1961–
　　John the Baptist : prophet of purity for a new age / Catherine M. Murphy.
　　　　p. cm. — (Interfaces)
　　"A Michael Glazier book."
　　Includes bibliographical references and index.
　　ISBN 0-8146-5933-0 (alk. paper)
　　　1. John, the Baptist, Saint. I. Title. II. Interfaces (Collegeville, Minn.)
　　BS2456.M87 2003
　　232.9'4—dc21　　　　　　　　　　　　　　　　　　　　　　　　2003044615

Dedicated to my mother,
Gertrude Blake Murphy,
in her seventieth year

CONTENTS

LIST OF FIGURES

PREFACE

The book you hold in your hand is one of six volumes in a new set. This series, called INTERFACES, is a curriculum and scholarly adventure, a creative opportunity in teaching and learning, presented at this moment in the long story of how the Bible has been studied, interpreted, and appropriated.

The INTERFACES project was prompted by a number of experiences that you, perhaps, share. When I first taught undergraduates the college had just received a substantial grant from the National Endowment for the Humanities, and one of the recurring courses designed within the grant was called Great Figures in Pursuit of Excellence. Three courses would be taught, each centering on a figure from some academic discipline or other, with a common seminar section to provide occasion for some integration. Some triads were more successful than others, as you might imagine. But the opportunity to concentrate on a single individual—whether historical or literary—to team teach, to make links to another pair of figures, and to learn new things about other disciplines was stimulating and fun for all involved. A second experience that gave rise to the present series came at the same time, connected also with undergraduates. It was my frequent experience to have Roman Catholic students feel quite put out about taking "more" biblical studies since, as they confidently affirmed, they had already been there many times and done it all. That was, of course, not true; as we well know, there is always more to learn. And often those who felt most informed were the least likely to take on new information when offered it.

A stimulus as primary as my experience with students was the familiarity of listening to friends and colleagues at professional meetings talking about the research that excites us most. I often wondered: Do her undergraduate students know about this? Or how does he bring these ideas—clearly so energizing to him—into the college classroom? Perhaps some of us have felt bored with classes that seem wholly unrelated to research, that rehash the same familiar material repeatedly. Hence the idea for this series of books to bring to the fore and combine some of our research interest with our teaching and learning. Accordingly, this series is not so much about creating texts *for* student audiences, but rather about *sharing* our scholarly passions with them. Because these volumes are intended each as a piece of original scholarship they are geared to be stimulating to both students and established scholars, perhaps resulting in some fruitful collaborative learning adventures.

The series also developed from a widely-shared sense that all academic fields are expanding and exploding, and that to contemplate "covering" even a testament (let alone the whole Bible or Western monotheistic religions) needs to be abandoned in favor of something with greater depth. At the same time the links between our fields are becoming increasingly obvious as well, and we glimpse exciting possibilities for ways of working that will draw together academic realms that once seemed separate. Finally, the spark of enthusiasm that almost always ignites when I mention to colleagues and students the idea of single figures in combination—interfacing—encourages me that this is an idea worth trying.

And so with the leadership and help of Liturgical Press Academic Editor Linda Maloney, as well as with the encouragement and support of Managing Editor Mark Twomey, the series has begun to take shape.

Each volume in the INTERFACES series focuses clearly on a biblical character (or perhaps a pair of them). The characters are in some cases powerful (King Saul, Pontius Pilate) and familiar (John the Baptist, Joseph) though in other cases they will strike many as minor and little-known (the Cannibal Mothers, Herodias). In any case, each of them has been chosen to open up a set of worlds for consideration. The named (or unnamed) character interfaces with his or her historical-cultural world and its many issues, with other characters from biblical literature; each character has drawn forth the creativity of the author, who has taken on the challenge of engaging many readers. The books are specifically designed for college students (though we think suitable for some graduate work as well), planned to provide young adults with relevant information and at a level of critical sophistication that matches the rest of the undergraduate curriculum. In fact, the expectation is that what students are learning in other classes on historiography, literary theory, and cultural anthropology will find an echo in these books, each of which is explicit about at least two relevant methodologies. It is surely the case that biblical studies is in a methodology-conscious moment, and the INTERFACES series embraces it enthusiastically. Our hope is for students (and teachers) to continue to see the relationship between their best questions and their most valuable insights, between how they approach texts and what they find there. The volumes go well beyond familiar paraphrase of narratives to ask questions that are relevant in our era. At the same time the series authors have each dealt with the notion of the Bible as Scripture in a way that is comfortable for them. None of the books is preachy or hortatory, and yet the self-implicating aspects of working with the revelatory text are handled frankly. The assumption is, again, that college can be a good time for students to rethink their beliefs and assumptions, and they need to do so in good company.

The INTERFACES volumes are not substitutes for the Bible. In every case they are to be read with the text. Quoting has been kept to a minimum for that very reason. The volumes, when used in a classroom setting, are accompanied by a companion volume, *From Earth's Creation to John's Revelation: The INTERFACES Biblical Storyline Companion,* which provides a quick, straightforward overview of the whole storyline into which the characters under special study fit. Web links will also be available through the Liturgical Press website: www.litpress.org.

The series challenge—for publisher, writers, teachers, and students— is to combine the volumes creatively, to "interface" them well so that the vast potential of the biblical text continues to unfold for all of us. The first six volumes: in Old Testament/Hebrew Bible featuring Saul, the Cannibal Mothers, and Joseph; in New Testament focusing on John the Baptist, Herodias, and Pontius Pilate, offer a foretaste of other volumes currently in preparation. It has been a pleasure, and a richly informative privilege, to work with the authors of these first volumes as well as the series consultants: Carleen Mandolfo for Hebrew Bible and Catherine Murphy for New Testament. It is the hope of all of us that you will find the series useful and stimulating for your own teaching and learning.

Barbara Green, O.P.
INTERFACES Series Editor
June 29, 2002
Berkeley, California

ACKNOWLEDGMENTS

It is a great pleasure to be able to thank the people whose influence is manifest in these pages. Barbara Green, O.P., introduced me to the field of Biblical Studies in the mid-1980s at Dominican University in San Rafael. Her creative teaching and clear love for her field were infectious, and my budding interest in advanced study blossomed under her tutelage. When Barbara proposed the INTERFACES project over a year ago and invited me to join her, I could not pass up the opportunity to work closely with her again. Her style of teaching and sense of humor have long been models for me in this serious discipline, and I hope I have reflected her graceful pedagogy on these pages. I have also greatly enjoyed the opportunity to collaborate with Carleen Mandolfo of Colby College on the companion INTERFACES volume and on advance presentations.

My mentors at the University of Notre Dame will recognize their influence throughout this book. The first three chapters are particularly influenced by Harold Attridge (now at Yale Divinity School), Gregory Sterling, and John Donahue (now at St. Mary's Seminary and University in Baltimore). I never had the privilege of studying formally with John Meier but have learned much from him through his magisterial work on the Historical Jesus and through presentations at the Catholic Biblical Association meetings. Chapters 1 and 3 in particular rely heavily on his research. Jerome Neyrey introduced me to the social-scientific study of biblical texts, a study made all the more engaging by his boundless energy and personal graciousness. I hope this first attempt to cut my teeth on the method does justice to his guidance. I would also like to acknowledge Blake Leyerle and Mary Rose D'Angelo, whose constant and compelling questions about social context and reconstruction have stimulated my interest in these issues. Finally, Eugene Ulrich and James VanderKam together provided an apprenticeship in Dead Sea Scrolls studies that was rigorous, collegial, and utterly enjoyable.

I would also like to thank some of my colleagues at Santa Clara University: Joe Grassi for his bibliographic suggestions, Diane Jonte-Pace and David Pinault for their generous counsel and wonderful example as teaching scholars (some of my metaphors are really theirs!), and the undergraduate and graduate students who continue to teach me how to teach.

The editorial staff at the Liturgical Press has been wonderful to work with. My thanks to Managing Editor Mark Twomey, Academic Editor Linda Maloney, Production Manager Colleen Stiller, Polly Chappell, and the Liturgical Press staff for shepherding this volume so competently into production.

Finally, I am grateful, always, to Kate McNichols for her wisdom, her patience, and her sense of humor.

All of the translations from Josephus and the New Testament are my own unless otherwise indicated.

ABBREVIATIONS

AB   Anchor Bible (Commentary series)

ABRL   Anchor Bible Reference Library

ANF   Ante-Nicene Fathers

Ap. Jas.   *Apocryphon of James*

BETL   Bibliotheca ephemeridum theologicarum lovaniensium

BHT   Beiträge zur historischen Theologie

FF   Foundations and Facets

GBSNTS   Guides to Biblical Scholarship, New Testament Series

Gos. Eb.   *Gospel of the Ebionites*

Gos. Heb.   *Gospel of the Hebrews*

Gos. Naz.   *Gospel of the Nazarenes*

Gos. Thom.   *Gospel of Thomas*

JSNTSup   Journal for the Study of the New Testament Supplement

LTT   Library of Theological Translations

NPNF   Nicene and Post-Nicene Fathers

NTL   New Testament Library

NTTS   New Testament Tools and Studies

OBT   Overtures to Biblical Theology

OTM   Oxford Theological Monographs

PHSR   Prentice-Hall Studies in Religion

SAC   Studies in Antiquity and Christianity

SBLDS   Society of Biblical Literature Dissertation Series

SBLMS   Society of Biblical Literature Manuscript Series

SDSSRL   Studies in the Dead Sea Scrolls and Related Literature

SNTSMS   Society for New Testament Studies Monograph Series
SNTSU   Studien zum Neuen Testament und seiner Umwelt
STDJ   Studies on the Texts of the Desert of Judah
UCL   Universitas Catholica Lovaniensis
ZSNT   Zacchaeus Studies: New Testament

CHAPTER ONE

Will the Real Baptist Please Stand Up?

John the Baptist cuts an imposing figure in the opening pages of the New Testament. Wearing coarse camel's hair and leather, eating locusts and wild honey, shouting at the top of his lungs in a wilderness place to the penitents and the curious, John leaps out of the Gospel pages as the frightening first figure of a new age. He rants of the coming judgment when the unjust will be destroyed, he demands conversion, he washes those who've begun to change their lives, and he is ultimately beheaded by a ruler who would not repent. And some of the Gospels add to this picture that John himself baptized Jesus. John the Baptist inaugurates the good news of God's kingdom like a champagne bottle shattered against the hull of a new ship.

That much about John the Baptist may already be familiar to you if you've read the Gospels or attended church. John is a difficult character to forget. And like many of the characters in the Bible, he may seem so familiar to you that you find yourself wondering, on the first pages of this book, what new insights could possibly make these two hundred pages worth reading. Others of you who are less familiar with the Gospels may be wondering how a character like John, who after all is dead throughout most of the Gospel story, is worth reading about at all.

Texts keep people alive, or at least they shape the memory of people's characters for a new generation. This is true of any text that maintains an ongoing audience, such as the Scriptures chosen as canonical in the Christian tradition. These texts, and the characters portrayed in them, continue to function as models and voices as long as new generations consider them authoritative. And that is never entirely determined by an organized religion but by every individual who reads the text. The character remains authoritative for people as long as she or he remains a window, a mirror, and a path.

1

John the Baptist is a window for us onto first-century Judea, the world in which contemporary Judaism and Christianity had their roots. His concerns for purity and righteousness parallel the interests of certain groups within Second Temple Judaism that would, after the destruction of that Temple, become Rabbinic Judaism, the dominant form of Judaism to our day. He was a contemporary of Jesus, was somehow connected with Jesus, and was executed like Jesus by a political authority of that time. His message, his actions, and his death cannot help but shed light on the Judaisms Jesus and other Jews negotiated and on the political constraints under which these people operated. Our access to all this is, of course, not John himself but the texts that describe him, so our windows are really named Josephus and the evangelists Mark and Matthew and Luke and John rather than the Baptist. But the Baptist still provides the glass framed by these authors through which we can glimpse, however darkly, a world that changed the world.

The Baptist is also a mirror for us. As we look into the glass, we see John certainly, but also ourselves looking. We are aware that what we see is limited by what we are looking for, by what questions we raise, by what knowledge we have. And our interests, questions, and knowledge are changing constantly throughout our lives. This means that no matter what character we look at in the text, that character will continually change because *we* continually change. In that sense, what we see is always partly determined by who we are. And that is also why what you learned about the New Testament in grammar school or high school or Sunday school or at any stage of adulthood for that matter is never adequate—you change, and that makes your insights into, and questions about, the characters in Scripture different every time you look.

Finally, the Baptist provides us a way. For communities of faith, of course, this path is confessional: John points from Israel's tradition to the perceived fulfillment of that tradition in Jesus of Nazareth. As such, he voices the recognition to which all Christians are called: "See the Lamb of God who takes away the sin of the world" (John 1:29). But in a book like this, the path John provides is more modest and is open to all, no matter whether they consider themselves Christian or not. In the pages that follow, John will provide a way for us into the study of the Gospels and the first-century world. Through him we will apply certain tools to examine the sources, and we will experiment at placing him in the social context of his times.

All this reference to "the Baptist" may be somewhat misleading, however, for what we really find when we look at the evidence that remains of him is that there are as many Baptists as we have sources. So the immediate tasks in this chapter are to identify those sources and to deal with the essential problem they raise: How can you have a Baptist at all when the sources about him diverge from one another? How does a historian of the text deal with multiple portraits? As we shall see, the path to an answer has three stages of its own. The first stage is to read the evidence, the second is to set up the "game rules" for reconstructing history from the evidence, and the third is to choose which questions one will pose to the evidence that has now been filtered.

Reading the Evidence: The Sources for John the Baptist

There are six important early texts that mention John the Baptist, all arguably dated to the first century C.E. There are many later texts that mention John, including the Koran, but since these are mostly based on the first six, we will focus on the more original materials.[1] The first is a short passage found in an important work by the Jewish historian and apologist Josephus. The other five texts are the Christian Gospels Mark, Matthew, Luke, and John and an account of the history of the early Church by Luke named the Acts of the Apostles. Since Josephus will be unfamiliar to many readers of this book, and since the Gospels will receive detailed attention in Chapters 2 and 3, Josephus and Acts will receive the most attention here.

Josephus, Antiquities of the Jews *18.116-119*

Josephus was born sometime around the year 37/38 C.E., which would place him just after the time of Jesus (Jesus was crucified during the prefecture of Pontius Pilate, 26–36 C.E.).[2] He died around the year 100 C.E.

---

[1] John is referred to in the Qur'an as Yaḥyá and is considered a prophet; see 3:39; 6:85; 19:1-15; 21:89-90. Christian sources that mention John but postdate the canonical texts include the *Gospel of Thomas*, the *Gospel of the Ebionites*, the *Gospel of the Nazoreans*, and the *Protoevangelium of James*. These Gospels are available in *New Testament Apocrypha*, vol. 1, ed. Wilhelm Schneemelcher, trans. R. McL. Wilson (Louisville, Ky.: Westminster/John Knox, 1992; German original, Tübingen: J. C. B. Mohr [Paul Siebeck], 1989), and in a handy paperback published by the Jesus Seminar, *The Complete Gospels: Annotated Scholars Version*, ed. Robert J. Miller (San Francisco: Polebridge/HarperSanFrancisco, 1994). For a discussion of these sources and their historical value, see Walter Wink, *John the Baptist in the Gospel Tradition*, SNTSMS 7 (Cambridge: Cambridge University Press, 1968); Ernst Bammel, "The Baptist in Early Christian Tradition," *New Testament Studies* 18 (1971–1972) 95–128, W. Barnes Tatum, *John the Baptist and Jesus: A Report of the Jesus Seminar* (Sonoma, Calif.: Polebridge, 1994) 84–104; and Robert L. Webb, *John the Baptizer and Prophet: A Socio-Historical Study*, JSNTSup 62 (Sheffield: JSOT Press, 1991).

[2] We are on firm ground dating Pontius Pilate's prefecture to this period thanks to several sources, particularly Josephus (*Antiquities* 18–20); see also the Jewish philosopher

Josephus was Jewish and even served as a general in the Galilee during the First Jewish Revolt against Rome (66–74 C.E.), but apparently, and by his own account, he was not much of a leader or a rebel. He opted against a guerrilla campaign, which was the only effective strategy against Roman legions so capable of siege tactics. Even worse, at least from the Jewish standpoint, when he and his fellow generals were besieged at Jotapata and opted for a suicide pact rather than surrender, Josephus likely manipulated the lots to assure his survival. He then surrendered to the Romans and somehow ended up with land, books, Roman citizenship, and a Roman pension and was eventually adopted into the imperial Flavian family (hence his altered name, *Flavius* Josephus).[3] Josephus attributes this fabulous reversal of fortune to an incident that occurred soon after his capture, when he predicted that the Roman general in Judea, the Flavian Vespasian, and his son Titus would become emperors, predictions that proved accurate. In all likelihood, his elevation was due at least partly to the strategic support and translation services he offered the Romans in their ongoing efforts to vanquish the Jews. As you might imagine, this activity did not endear him to the Jewish people, and in fact there is no mention of Josephus in rabbinic literature. It would be Christians in the Roman Empire who would preserve Josephus's works, in part because of his brief references to John the Baptist, Jesus, and James the brother of Jesus.[4]

Once he had achieved his new station, Josephus used his privileged position to explain the Jews to the Romans in two extensive literary works. The first, a seven-volume opus entitled *The Jewish War*, was composed shortly after the revolt, with the intent of restoring Roman opinion of the Jews in the wake of that disastrous rebellion. The second was a leisurely (some would say long-winded) twenty-volume work, the *Antiquities of the*

Philo of Alexandria (*Embassy to Gaius* 299–305), the Roman Tacitus (*Annals* 2.42.5; 15.44.3), and the Christian Eusebius (*History of the Church* 1.9; 2.7.1, NPNF Second Series 1).

[3] *Life* §411-429; *War* 3 §316-408.

[4] This James is neither James son of Zebedee (a.k.a. "James the greater") nor James son of Alphaeus (perhaps the "James the less" mentioned in Mark 15:40), both mentioned as members of the twelve disciples closest to Jesus. This is rather James "the brother of the Lord," whose name occurs in several New Testament passages (Gal 1:1–2:14; 4:1-31; 1 Cor 9:4-5; 15:3-11; Mark 3:19-35 par. Matt 12:46-50 par. Luke 8:19-21 par. *Gos. Thom.* 99; Mark 6:3-4 par. Matt 13:54-58 par. Luke 4:16-30; John 7:1-13; 19:25-27; Acts 1:14; 12:17; 15:13-21; 21:17-26; Jude 1; James 1:1–5:20; cf. *Ant.* 20 §197-203). For the recently published ossuary or bone box inscribed with the Aramaic words "James, son of Joseph, brother of Jesus," see André Lemaire, "Burial Box of James the Brother of Jesus," *Biblical Archaeology Review* 28 (6 2002) 24–33, 70. For further information on the relatives of Jesus, see Richard Bauckham, *Jude and the Relatives of Jesus in the Early Church* (Edinburgh: T & T Clarke, 1990).

Jews, written well after the Jewish Revolt ca. 93 C.E., which sought to represent the entire history of the Jewish people to the Romans in order to demonstrate the venerability of Jewish tradition and customs. It is toward the end of this latter work, in Book 18, that Josephus mentions John the Baptist.

At this particular moment in the narrative, Josephus has just recounted the defeat of the Jewish ruler Herod Antipas, the tetrarch of Galilee and Perea, by the Nabatean King Aretas IV (37 C.E.).[5] As you read, remember that Josephus is not a Christian; in fact, as you will see, he never mentions Jesus in connection with John.

> §116. But to some of the Jews it seemed that Herod's army had been destroyed by divine vengeance—and quite justly, as a punishment for John who is called the Baptist.
> §117. For Herod killed him, although he was a good man and urged the Jews to practice virtue and justice toward one another and piety toward God, doing so to come together in baptism. In this way, it seemed to him, would the baptism indeed be acceptable—not used to gain pardon for some sins but rather for purification of the body, seeing that the soul had already been cleansed before by justice.
> §118. And when the others gathered together, they were lifted up to the greatest extent in the hearing of the words. Herod became alarmed that John's powerful ability to persuade men might cause some sort of revolt, for they seemed likely to do everything he counseled. So it would be much better to take the lead before he sparked a revolt than to wait until a change occurred and to regret [it] when he was engulfed in the circumstances.
> §119. And so, because of Herod's suspicion, John was sent in chains to Machaerus, the citadel previously mentioned; there he was killed. But to the Jews it seemed that the destruction of the army was in retribution for John, God wishing to inflict evil on Herod.

There are several important elements in Josephus's description of John. First, Josephus confirms that John was known as "the Baptist," no doubt because that was the activity that most characterized his work. This baptism is further described as a secondary act that cleansed the body after the deeper purification of behavior had already occurred. In Josephus's eyes, baptism does not effect a transformation of the will, but rather simply

---

[5] The capital of Nabatea was Petra, in contemporary Jordan, a site with amazing building façades carved in a cliff that you might remember from the movie *Indiana Jones and the Last Crusade*, directed by Steven Spielberg (1989).

marks that prior change on the body; however, this emphasis may reflect Josephus's tendency to adapt Jewish figures to a Hellenistic moral and philosophical framework. The soul, according to Josephus, has not simply been purified by individual moral rectitude, but rather by visible acts of justice, which suggests a social component. Furthermore, the baptism is presented as a kind of sacrifice; notice the concern that the baptism "be acceptable [to God]."

The account tells us several things beyond the nature of John's baptism. It alerts us that John was a persuasive speaker, that he engendered zealous adherence, that Herod felt threatened not only by John's rhetorical skill but also by his political power, and that therefore Herod arrested and executed him. Whether Herod's subsequent military defeat was an act of divine vengeance is, of course, beyond the historian's power to judge; but Josephus's report that many people believed this to be true is invaluable, for it indicates that John continued to exert an influence on people after his death.

The Gospels

The four canonical Christian Gospels provide the bulk of our information about John the Baptist. Our earliest manuscripts of Matthew, Mark, Luke, and John date from the second to the fourth centuries C.E., but it is likely that all the Gospel autographs, with the possible exception of John, date to the first century.[6] There are three chief reasons for this belief. The first is that by the mid- to late-second century, several works quote passages from written Gospels or even refer to the Gospels by name, a fact which would suggest that the Gospels had been around long enough to circulate and achieve special status.[7] Second, several of these Gospels describe the destruction of Jerusalem so accurately that they almost certainly were written soon after those events (70 C.E.). Third, it is clear from the earliest strands of the New Testament, the Pauline epistles, that the first use

---

[6] Christian tradition associates the Fourth Gospel with one of the twelve disciples closest to Jesus, John. This is not John the Baptist, but a John who followed Jesus during his lifetime. In order to help keep track of the Baptist, the Gospel of John will almost always be referred to in this book as "the Fourth Gospel." All the names attributed to the Gospels are problematic (see note 15), but for convenience they will be used in this book interchangeably to refer to the Gospels and their authors.

[7] *2 Clement; Shepherd of Hermas*; Polycarp of Smyrna's *Letter to the Philippians;* Justin Martyr's two *Apologies* and his *Dialogue with Trypho;* Irenaeus's *Against Heresies* 3.1.1, preserved in Eusebius, *History of the Church* 5.8.2-4; and the testimony of Papias preserved in Eusebius, *History of the Church* 3.39.14-16.

of the term "gospel" was reserved to the oral preaching of Jesus' death and resurrection, and it makes sense that, once the first generation of witnesses to those events began to die, Christians would want to preserve their loose preaching in written form.[8] There are some other considerations that help to establish the dates of the texts, for example, the literary relationships alleged to exist between the Gospels, various internal clues, and presumptions about developments in the early Church's Christology, moral practice, theology, and internal polity. Together, these traces have yielded the consensus that Mark was composed ca. 65–75 C.E., Matthew ca. 80–90 C.E., Luke ca. 80–85 C.E., and John ca. 90–95 C.E.

There are so many passages that refer to John in these Gospels that they cannot all be presented here in the Introduction; instead, they will each be cited and discussed in some detail in Chapter 3. Their general character, however, can be presented and compared against Josephus to set up the promise and problems of our evidence.

All four Gospels locate John in the wilderness and associate his appearance in that location with a prophecy from the Jewish Scriptures: "A voice cries out: 'In the wilderness make ready the way of the Lord, make straight in the desert a highway for our God'" (Isa 40:3). Josephus does not tell us where John operated and does not refer to any specific prophecies that either he or other Jews believed to be fulfilled in John.

All four Gospels indicate that John was extremely popular. In Mark and Matthew, all the Judean region and Jerusalemites were going out to him, and Matthew adds that Pharisees and Sadducees, represented as leading Jewish groups, came as well. In Luke there are crowds of Jews, tax collectors, and soldiers, but no Jewish leaders. In the Fourth Gospel, we can presume that people came to John when we read that he was baptizing and that he had disciples, but there are few named characters or groups that interact with him—only Jesus, Andrew, and the priests who come out to question John. Josephus likewise reports John's popularity but gives no indication that any Jewish leaders apart from Herod felt particularly threatened by him.

All four Gospels associate John with the inauguration of Jesus' ministry. In Mark and Matthew, John baptizes Jesus (though in Matthew, he is reluctant to do so). In Luke, John is imprisoned before Jesus comes to be baptized, but he had met him already as a fetus, leaping in his mother's

---

[8] For further background on the formation of the Gospel tradition and the manuscript history of the Gospel texts, see respectively Helmut Koester, *Ancient Christian Gospels: Their History and Development* (Philadelphia: Trinity Press International, 1990); and Bruce M. Metzger, *The Text of the New Testament: Its Transmission, Corruption, and Restoration*, 3rd ed. (New York: Oxford University Press, 1992).

womb at the arrival of Jesus' pregnant mother Mary. The Fourth Gospel has no such infancy story, but, like Luke's Gospel, never narrates that John baptized Jesus. John does baptize, but his relationship to Jesus is to testify to him. Josephus never reports any of this, either in his description of John or in the two passages in which he mentions Jesus.

Mark, Matthew, and Luke refer to John as "the Baptist" or "the Baptizer," although the Fourth Gospel uses no such epithets. Mark, Matthew, and Luke refer to the purpose of John's baptism as an acknowledgment of conversion leading to the forgiveness of sins, similar to Josephus's comment that the baptism simply purified the body after a prior purification by justice (but notice that the notion of forgiveness of sins is unique to the Gospels). Only the Fourth Gospel indicates that Jesus himself, or at least his disciples, began a baptizing ministry in Judea, at the same time that John was still baptizing. The other Gospels and even the Fourth contrast John's baptism with water and the baptism with the Holy Spirit that Jesus will offer at some point in the future. Josephus, who tells us so much about John's ministry of purification, makes no such comment about Jesus' ministry of baptism.

The Gospels all agree that Herod arrested John, and all but the Fourth Gospel explain further that Herod executed him, and that the reason for this was John's condemnation of Herod's marriage to his sister-in-law. Josephus agrees that Herod Antipas arrested and killed John, but he offers a different explanation, as we have seen. As Josephus describes it, John had the power to foment revolt against Herod, so the arrest and execution were preventive measures. This does not preclude the Gospel claim, since marital relations outside the bounds of Jewish law were hotly contested in that period. But neither does Josephus confirm the Gospel accounts.

The remaining Gospel passages about John deal with the relationship of John and Jesus—which figure is greater, which endtime figures both men are thought to be, which baptism both men offer. None of this, as we have seen, comes up in Josephus.

There is a further and related disparity between the Gospel accounts and Josephus. The Gospels imbue John's ministry with endtime significance: He preaches of preparing for God's coming judgment, and he is depicted as the endtime prophet who will prepare God's way. In contrast, Josephus never refers to this eschatological notion of coming judgment in his account of John. Perhaps he alludes to something similar when he reports that many people saw in Herod's defeat a kind of divine retribution for Herod's evil act. But this cosmic justice was not specifically eschatological; Josephus does not present it as having implications for the end of the present world and the beginning of a new one.

The Acts of the Apostles

The Acts of the Apostles is the second volume written by Luke and functions as a kind of sequel to his Gospel.[9] The author picks up where the Gospel leaves off, recounting what the followers of Jesus did after Jesus' resurrection and ascension. Because both works were written by the same author, the dates offered for the composition of the Gospel suffice for Acts as well (ca. 80–85 C.E.).

There are seven references to John the Baptist in Acts. These can be grouped into two categories: those dealing with criteria for apostles and those contrasting John's baptism with that of Jesus. Let us look at these passages in greater detail.

The first category of passages about the Baptist includes two passages that present the criteria for apostleship. Jesus had selected twelve close disciples in the Gospels, but one of them, Judas Iscariot, had betrayed Jesus to the authorities and then committed suicide. Acts opens with the remaining eleven seeking to round out their number as they prepare to receive the Holy Spirit, which Jesus had promised to send to guide them.[10] In Acts 1:21-22, Peter opens the discussion by laying out the criteria for distinguishing who, out of all of Jesus' disciples, might be considered for the replacement position:

> Therefore it is necessary one of the men who traveled with us in all the time during which the Lord Jesus came and went among us, beginning with the baptism of John until the day on which he was taken up from us, become with us a witness of his resurrection.

John's baptism is here understood as the beginning of Jesus' ministry, and apostles are those who are eyewitnesses to that entire ministry.

A second passage, Acts 10:36-39, presents the same criterion. Here Peter again is speaking, but to a very different audience. Peter has now

---

[9] Most scholars consider Luke-Acts to be a unified work, though there are some dissenters. The classic argument for unity is H. J. Cadbury, *The Making of Luke-Acts* (New York: Macmillan, 1927); see also Robert C. Tannehill, *The Narrative Unity of Luke-Acts: A Literary Interpretation*, 2 vols., FF (Minneapolis: Fortress, 1991–1994), and *The Unity of Luke-Acts*, ed. J. Verheyden, BETL 142 (Leuven: Leuven University Press/Peeters, 1999).

[10] The number twelve had important biblical associations with the twelve original tribes of Israel. Luke portrays the early Church as the "new Israel," and so synchronizes the number of its leaders with the organization of the "old Israel." The conflation of old and new predates Luke and likely dates to the historical Jesus himself (see John P. Meier, "Jesus in Relation to His Followers: The Existence and Nature of the Twelve," in *A Marginal Jew: Rethinking the Historical Jesus*, vol. 3, *Companions and Competitors*, ABRL [New York: Doubleday, 2001] 125–197).

been led out of Jerusalem to the house of a Gentile named Cornelius. To this point in Luke-Acts only Jews have been baptized by John and Jesus. But Peter has had a revelatory dream indicating that it is now time for Gentiles to become part of the Christian community, and Cornelius and his household will be the first converts. So before these Gentiles receive the Holy Spirit and then the water baptism in Jesus' name, Peter shares the good news with them:

> The word which [God] sent to the sons of Israel, proclaiming peace through Jesus Christ, who is Lord of all: You know the things that have happened all over Judea, beginning from the Galilee with the baptism John preached, how God anointed Jesus of Nazareth with the Holy Spirit and with power, who went around doing good and healing everyone controlled by the devil, that God was with him. And we are witnesses of everything he did in the region of Judea and in Jerusalem.

Once again, the work of Jesus is presented as beginning in the work of John. Of even greater interest is that the water baptism is still performed, but only after the Spirit baptism, and then in Jesus' name rather than John's. The water baptism is generally associated in the Gospels with John and is understood to be preliminary to the baptism Jesus offers, but here they are reversed.

The second category of passages that mention John is those that contrast the baptisms of John and Jesus more pointedly. There are five such passages.

In the first, Jesus is speaking to his apostles just before his ascension: "[For] this is what you heard from me, that John baptized with water, but you in the Holy Spirit will be baptized not many days from now" (Acts 1:4-5). As we will see in Chapter 3, this sequence parallels Jesus' own "baptisms," first in water and then by the descent of the Holy Spirit, which propelled him into his ministry (Luke 3:21–4:30). Now in Acts the apostles will also be propelled into ministry by the "baptism" of the Holy Spirit, which is uniquely Jesus' to offer.[11]

In the second passage, Peter is reporting Cornelius's baptism to skeptical "circumcised believers" who are not yet ready to accept Gentiles into the Christian community. He narrates to these Jews what happened after he

---

[11] It is never mentioned in the Gospels that any of the Twelve were baptized by John, except in the Fourth Gospel, where Andrew and another unnamed disciple leave John to follow Jesus (John 1:29-42). The unnamed disciple may be Philip; compare vv. 40-42 with vv. 43-46 and note the repetition of the command "Come and see" in vv. 39 and 46 (Meier, *A Marginal Jew*, 3.194, n. 68).

told Cornelius of John's baptism and Jesus' ministry: "And as I began to speak, the Holy Spirit fell on them just as on us in the beginning. And I remembered the word of the Lord, who said, 'John baptized with water, but you will be baptized in the Holy Spirit'" (Acts 11:15-16). This reads at first glance like mere repetition of the first passage. But one important thing has changed. Cornelius is not one of the apostles, present from the baptism of John. He is a Gentile, but nevertheless the Spirit of the Jewish Jesus and the Jewish God falls upon him. In Peter's words, this makes Cornelius the Gentile indistinguishable from the Jewish followers. Furthermore, the Spirit baptism precedes the water baptism, a reversal of order that authorizes the extension of both baptisms to the Gentile community. As Peter says in Acts 10:47, "Can anyone withhold the water for baptizing these people, who have received the Holy Spirit even as we have?" And something subtler is at play. This turn to the Gentiles, which is so fundamental a shift that Peter will have to explain it on three separate occasions, is justified by reference to that earlier shift from John's baptism to that of Jesus. Just as there is more now than mere baptism in water, there are more people now than merely the Jews who will benefit from it. If the one transition is allowed, the other must be as well.

The remaining passages take us out of Israel completely and into the Gentile world. The protagonist of this part (the bulk) of Acts is Paul, a Jewish Pharisee committed to evangelizing the Gentiles.[12] Our third passage is set in Pisidian Antioch. Paul has gone to the Jewish synagogue on a Sabbath and is summarizing God's saving acts for the Jews and Gentile God-fearers who have assembled there:

> From before [Jesus'] coming John had preached a baptism of conversion to all the people of Israel. And as John was completing the course, he said, "What do you suppose me to be? I am not [that]; but see he comes after me, the one regarding whom I am not worthy to untie the sandals of his feet" (Acts 13:24-25).

Here it is not so much John's baptism that is compared with that of Jesus but John himself who is compared to Jesus. This passage quotes material in Luke 3:15-16, where John's final comments are indeed these very words. In this context, however, the meaning changes, or perhaps just becomes

---

[12] Paul considers himself an apostle, and Luke calls him one in Acts, even though Paul doesn't meet the earlier criteria of Acts, because he was not present from the baptism of John. Rather, his claim to the title is based on the revelatory experience he had of the risen Christ and the commission he received. See Rom 1:1; 11:13; 1 Cor 1:1; 9:12; 15:8-11; Gal 1:1–2:21; Acts 14:4, 14.

more transparent. There would be no need for Paul to make this statement in Pisidian Antioch if people there had never heard of John. It is likely therefore that Paul (or rather Luke) needed to make this statement because there were people who had not only heard of John but thought him to be the messiah and/or greater than Jesus. Luke's Paul then tells them they are wrong, that Jesus is the greater figure, and he proves this convincingly by quoting the very witness whom these people would find most compelling—John himself.

This possibility would be highly speculative were it not for our fourth and fifth passages. Here the contrast between John and Jesus is even more pointed. We hear that John's baptizing ministry has produced disciples who, like the apostles, are traveling the Mediterranean to spread the baptism and its accompanying message. The competition is focused around the figure of Apollos, who is presented as learned and eloquent, but deficient in his knowledge of baptism.[13] Therefore Paul's companions and co-workers, a married couple named Priscilla and Aquila, have to retrain Apollos, and Paul himself will have to return to Asia Minor to clean up the mess Apollos has left behind:

> A Jew named Apollos, by origin Alexandrian, an eloquent man, arrived in Ephesus; he was competent in the Scriptures. This one had been instructed in the way of the Lord and, fired up by the Spirit, was speaking and teaching accurately the things concerning Jesus, knowing only the baptism of John; he began to speak fearlessly in the synagogue. When Priscilla and Aquila heard him, they took him aside and explained the way of God more accurately to him (Acts 18:24-26).

It sounds as if Apollos believes in Jesus, and he appears to be an amenable student. But it is clear that he hasn't understood Jesus well enough in our final passage. When Paul returns to the area, he has to complete the job Apollos left undone:

> And while Apollos was in Corinth, Paul came through the upper regions and came to Ephesus and found some disciples. He said to them, "Did you receive the Spirit when you became believers?" And they (said) to him, "But we did not hear that there is a Holy Spirit." He said, "So in what were you baptized?" They said, "Into the baptism of

[13] For references to Apollos in Paul's own letters, see 1 Cor 1:12; 3:4-6, 22; 4:6; 16:12 (also the deutero-Pauline Titus 3:13). Priscilla and Aquila are also mentioned in Paul's letters (Rom 16:3; 1 Cor 16:19; and the deutero-Pauline 2 Tim 4:19, where the woman's name is spelled Prisca).

John." And Paul said, "John baptized a baptism of conversion, saying to the people that they should believe in the one coming after him, that is in Jesus." Hearing (this), they were baptized in the name of the Lord Jesus, and when Paul placed hands on them, the Holy Spirit came on them, and they spoke in tongues and prophesied (Acts 19:1-7).

Apollos's knowledge of Jesus is deficient because it is limited to a behavioral conversion, and his knowledge of John's baptism lacks awareness that it was preparatory rather than sufficient. Full participation in Christian community, in Luke's eyes, requires more than adherence to a moral code; it includes submission to Jesus and the gift of the Holy Spirit, manifest in charismatic gifts. John could not offer this, so while his baptism is legitimated and valued, it is not enough.

The Promise and the Problem of the Sources

It is obvious by this point that our sources both agree and disagree. And this means that the sources are somewhat compromised as windows onto the first-century world. If the accounts were historically accurate portraits of the Baptist, they would all agree, or at least they would not *disagree*. But some lack material found in others, and sometimes they conflict outright. Will the real Baptist please stand up?

The "Game Rules" for Reconstructing History from Ancient Witnesses

This cursory introduction to the sources on the Baptist has led us to a basic question: Can historically accurate data be drawn from disparate accounts? And why are accounts about the same person different in the first place?

Means, Motive, and Opportunity: Why Texts Differ

The historian approaches ancient texts like the forensic detective approaches a criminal investigation, though of course most historians don't think of ancient authors as criminals, no matter how creative their writing style.[14] The historian instead presumes that texts will differ from each other,

[14] One famous exception is Hermann Samuel Reimarus (1694–1768), who was convinced that the disciples stole Jesus' body to fake the resurrection so that they could create a success out of Jesus' failure. Reimarus believed that the disciples perpetrated a further fraud by deceiving others into believing that Jesus had risen and would soon return. The Gospels are the chief

even if reporting the same story, because the authors' means, motives, and opportunities differ.

Most of us know what these terms mean in a criminal context: *Means* refers to how the act was done, including techniques, weapons, and *modus operandi,* while the *motive* provides the "why," and the *opportunity* is the "when/where"—was the criminal near the crime scene at the right time, or does she or he have an alibi?

Step out of the criminal context now and into the world of biblical and literary study. In this world the authors' means are anything relevant to how the account got written. Now, an author cannot write a text about someone unless he or she was an eyewitness and/or has some sources about the person. Moreover, a person cannot write at all without having learned to do so, and this is not to be taken for granted in antiquity, when literacy rates were low. A person's education and exposure to literature and rhetoric would have provided a toolbox of literary genres, techniques, allusions, commonplaces, and stylistic options that could serve well as the gear for any writing project undertaken. And authors might select different tools depending upon the audience to whom they are speaking, pitching their message in a manner most likely to gain them an audience.

This leads us naturally to the motives an author might have for writing. The writer, the social groups with whom he or she interacts, and the patron commissioning the author to write might all have their reasons why the literary work should be produced. Motives can be detected in several forms. There is simple bias, when a viewpoint is advanced without argument. There are themes, which are more complex teachings that the work is designed to render persuasive to the reader through repetition or narrative placement or rhetorical argument or literary beauty. There are apologetic interests, whereby the author attempts to explain a position as a form of defense, for internal or external audiences. And there are historical considerations that may prompt an author to write, such as the evangelists' concern to record the firsthand experiences of Jesus before all of the eyewitnesses had passed away.

Finally, there is the element of opportunity. For the author, as opposed to the criminal, opportunity refers not to when and where he was relative to the historical events recounted in the story, but rather when and where he was when the need for the story arose. Who enabled him to write? A community of believers? A solitary patron? Someone had to finance the author through the project, paying for his services, for his board and keep, and for

---

vehicles of this deception. See Charles H. Talbert, ed., *Reimarus, Fragments*, trans. Ralph S. Fraser (Chico, Calif.: Scholars Press, 1985; original, Philadelphia: Fortress, 1970).

the written sources he would need to use. Did social forces and historical events converge to present an opportunity or imperative to write?

Means, motive, and opportunity. Each has its own range of variables, and each of these will likely differ from author to author. There are enough permutations possible in the arrangement of these factors that it suffices to explain why documents about the same events can differ markedly from one another.

So what is the historian to do? Can any distinctions be made between the relative value of various traditions?

The Criteria of Historicity

Given these variations between our sources, our inability to determine the authors' situations exactly, and the accidental quality of what has survived to our own time, we could throw up our hands entirely at the prospect of ever discovering anything historical in the few sources we still have. Yet the situation is not really that bleak. It is analogous to a criminal trial in which the jury must try to decide guilt or innocence on the basis of sometimes conflicting or incomplete evidence and on the basis of the competing interpretations of the evidence proffered by the attorneys for the prosecution and the defense. If it were outright impossible to determine what happened, no one would bother with jury trials; but in fact there are several criteria the judge offers the jury to help them weigh the evidence and reach their verdict. For example, do the witnesses corroborate one another? Are they sufficiently independent of one another to count as separate witnesses, or might one have influenced the other? What motives might the witnesses have to testify or not to testify? If they fear reprisal and nevertheless testify, their testimony can be accorded greater credibility than words that cost the witness nothing. On the other hand, if they have something to gain from speaking, then we might doubt the veracity of their remarks.

These criteria are quite similar to those used by historians who try to reconstruct events from the biblical texts. Of course, the biblical historian is looking at silent, ancient texts rather than live witnesses, and so there are perhaps fewer clues to work with and gaps that may be more easily filled with the historian's own biases and motives. And every student of Scripture, no matter what level, cannot help but bring biases and perspectives to the text that intentionally or unconsciously color their interpretations.

The criteria of historicity offer a counterweight to these limitations. They help us to assess the degree of likelihood that something happened, whether an event, word, issue, character, or theological formulation. All they can help us to establish is a degree of likelihood rather than absolute certainty, but when two thousand years separate us from our subject, this limitation is to be expected. Think of these criteria as the ground rules for the game of historical reconstruction. And understand at the outset that their yield will be modest: We are not claiming to reconstruct what really happened but only what elements in our surviving texts most likely happened. Thus our results will be limited by several factors: (1) which texts were selected for preservation in antiquity, thus increasing the likelihood that they would be copied and then survive? (2) which texts actually did survive? (3) which elements in the surviving texts meet the criteria? and (4) our ignorance of the cultural context of Jesus' time, which will impede the application of some of the criteria. These are serious limitations that reveal how modest we must be as we move forward in our study of John the Baptist or any figure from antiquity.

And now to the criteria themselves. *Rule Number 1:* An argument from silence is "the weakest link." The absence of evidence may be more easily explained as accidental rather than intentional. More importantly, it is difficult to argue about something that does not exist, unless you can demonstrate that the author chose to exclude it from his or her source. For example, Josephus discusses John the Baptist at greater length than he discusses Jesus, and he never places the two in any relationship. Does this mean that the Baptist and Jesus never met? We can't really say, since Josephus might not have mentioned this for any number of reasons (for example, it didn't happen; his sources make no mention of it; he didn't think it significant enough to include; he included it, but that part of his text subsequently was lost or corrupted).

Rule Number 2: The strongest testimony is eyewitness testimony. This might make it appear that the Gospels of Matthew and John are the most reliable, since early Christian tradition held that these two Gospels had been written by two of Jesus' twelve disciples.[15] But how historical are these traditions? In contrast to this early Church testimony, the scholarly consensus today is that these two Gospels, and indeed all the Gospels, were composed at least one generation after the lifetime of Jesus and the

---

[15] There are two early sources that mention the authorship of the Gospels. Papias, who wrote in the early second century C.E., traced Mark's Gospel to the disciple Peter's reports about Jesus and Matthew's Gospel to one of Jesus' disciples (Eusebius, *History of the Church* 3.39.14-16; NPNF Second Series 1.172-3). The second-century C.E. Muratorian Fragment preserves a partial list of the canon of documents in the New Testament (ANF 5.603-604). It traces Luke's Gospel to Paul's witness and John's Gospel to the disciple John; see Samuel P. Tregelles, *Canon Muratorianus: The Earliest Catalogue of the Books of the New Testament* (Oxford: Clarendon, 1867); and Geoffrey M. Hahneman, *The Muratorian Fragment and the Development of the Canon*, OTM (New York: Oxford University Press, 1992).

eyewitnesses who accompanied him. The canonical Gospels certainly depend upon traditions passed down to their authors by eyewitnesses, but the finished texts we have before us are not eyewitness accounts. Thus by its very nature our evidence prevents us from applying this criterion easily.

Rule Number 3: The strongest evidence for the historicity of a saying or event is when multiple, independent sources attest to something, and/or when something is found in more than one literary form.[16] In courtrooms witnesses are not allowed to hear each other testify so that their comments will not unduly influence other witnesses' recollections. In the same way, we're on firmer ground in reading ancient evidence if we have separate authors who did not read each others' work reporting the same events. We have four independent sources in the case of John the Baptist, namely, Josephus and three Gospel-related witnesses that will be introduced in Chapter 2 (Q, Mark, and the Fourth Gospel). The second part of this criterion is that an event or saying is more reliable if it is found in more than one literary form. Literary forms one finds in the Gospel material include aphorisms (short, witty sayings), *chreiai* (short stories culminating in an aphorism), parables, dispute stories, miracle stories, beatitudes, and prayers. The fifteen vignettes that explicitly mention John the Baptist are indeed distributed across several forms or genres, for example infancy narrative (Luke 1–2), prophetic prologue (Mark 1:2-6), controversy story (Mark 2:18-22; 11:27-33; John 3:22–4:3), and parable (Matt 11:16-19 par. Luke 7:31-35). This criterion is only capable of ruling material *in;* it cannot rule material out, because it is still theoretically possible that an event narrated in only one Gospel is historical—we simply can't use this criterion to demonstrate it. For example, only Luke tells us that John taught his disciples how to pray (Luke 11:1-4), and only John tells us that baptism was part of Jesus' ministry and that there was some competition between the "baptisms" (3:22–4:3; but see Acts 18:24–19:7; 1 Cor 1:11-17). There may be a kernel of truth in these accounts, and so we would have to use other criteria to determine their historical likelihood.

Rule Number 4: Another strong argument for the historicity of an event is advanced when the author reports something awkward or embarrassing. This can usually be identified by textual clues. For example, does the author spill some ink trying to explain the saying or event? Do later authors add further explanations or otherwise mitigate the problem? If an author reports something that is awkward and has to be explained, and he

---

[16] At this point I begin to follow the criteria developed in historical Jesus research; see Meier in *A Marginal Jew*, vol. 1, *The Roots of the Problem and the Person*, ABRL (New York: Doubleday, 1991) 167–195.

would have every reason not to report it but must anyway, it's likely that it happened. That is true, as we shall soon see, with the account of Jesus' baptism. Why would Jesus, whom the Gospel authors identify as greater than John, need to bend down before John to be baptized? And why would Jesus need to be baptized in the first place, if the purpose of baptism is conversion and Jesus does not need to repent for anything? The fact that the event is narrated in some form in all four Gospels despite these awkward elements makes a good case for the historicity of the event; and as we shall see, the later authors try to diminish the embarrassing elements in various ways. This is not a foolproof criterion on its own. What if an event actually occurred that was not so embarrassing? This criterion would lead us to judge the report less historical simply because of its pedestrian nature. Then, too, how can we, at a two-thousand-year remove from these events, know for certain what would have been embarrassing to a first-century author or audience? These considerations alert us once again that no single criterion is adequate to establish the historicity of an event.

Rule Number 5: If the saying or event is unusual or unexpected given what we know of the various Judaisms of Jesus' day or the various forms of early Christianity, then our authors have likely preserved something historical. This criterion is called "discontinuity" or "dissimilarity." The idea is that the matter is so unusual that it was likely noticed and preserved, even though Christian communities may have developed in different directions thereafter. This rule, too, has some built-in problems. If it were our only criterion, it would render a portrait of John the Baptist or Jesus so unique that they would appear divorced from their culture, and in Jesus' case this would have dangerous and even heretical implications. Jesus and John the Baptist were Jewish men, and if they did not speak in the idiom of their culture, no one would have understood them well enough to follow them, let alone to report anything about them. This criterion is completely incapable of identifying those features of either man's life and teachings that were continuous with the Judaisms of their day, or with early Christianities for that matter. So once again, caution is warranted in the application of this rule.

Rule Number 6: A passage may be considered historical if it is coherent or consistent with other material established as historical by the previous criteria. To apply this criterion, we need to have a kind of database of such established historical passages against which we can compare a given text. And, once again, this criterion can rule in but not out the historicity of the new text, because human beings are not entirely consistent.

Rule Number 7: For an event about Jesus to be historical, it must somehow be consistent with his eventual rejection and execution. This criterion might be applicable to other characters as well, and particularly John the Baptist. John is present at the inauguration of Jesus' ministry, and prefigures his end as well when he himself is arrested and executed. Like Jesus, he must have been a controversial figure, his very popularity a threat. So we can judge as more historical those accounts that present his popularity and his threatening message. Portraits of him that would present him on the margins of Jewish society rather than at its center and preaching an uncontroversial message would be historically unlikely.

Rule Number 8: Prescriptive and hortatory passages indicate behaviors. A prescriptive passage is one that lays down a law about something, while a hortatory text is one that encourages or persuades an audience to some course of action. The principle here is that laws and persuasion are not necessary if the audience is already doing the thing the law commands or the exhortation encourages. At the very least, the audience needs encouragement to behave a certain way; at most, they may be behaving in a completely unacceptable way already, so that the author feels the need to command them to some other course of action. This rule is most easily applied to rhetorical texts, such as speeches, letters, and legal pronouncements. These genres are by nature hortatory or prescriptive (or both). But it can be adapted usefully to our project for narrative texts as well. If, for example, our authors keep generating stories to demonstrate that Jesus is greater than John the Baptist, our suspicion should be aroused that he was not—at least in some people's eyes. After all, there's no need to state something, let alone repeat it over and over again, if it's true and generally accepted. We know that John was extremely popular from the Gospel texts themselves, which recount that all of Judea and Jerusalem was going out to him for baptism and which narrate that Herod considered John's influence threat enough to have him beheaded. Moreover, as we have seen, there are texts outside the Gospels that indicate the ongoing baptizing activity of John's disciples and some degree of competition between the baptisms of Jesus and John. So when we find regular questions in the Gospels about the relationship of these two figures, we should read these passages as evidence that the men's relationship was still contested in the author's day. This criterion demonstrates the historicity of an issue in the author's context; it does not necessarily determine the historicity of an event in the time of Jesus and John.

So to summarize, a saying or event reported about John the Baptist in the text is more likely to be historical if it is:

1. *In the text*, and not an argument from silence ("the weakest link")
2. *Eyewitness testimony* rather than a derivative witness

3. *Multiply attested* in independent witnesses and various literary forms
4. *Embarrassing* to the author
5. *Discontinuous* with known Jewish or Christian traditions
6. *Coherent* with other events/sayings established as historical
7. *Consistent* with the fact that the Baptist is arrested and executed
8. *Persuasive or Prescriptive*, because these indicate behavior and issues, at least in the time of the author

From Criteria to Critical Methods

The criteria of historicity alone will not yield us very much. All they can do is offer a modest final picture of what likely happened before the text was written. But what about what was going on *when* the text was written? And are there other sources beyond those that mention John the Baptist that can help us flesh out what his world was like? These are the two central questions that will guide our study from here on.

Just as contemporary forensic detectives use a variety of tools and techniques to reconstruct a crime scene, so the historical detective must use several different techniques to approach the limited evidence from antiquity. Biblical scholars refer to their techniques as "critical methods," because they are methods of posing questions to texts and of developing answers to those questions (from *krino,* meaning "to judge, discern"). We have already met one of these critical methods here in Chapter 1—the basic historical critical method that attempts to reconstruct history from literary accounts. We will have recourse to this fundamental technique throughout this book. In addition to historical criticism, we will apply two other critical methods to our texts on John. Each of them begins from a question and then follows certain steps to answer that question. As we saw with the criteria of historicity, each method yields limited results because it begins with a limited range of assumptions and questions and must then work within the constraints of its steps.

The first questions we will pose to the portraits of John the Baptist in this book are how and why the accounts most similar to each other, namely Mark, Matthew, and Luke, nevertheless diverge. This question yields the critical method of redaction or editorial criticism. This method begins with a claim about the means used by these authors, which is that Mark's Gospel was the first to be written and that Matthew and Luke used it and some other sources in the composition of their texts. The method then examines the changes each later author introduces to determine patterns in the motives of the author, that is, the teachings he is emphasizing. From these patterns, conclusions can be drawn about the audience and social location of the author.

The second critical method we will use to explore the Baptist traditions steps outside the world of the text to the world that produced the text. Social-scientific criticism employs techniques drawn from the social sciences (for example, archaeology, anthropology, sociology) to gain a better sense of the material culture, conceptual stereotypes, social networks, political paradigms, persuasive techniques, and religious beliefs of the world that produced John the Baptist and the accounts about him. In this section of the book we will explore the new religious movement John inaugurates within the social context of Judea in the first century C.E. John's appearance coincides with parallel social and religious developments, such as the growth of the community at Qumran, the rise of the Zealots, the interference of Rome in Judean politics, and the periodic rebellions against Rome culminating in the First and Second Jewish Revolts (66–74 C.E. and 132–135 C.E., respectively). What information can social-scientific analysis of these social movements and socioeconomic circumstances yield that will help us to understand the rise of John and the perspectives of our authors?

These methods together will still only yield a partial picture of the historical Baptist and the redacted Baptists. But in the process of applying the methods, we will see John more clearly through the window of our texts, we will be able to see ourselves looking as we consciously apply our methods, and we will forge at least a few paths into the fascinating detective work of biblical studies.

CHAPTER TWO

Redaction Criticism:
How and Why Authors Shape Their Stories

The first chapter dwelt on the kinds of questions a historian poses to a text when she or he wants to know the historical possibility that a character lived or an event happened. That is always a fundamental question, and one to which we will return periodically. We saw that a significant obstacle to answering that question is posed by multiple, conflicting accounts. But those accounts represent a bonanza for the historian if her lens is focused on the world *of* the text rather than on the world *behind* the text. That is, each text yields a rich vein of material on the circumstances in which its author wrote, on the means, motives, and opportunities that converged to produce his particular text. The means will always include earlier material on which the author based his work, so that there is always some potential to dig for the history behind the lives of the characters in the story. But the motives of the author who finally pulls those sources together, adding new material and shaping the final product—these "fingerprints" of the author are all over his work, and they are not so difficult to discern.

Redaction criticism is a method of analysis that dusts the text for its author's prints. It is easiest to do when the critic knows something about the means at the author's disposal, that is, the sources the author used. Imagine that ancient authors lined up sources on the table before them, much as one might when writing a research paper, and then laid out a new piece of parchment for their own account. If we knew what their sources were, we would know just where and how this final author used, edited, and adjusted them for his own purposes. More than that, all those changes would indicate to us just what his purposes were. Well, it happens that we *do* have a good sense what the sources were for the first three Gospels, all based on clues in those texts, and from this theory of literary sources we can begin to analyze the changes later authors made as they edited the material. "Redaction" is a term coined from the German word for "editing," so redaction criticism is simply a critical method that analyzes the editorial activity of an author in order to isolate his theological motives and social circumstances.

Again, redaction criticism works best when you have some concrete evidence of the resources an author used. Since we have only the final texts the authors produced, that will take some imaginative reconstruction. But there are clues in the texts to guide our work, and that is especially true for the first three Gospels, Matthew, Mark, and Luke. These three are often referred to as the "Synoptic Gospels," because they tell the story of Jesus in largely the same way (in Greek, *sunoptos* means "viewable together"). These three Gospels present the same stories in roughly the same order and sometimes even with the exact same vocabulary. Now that is an unusual phenomenon! If three separate accounts had been written by different people at different times so long after Jesus' death, one would expect them to differ more substantially, as Josephus and Acts do, for example. Matthew, Mark, and Luke, on the other hand, present quite a different picture. When one encounters three texts that are so alike, and in fact verbatim at points, the hypothesis that best fits the evidence is that somebody copied, with component sources and/or one of the texts itself serving as the common base text(s). That at least is the hypothesis with which we will begin our study of redaction criticism and the Synoptic Gospels.

The Synoptic Problem in the Account of the Baptism of Jesus

The Synoptic Gospels have barely been introduced and already there's a problem. These three Gospels are indeed very much alike. But they also differ, and therein lies the problem. The best way to apprehend the problem is to see the evidence, and the best way to see the evidence is to look at the three Gospel versions of the same event side by side. Just as the Gospels are called "synoptic," any multi-column layout that presents related passages alongside each other is called a "synopsis." Here is a synopsis of the accounts of the baptism of Jesus:

Mark 1:9-11	**Matthew 3:13-17**	**Luke 3:21-23**
And it was in those days that Jesus came from Nazareth of the Galilee	Then Jesus arrived from the Galilee to the Jordan, to John to be baptized by him. But John prevented him saying, "I need to be baptized by you, and you would come to me?" But Jesus answered and said to him, "Permit it now, for in this way it is fit-ting for us to fulfill all righteousness." Then he permitted him.	Now it was when all the people had been baptized
and was baptized in the Jordan by John. And im-mediately as he was coming up from the water, he saw the heavens tearing	And when Jesus was baptized　immediately he came up from the water; and see, the heavens were opened [to him]	and Jesus had been bap-tized, and was praying,
and　　the Spirit	and he saw the Spirit of God descend	the heaven was opened and　the Holy Spirit descended on him in
like a dove coming down to him. And　a voice was from the heavens, "You are my son, the beloved; in you I am well pleased."	like a dove and come on him; and see, a voice from the heavens saying, "This is my son, the beloved, in whom I am well pleased."	bodily form like a dove, and　a voice came from heaven,　"You are my son the beloved, in you I am well pleased."

A mere glance at the synopsis would tell us both that somebody copied and that whole chunks of material were either added to or deleted from the tradition. A closer look would yield more subtle differences—in geographic detail, vocabulary, characters, and events. The first step in redaction criticism is this kind of close analysis. And the best way to do it is to mark every similarity and difference found in the text, and then to make a list of the most significant phenomena. We are not going to ask yet who changed whom; all we want to do now is to become familiar with the evidence.

A recommended method for analyzing the text is to mark it with col-ored pencils. That can be done right in this book. We might use one color to underline words that we find in multiple columns to help our eye see them quickly thereafter. If one of the authors uses a slightly different word, we would use a different style of underline in the same color for that word. If an author has a substantial chunk of material not found elsewhere, we might box it in red—these differences will be important. If only one author has a detail that the others lack, we use yet another style of line or box to mark it. We must be alert to changes in terminology, verb person or tense, location, time, causation, or explanation. If we try this for the baptism story above, we might end up with a synopsis that looks like this:

Figure 1. Redaction-Critical Mark-Up of the Account of Jesus' Baptism

Mark 1:9-11	Matthew 3:13-17	Luke 3:21-23
And it was in those days that <u>Jesus came from</u> Nazareth of <u>the Galilee</u>	Then <u>Jesus arrived from the Galilee</u> to the Jordan,	Now it was <u>when all the people had been baptized</u>
	to John to be baptized by him. But John prevented him saying, "I need to be baptized by you, and you would come to me?" But Jesus answered and said to him, "Permit it now, for in this way it is fitting for us to fulfill all righteousness." Then he permitted him.	
<u>and was baptized in the Jordan by John</u>. And <u>immediately as he was coming up from the water,</u> ⇔	<u>And when Jesus was baptized immediately he came up from the water;</u> and see,	and <u>Jesus had been baptized, and was praying,</u>
<u>he saw</u> the heavens tearing and the Spirit like a dove coming down to him. And a voice was from the heavens, "<u>You are</u> my son, the beloved; in <u>you</u> I am well pleased."	the heavens were opened [to him] and <u>he saw</u> the Spirit of God descend like a dove and come on him; and see, a voice from the heavens saying, "<u>This is</u> my son, the beloved, in <u>whom</u> I am well pleased."	the heaven was opened and the Holy Spirit descended on him in bodily form like a dove, and a voice came from heaven, "<u>You are</u> my son the beloved, in <u>you</u> I am well pleased."

Clearly, this is a good synoptic passage in that all three Gospels have some version of the event. In all the accounts, baptizing activity associated with John is going on (we'd have to have read a few verses prior in Luke to know that John had started the practice). Jesus comes to be baptized, *is* baptized, and then a revelatory experience occurs that announces Jesus to be God's son. That is a lot of similar material, and the vocabulary is often quite similar as well. That proves well enough why these Gospels are called "Synoptic."

But now we turn to the problem. There are some real differences. The first and perhaps the most glaring one of all is that John does not want to baptize Jesus in Matthew's Gospel. This story is not recounted in either Mark or Luke. Jesus has to talk John into it. Then we get to the baptism itself: in Mark and Matthew, John does it, but not in Luke. Luke frames it in the passive voice: "Jesus had been baptized." Had we read the few verses prior to this passage in Luke, we would know that John could not possibly have baptized Jesus, because John had already been imprisoned by Herod. And then there's the curious revelation from the heavens. In Mark, the heavens tear, while in Matthew and Luke they are opened. In all three, the Spirit of God/Holy Spirit descends upon Jesus in the form of a dove (or pigeon; we don't have enough occurrences in Greek to really settle the definition of the term). In Mark, the combination "He saw" and God's second-person address "You are" suggests that only Jesus was privy to the revelation, whereas subtle shifts in Matthew and Luke suggest that others besides Jesus and the Gospel audience see or hear as well. You may have picked up on other differences yourself. For example, compare the introduction of the voice in Mark ("And a voice was from the heavens") with the versions in Matthew ("And see, a voice from the heavens saying") and Luke ("and a voice came from heaven"). Assume as you analyze that everything *may* be significant and mark it.

After marking the text, draft a list of what seem to be the most significant of the similarities and differences you have found. Our list for the Synoptic baptism scene would look something like this:

Similarities
1. Baptizing activity associated with John is occurring.
2. Jesus comes to be baptized.
3. Jesus is baptized.
4. Revelatory experience
   - heavens tear/open
   - Spirit of God descends like a dove
   - heavenly voice names Jesus "my son, the beloved" in whom the speaker is well pleased.

Differences

1. John baptizes Jesus in Mark, he baptizes him reluctantly in Matthew, and he does not baptize him at all in Luke.
2. In Mark, the heavens tear open, whereas in Matthew and Luke they simply open.
3. In Mark, only Jesus seems to hear the voice, whereas in Matthew and Luke some part of the revelation is accessible to other characters in the story (the voice in Matthew, the Spirit's descent in Luke).
4. Different verbs are used to describe the heavenly voice: in Mark, it "was," in Matthew, it is "saying," in Luke, it "came."
5. Matthew has a unique conversation between John and Jesus, in which John expresses reservations about baptizing Jesus, and Jesus tells him to do it in order to "fulfill all righteousness."
6. Luke alone speaks of "all the people" being baptized and portrays the heavenly revelation in the context of Jesus praying.

Now that the work of gathering the evidence is complete, we need to begin to generate hypotheses based on the evidence to account for the similarities and differences. The first hypothesis we will generate will attempt to explain the literary relationship of the three Gospels. This theory will solve the "Synoptic Problem" for us by accounting for the literary relationships between the three Gospels. Once that step is accomplished, we will move on to the focal task of redaction criticism, which is to analyze the patterns of changes that later editors make to earlier source material in order to derive a picture of those editors' theological motives and social circumstances.

Before we go any further, you might want to dog-ear or tag both page 26 (Figure 1) and page 28 (the list of differences) so that you can refer back to them easily through the rest of this chapter.

A Solution to the Synoptic Problem: The Two-Source Hypothesis

The similarities between the accounts of John's baptism, and the almost verbatim agreements between Mark and Matthew at several points and all three Gospels in the climactic revelatory experience, are most easily explained by the hypothesis that one of the three accounts was copied by the other two authors. But which one came first? And how would we even decide?

The criteria of historicity, and particularly the criterion of embarrassment, will be particularly useful to us as we try to answer that question. You will recall that this rule says that an event likely occurred if an author reports it even when he'd have every reason *not* to. And you can tell that the author would rather not report an event when the author himself tries to explain it away. The entire story of Jesus' baptism by John is likely historical for that very reason—it was embarrassing, but nevertheless all three Synoptics, and the Fourth Gospel for that matter, report it.[1] But now the differences listed above come into play. Our authors do not all report the event in the same way. Mark simply tells us that Jesus was baptized by John, but Matthew and Luke qualify the account: Matthew's Jesus first has to give John permission, and Luke's Jesus is not baptized by John at all. What can we make of these differences?

The portrait of John in each Gospel can act as our guide. In Matthew's Gospel, John voices his concern: "I need to be baptized by you, and you would come to me?" Here John is acknowledging his inferiority to Jesus and his consequent discomfort at Jesus' making the inferior's gesture of bowing under John's baptizing hands. In Luke's Gospel, John does not baptize Jesus. Both of these Gospels indicate in their own way that the relationship of Jesus and John is at issue here. Matthew is perhaps clearest; the baptism of Jesus by John is a problem because Jesus should be superior to John. Matthew resolves the problem by allowing John to acknowledge his lower status, which in turn allows Jesus to control the action when he tells John, "Permit it now." Luke resolves the problem by taking John out of the action altogether and shifting the narration into the passive voice: John is imprisoned already, and Jesus "had been baptized." Luke's adjustment of the verbal tense is also interesting: the baptism is reported as something that took place prior to the present action being narrated, the revelatory experience. This has the effect of relegating the baptism to the back burner in terms of the verbal action in the sentence and focusing the energy of the sentence on the revelation of Jesus' unique identity. Luke's two strategies—the removal of John and the verbal focus on the revelatory experience—together displace the problem of the Jesus-John relationship entirely. Note, too, difference no. 3: both Matthew and Luke find a way to have more characters in the story hear from heaven that Jesus is the son, the beloved, which clearly sets his status above that of John.

There is a further embarrassment in the account of Jesus' conversion. The baptism of John is reported in all the Synoptics to be a baptism of conversion for the release (or forgiveness) of sins. Why, then, would *Jesus*

---

[1] The Fourth Gospel is not normally invoked in redaction critical studies, because it is thought to depend on sources entirely different from those of the Synoptic Gospels. Nevertheless, the close study of the Baptist traditions in Chapter 3 will at least present the Fourth Gospel "parallels" in notes, because these correlations provide important evidence of multiple attestation.

need to be baptized? John's baptism, according to Josephus and the Synoptics, was a purification symbolizing a prior conversion toward a just lifestyle. But nothing in the Synoptic accounts of Jesus, either before the baptism story or after it, would indicate that Jesus ever needed to convert or ever did convert from an unjust or sinful past. So why receive the purification? The fact that all our evangelists report the baptism despite this awkward *non sequitur* is once again evidence for its historicity *and* provides a clue as to which Gospel came first.

Now, it is theoretically possible that any one of these Gospels was written first and that the other two borrowed from it and made their changes. But it is much easier to imagine that a later author cleaned up an embarrassing detail than to suppose that a later author made the account more embarrassing.

Mark's account is the most embarrassing. He has John baptize Jesus with little concern for the challenges this poses to Jesus' superior status and sinless behavior. Both Matthew and Luke attack the challenges head on, and for that reason it is logical to argue that they were written after Mark and used his Gospel as a source. We can make the case for dependence on Mark in every passage where an event is reported by the "triple tradition," that is, by Matthew, Mark, and Luke.

Incidentally, this also explains some minor differences of grammar, syntax, and diction that we find in many passages. Mark's Gospel is written in rather rough Greek, and Matthew and Luke often clean it up, as one of your friends or professors might do with a first draft of a research paper you've written. This explains our difference no. 4 above, where Mark uses a generic verb that means "to be or become" to describe the presence of the heavenly voice, and Matthew and Luke supply the more descriptive verbs of movement or speaking. Many of these types of differences, however, are only visible in the original Greek and in the apparatus of the critical edition, where you can follow the trail of copyists' corrections in later manuscripts of the same Gospel. Another example from the baptism scene that is clear even in English is the verb choice about how the heavens release the voice: In Mark they "tear" open, while Matthew and Luke replace the violent verb with the more gentle "open." Mark may have his own reasons to use "tear"—it is, after all, the same thing that happens to the sanctuary curtain in the Temple at the moment of Jesus' death, after which a Roman centurion's voice will say, "Truly this man was a son of God" (15:37-39). That is too close a parallel and the moments too climactic for this correspondence to have been sheer coincidence.

This section had in its title the words "the Two-Source Hypothesis," and so far we have identified one of the two sources: Mark is the source of

Matthew and Luke in all cases of the triple tradition. The textual clues indicating the presence of the *other* source will require the presentation of another passage and acceptance of the fact that there are many passages in the Synoptic Gospels that look just like it. Once again, we will use one of the passages in which John the Baptist is mentioned. This account is set well after John's execution, as Jesus' own execution draws near:

Matthew 11:7-15	**Luke 7:24-30**
As they were going away Jesus began to speak to the crowds about John: "What did you go out into the desert to look at? A reed shaken by the wind? But what did you go out to see—a man clothed in soft (things)? See, those wearing soft things	When the messengers of John had left, he began to speak to the crowds about John: "What did you go out into the desert to look at? A reed shaken by the wind? But what did you go out to see—a man clothed in soft garments? See, those who are in glorious clothing
are in the houses of kings. But what did you go out to see? A prophet? Yes, I tell you, and one even greater than a prophet. This is the one about whom it is written, 'See, I send my messenger before you, who will prepare your way before you.' Truly, I tell you: There has not arisen from those born of women one greater than John the Baptist; but the least one in the kingdom of the heavens is greater than he. From the days of John the Baptist until now the kingdom of the heavens has been constrained and violent people take it by force. For all the prophets and the law prophesied until John; and if you wish to accept it, this man is Elijah, the one who is to come. He who has ears, let him hear."	and luxury are in palaces. But what did you go out to see? A prophet? Yes, I tell you, and one even greater than a prophet. This is the one about whom it is written, 'See, I send my messenger before you, who will prepare your way before you.' I tell you: There is no one greater of those born of women than John. But the least one in the kingdom of God is greater than he. The law and the prophets were until John; from then, the good news of the kingdom of God is proclaimed and everyone takes it by force."

In this case we do not need to do a close analysis to see which words and ideas have been changed because, apart from the beginning and end of the passage, very little differs. In fact, the core speech of Jesus is reproduced almost verbatim in both Gospels. And this phenomenon repeats itself across these two Gospels, not in just a few places but in fully sixty-eight passages. The phenomenon is so remarkable that it has been dubbed the "double tradition." It simply cannot be sheer coincidence and must indicate verbal dependence. Moreover, most of these passages are generically similar; they are sayings, most often spoken by Jesus. You'll notice that in the above passage the narrative set-up is unique to each author, but the saying of Jesus is repeated almost verbatim.

There are several theories we could propose to explain the verbal relationship. It is possible that Matthew used Luke or that Luke used Matthew. But these hypotheses are not entirely satisfactory, because if each knew the other Gospel in the form that we now have them, it would mean that they would have chosen to exclude some passages that are literary and pedagogical gems, like Luke's parables of the good Samaritan and the prodigal son (10:29-37; 15:11-32) or Matthew's dramatic final judgment scene (25:31-46). There is one other possibility, and that is that Matthew and Luke both used a single literary source to which they both had access. This thesis is supported by the generic similarity of most of these shared passages. It is easy to imagine that a list of Jesus' sayings was written down early in the life of the Church as an aid to preaching and catechesis. The list would have grown and could have become somewhat standardized, so that by the time Matthew and Luke sat down to compose their Gospels, they might well have had copies of the same document laid out before them.

No one has ever found this document, although the discovery of the *Gospel of Thomas* in 1945 among the Nag Hammadi codices from Egypt lent credence to the theory that a sayings gospel may have existed.[2] For now, this "second source" of the Synoptics, or more properly of Matthew and Luke, remains a hypothetical document. Since German Scripture scholars developed the hypothesis of the two sources—Mark and this sayings source—we follow their convention in designating the latter "Q," from the German *Quelle,* meaning "source."[3]

---

[2] See the edition by Helmut Koester and Thomas O. Lambdin in *The Nag Hammadi Library*, rev. ed., ed. James M. Robinson (San Francisco: Harper & Row, 1978) 124–138, and the discussion by Henri-Charles Puech in *New Testament Apocrypha*, 2 vols., ed. Wilhelm Schneemelcher, trans. R. McL. Wilson (Louisville, Ky.: Westminster/John Knox, 1992; German original, Tübingen: J.C.B. Mohr [Paul Siebeck], 1989) 1.278–307 (pages in the 1963 edition), or the more accessible paperback, *The Complete Gospels: Annotated Scholars Version*, ed. Robert J. Miller (San Francisco: Polebridge/HarperSanFrancisco, 1994) 301–329.

[3] See the definitive edition by James M. Robinson, Paul Hoffmann, and John S. Kloppenborg, *Critical Edition of Q*, Hermeneia Supplement (Minneapolis: Fortress, 2000), as well as the translation in *The Complete Gospels*, 249–300. Designations of Q passages follow the Lukan chapter and verse. In addition, see several studies by Kloppenborg: *Q Parallels: Synopsis, Critical Notes and Concordance* (Sonoma, Calif.: Polebridge, 1988); *Excavating Q: The History and Setting of the Sayings Gospel* (Minneapolis: Fortress, 2000); and *The Formation of Q: Trajectories in Ancient Wisdom Collections*, SAC (Philadelphia: Fortress, 1987). The first person to designate the Q source was Paul Wernle, *Die synoptische Frage* (Freiburg: J.C.B. Mohr [Paul Siebeck], 1989).

The Two-Source Hypothesis

We have now identified four common phenomena in the Synoptic texts:

1. In some passages, Mark = Matthew = Luke; we call this the "triple tradition."
2. In other places, Matthew = Luke, but Mark is lacking; we call this the "double tradition."
3. There are quite a few unique Matthean passages, like the judgment scene.
4. There are many unique Lukan passages, like the parables mentioned above.[4]

The Two-Source Hypothesis explains all these phenomena. It states that Matthew and Luke both used two of the same sources when compiling their accounts, namely, Mark's Gospel and Q, the hypothetical sayings source (hence the "Two-Source" Hypothesis). In addition to these two shared sources, Matthew and Luke each had material unique to them that they integrated in their Gospel accounts (this explains, respectively, points 3 and 4 above).

Now, when you see a synopsis in which all three columns are filled, you can assume with the majority of biblical scholars that it is a case of the triple tradition and that Matthew and Luke based their versions of the event on Mark's account.[5] When you encounter a synopsis in which only Matthew's and Luke's columns have text and that material is similar, you will know that it is an example of the double tradition and thus a case of dependence on Q. And if you come across a passage in Matthew or Luke with no parallel in the other Synoptics, you are likely in the presence of each author's unique source (designated "M" or "L" respectively).

---

[4] By the way, there are very few Markan passages that are unique to Mark: 1:1-3 and 2:1-2 are both transitional; 3:19b-21 narrates how Jesus' family thought he was insane; and 4:26-29 is an obscure parable about seed growing secretly. In each case it is easy to argue why Matthew and Luke might have chosen to omit the material.

[5] There are scholars who dispute the Two-Source Hypothesis. The chief competing theory is the "Two-Gospel (or Griesbach) Hypothesis," which argues that Mark used Matthew and Luke as sources (and Luke had used Matthew), conflating the two intentionally to produce a document that would appeal to both Jewish and Gentile Christians. See William R. Farmer, *The Synoptic Problem. A Critical Analysis* (New York: Macmillan, 1964; rept. Dillsboro, N.C.: Western North Carolina Press, 1976); Christopher M. Tuckett, *The Revival of the Griesbach Hypothesis: An Analysis and Appraisal* (New York: Cambridge University Press, 1963); and the collection of essays in *The Two-Source Hypothesis: A Critical Appraisal*, ed. Arthur J. Bellinzoni, Jr. (Macon, Ga.: Mercer, 1985).

The Two-Source Hypothesis is often sketched in the following way:

Figure 2. The Two-Source Hypothesis

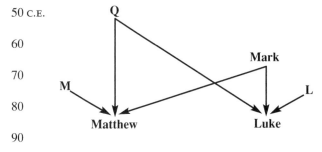

The timeline along the left indicates the dates that have generally been assigned to the sources Q and Mark and the Gospels Matthew and Luke. The "dates" for the special Matthean material "M" and the special Lukan material "L" are arbitrary; all that can be said is that they must have predated the final editions of these Gospels.

Summary: The View from the Evidence
and the View from the Solution

Synoptic alignments of Mark, Matthew, and Luke yield evidence of the triple tradition (Mark = Matthew = Luke), the double tradition ([Matthew = Luke] ≠ Mark), unique Matthean material (Matthew ≠ [Mark or Luke]), and unique Lukan material (Luke ≠ [Mark or Matthew]). This evidence must be explained in terms of literary dependencies, and the Two-Source Hypothesis offers one theory for these relationships: Mark was the source of Matthew and Luke for cases of the triple tradition; Q was the source of Matthew and Luke in cases of the double tradition; a source unique to Matthew explains many passages unique to that Gospel; and a source unique to Luke accounts for much of the special Lukan material. Thus Matthew used three sources for his Gospel: Mark, Q, and a special source. Likewise, Luke used three sources: Mark, Q, and a special source unique to him. Mark certainly used sources as well, but since his was the first Gospel, we cannot identify them in precisely the same way.[6]

[6] The way to identify them would be through form criticism, which seeks to isolate discrete literary forms (miracle stories, parables, etc.) and posit their original *Sitz im Leben*, or "setting in life"; see Martin Dibelius, *From Tradition to Gospel*, trans. Bertram Lee Woolf, LTT (Cambridge: James Clarke, 1971 [from the 2nd rev. ed.]; German original, Tübingen:

Redaction Criticism

Now that we have a working hypothesis for the literary relationships between the Synoptic Gospels, we are prepared to employ the method of redaction criticism to determine the theological interests and social situation of our later editors. Recall that "redaction" is simply a fancy word for "editing," and you will now know which of the Synoptic authors we will be examining. Matthew and Luke edited sources we can define. By laying Matthew and Luke alongside each other and against their common source Mark, we can see these editors' hands at work in the ways they collected, arranged, edited, and modified their sources.

The process of redaction criticism began earlier in this chapter when we analyzed the synopsis of the baptism scene. Let us return to that scene now. It will be easiest if you've dog-eared page 28, because frequent reference will be made to the list of differences presented there as the steps of redaction criticism are introduced below. [7]

Step 1. Analyze the text.

The first step of redaction criticism is to lay out the passage in synoptic fashion or to use a published synopsis that does this.[8] Mark the text as we did earlier in the chapter, highlighting similarities and differences.

J.C.B. Mohr [Paul Siebeck], 1919); and Rudolf K. Bultmann, *The History of the Synoptic Tradition*, trans. John Marsh (Peabody, Mass.: Hendrickson, 1994 [from the 5th ed.]; German original, Göttingen: Vandenhoeck & Ruprecht, 1921). Once these units are identified, the redaction critic can discern Mark's theological orientation and social circumstances in the narrator's voice and in the structure and placement of the component passages. A classic work that positioned Markan studies for redaction criticism was William Wrede, *The Messianic Secret*, trans. J.C.G. Greig, LTT (Cambridge: James Clarke, 1971; German original, Göttingen: Vandenhoeck & Ruprecht, 1901). For a comprehensive redaction-critical study of the Gospel, see Willi Marxsen, *Mark the Evangelist: Studies on the Redaction History of the Gospel*, trans. James Boyce (Nashville, Tenn.: Abingdon, 1969; German original, Göttingen: Vandenhoeck & Ruprecht, 1956).

[7] For a more complete introduction to redaction criticism, see Norman Perrin, *What Is Redaction Criticism?*, GBSNTS (Philadelphia: Fortress, 1969).

[8] The standard synopsis is Kurt Aland, ed., *Synopsis of the Four Gospels: English Edition* ([n. l.]: United Bible Societies, 1982), but see also Robert W. Funk, *New Gospel Parallels* (Philadelphia: Fortress, 1985), and Burton H. Throckmorton, Jr., ed., *Gospel Parallels: A Synopsis of the First Three Gospels*, 5th ed. (Nashville, Tenn.: T. Nelson, 1992). Students with facility in Greek will want to use Kurt Aland, ed., *Synopsis of the Four Gospels: Greek-English Edition of the Synopsis Quattuor Evangeliorum*, 9th ed. (Stuttgart: German Bible Society, 1989). The Aland editions reproduce the Fourth Gospel as well, which is instructive.

Step 2. List the similarities and differences.

Next, draw up a list of what seem to be the most significant differences. Assume the Two-Source Hypothesis and focus on how Matthew and Luke change Mark or, if it is a passage from the double tradition, how Matthew and Luke differ from each other (see the dog-eared page 28). A further exercise as you become more familiar with the Gospels is to look up each version of the passage in its original context to determine whether Matthew and Luke moved the account into a different chronological, geographic, or narrative context.

Step 3. Discern patterns of differences.

Perform this exercise on a group of passages so that you can begin to develop a kind of database of differences. From this you will begin to be able to discern patterns in the alterations introduced by the later editors. Reconsider the effects of location; if Matthew or Luke moved a passage, what effect does this have on the meaning of the piece, and does that fit the patterns you are beginning to discern?

If you only have time to research one passage or pericope, you can still perform this step by consulting a good biblical commentary. Biblical commentaries provide verse-by-verse analysis of a given biblical book. Although there are single-volume commentaries that cover the entire Bible, the more useful commentaries for this critical method are those series that devote one volume to each book of the Bible, because each volume can achieve greater depth.[9] Consult in particular the exegesis of your chosen passage, which will help you to identify alterations and key terms. Review also the introduction to the commentary, which will discuss the overarching structure of the Gospel, its key themes, and the author's theological interests and audience.

[9] Four examples of the single-volume commentary on the entire Bible are Raymond E. Brown and others, *The New Jerome Biblical Commentary* (Englewood Cliffs, N.J.: Prentice-Hall, 1990); John Barton and John Muddiman, eds., *The Oxford Bible Commentary* (New York: Oxford University Press, 2001); Charles M. Laymon, ed., *The Interpreter's One-Volume Commentary on the Bible* (Nashville, Tenn.: Abingdon, 1971); and Carol A. Newsom and Sharon H. Ringe, eds., *The Women's Bible Commentary* (Louisville, Ky.: Westminster/John Knox, 1992).

Your professor can introduce you to the commentary series that he or she uses for Scripture study, which might include the Anchor Bible Commentary (New York: Doubleday); Black's New Testament Commentary (Peabody, Mass.: Hendrickson); Hermeneia (Minneapolis: Fortress); the New International Commentary on the New Testament (Grand Rapids, Mich.: Wm. B. Eerdmans); The New Interpreters Bible (Nashville, Tenn.: Abingdon); Sacra Pagina (Collegeville, Minn.: The Liturgical Press); and Word Biblical Commentary (Nashville, Tenn.: Word).

It is possible and preferable to discover these features yourself, however, before consulting a biblical commentary or other secondary works. Let us take the Synoptic account of the baptism and see what we can do with it ourselves. We are especially concerned here to identify features found only in Matthew or Luke. For example, recall our difference no. 5, Matthew's unique conversation between Jesus and the Baptist. Matthew's Jesus tells John that Jesus' submission must be permitted, "for in this way it is fitting for us to fulfill all righteousness." If we repeated this exercise across multiple passages or took the shortcut of checking a concordance for these key terms, we would find that the terms "fulfill" and "righteousness" recur regularly in Matthew and are used much more frequently there than in the other Gospels.[10] Turning to Luke, we will note his unique phrases that "all the people had been baptized" and that Jesus' revelatory experience happened while he was at prayer (difference no. 6). A survey of other synopses would demonstrate that Luke often broadens Mark's references to crowds or Jews to include more generic groups of people, and sometimes explicitly Gentiles. Luke also presents his characters, particularly Jesus, in prayer more than any other Gospel.

Step 4. Develop a hypothesis regarding the editor's interests and/or social situation.

The final stage in redaction criticism is to move from pattern to hypothesis. In this stage we want to do two things: identify the themes visible in the patterns of editorial changes and develop a thesis that explains why the editor might have wanted to advance those themes (the social situation or audience).

In Matthew's version of the baptism, we saw that his unique emphasis was on "fulfilling all righteousness." These are words only and not yet themes. A theme has to be a sentence rather than a word, a teaching that a

---

[10] A concordance lists every word that occurs in a text or corpus, and every citation where that word occurs. If you have a hunch that a particular term in your passage is significant, you can look up the word in the concordance and discover immediately where that term occurs within your chosen book and across the Bible. Since every version of Scripture makes different translation choices, it is important to use the concordance that complements the version of the Bible you are using. For example, if you have the New Revised Standard Version of the Bible (NRSV), you will want to use John R. Kohlenberger III, *The NRSV Concordance Unabridged* (Grand Rapids, Mich.: Zondervan, 1991); if you have the New American Bible (NAB), you will want to use *Nelson's Complete Concordance of the New American Bible*, ed. Stephen J. Hartdegen (Nashville, Tenn.: Thomas Nelson, 1977; an updated edition may be prepared after the NAB revision of the Old Testament is completed in 2004–2005 [revisions of the New Testament and the Psalter preceded in 1986 and 1991, respectively]).

work is designed to render persuasive to the reader, and it becomes visible not only in solitary words like these but in the larger design of the Gospel (repetition, explicit teaching, location of topics at key points). If we had time to scan several synopses and read through Matthew's Gospel, we would find that his concern for fulfillment and righteousness are repeated often and at key moments. We could then discern more clearly some key Matthean themes, for example, that Jesus fulfills rather than abolishes the Jewish law and prophets, thus exemplifying in a special way the righteousness that had always been manifest in God's revelation to the Jews. This then would be one of the theological interests that redaction criticism aims to identify, and it would tip us off that Matthew is likely writing to Christians who identify deeply with Jewish tradition.[11]

In Luke's account of the baptism, we found that he emphasizes the presence of "all people" and Jesus at prayer, patterns that repeat throughout the Gospel and at some of its most critical moments. The themes we could draw from these patterns are that the Gospel has been broadened to include the Gentiles more explicitly and that prayer is an important part of the life of faith. These are theological interests or claims, and the first one at least suggests that Luke's audience included and may have been dominated by Gentile Christians.[12]

The steps of redaction criticism can be summarized as follows:

1. *Analyze the text.* Mark every similarity and difference you find.
2. *List the similarities and differences.* Be alert to the following literary elements that might be changed and to the types of changes that may be made:
   a. Literary Elements
      • Vocabulary

---

[11] For a comprehensive redaction-critical study of Matthew's Gospel, see Günther Bornkamm, Gerhard Barth, and Heinz Joachim Held, *Tradition and Interpretation in Matthew*, trans. Percy Scott, NTL (London: SCM, 1963; German original, Neukirchen: Neukirchener, 1960). See also Jack Dean Kingsbury, *The Parables of Jesus in Matthew 13: A Study in Redaction Criticism* (London: Society for Promoting Christian Knowledge, 1969), and Krister Stendahl, *The School of Matthew and Its Use of the Old Testament*, 2nd ed. (Lund: CWK Gleerup, 1968).

[12] For a comprehensive redaction-critical study of Luke's Gospel, see Hans Conzelmann, *The Theology of St. Luke*, trans. Geoffrey Buswell (Philadelphia: Fortress, 1961; German original, Tübingen: J.C.B. Mohr [Paul Siebeck], 1954). For more general redaction-critical studies of the Synoptics, see Joachim Rohde, *Rediscovering the Teachings of the Evangelists*, trans. Dorothea M. Barton (London: SCM, 1968; German original, Hamburg: Furch, 1966); and Joachim Jeremias, *The Parables of Jesus*, 2nd rev. ed., trans. S. H. Hooke (New York: Scribner, 1972).

- Structure: syntax of sentences, arrangement of clauses and sentences within passage; narrative set-up and conclusion of core material
- Placement: location of pericope in larger narrative, with special attention to passages just before and just after

b. Types of Changes
- Omission: Editor might delete unnecessary detail, problematic stories or phrases, contradictions in text
- Addition: Editor might add words, phrases, proofs, explanations, translations, insight into characters, and entire passages to augment narrative
- Alteration: Editor might clean up diction or grammar, harmonize parallel passages, conflate two stories into one
- Relocation: Editor might move the story to introduce more order in the sequence or to alter the meaning

3. *Discern patterns of differences.* Examine enough passages to build a "database" of terms and teachings that are repeated or located at critical moments of the Gospel (these are clues to "themes," teachings that the work is *designed* to render persuasive to the reader).

4. *Develop a hypothesis regarding the editor's interests and/or social location.*
   a. Identify the themes visible in the patterns of Step 3.
   b. Develop a thesis that explains why this editor advanced these themes; consider social and theological developments that might have influenced him as well as the composition of his audience.

Both Matthew and Luke alter the Markan image of the Baptist. Neither editor can ignore the embarrassing fact that Jesus' ministry began somehow with John's baptism. But both authors diminish John's presence through John's voice (Matthew) or by removing him from the scene (Luke). As we now turn to a redaction-critical examination of the entire Synoptic record of the Baptist in Chapter 3, we shall have to see whether this pattern of diminishment is repeated and what new patterns emerge. That will allow us by the end of that chapter to account anew for the theological motives and social circumstances revealed by the editorial activity of Matthew and Luke.

CHAPTER THREE

Baptist Vignettes in the Gospels:
A Redaction-Critical Approach

John the Baptist is imprisoned or dead during most of the story time of the Gospels, yet his name and memory keep cropping up throughout the narrative of Jesus' life. Add to this phenomenon the fact that the Synoptic Gospels were written thirty to sixty years after the death of both John and Jesus, and it becomes even more curious that our authors find it necessary to define Jesus in relationship to John. Clearly the memory of both men continued to exert influence on their followers well after their lives, a fact we take for granted in Jesus' case but may be more surprised to find true of John as well. Recall that Josephus, writing just after the Synoptic Gospels were penned, writes more about John than about Jesus, and that accounts of the early Church refer to the popularity and spread of "John's baptism" (as distinct from that of Jesus), and it begins to appear that outside Christian circles John was even more widely renowned than Jesus in the earliest period of the Church's history.

Whether that is the case or not, the sheer number of references to John in the New Testament Gospels indicates that the evangelists were keen to negotiate the relationship between these two figures. As we might expect from the Two-Source Hypothesis, Matthew and Luke largely follow Mark in the portraits they present of the Baptist, but they also diverge dramatically from their source at several points. In this chapter we will explore carefully the similarities and differences in the Synoptic accounts of John. First, we will look at the fifteen short stories in the Synoptics in which John is mentioned explicitly. Then we will summarize our results from the vantage point of the redactors, Matthew and Luke. Finally, we will read the evidence in the other direction to distinguish the historical Baptist from the redacted Baptist.

Fifteen Vignettes

The first references to John the Baptist are the most obvious ones, that is, those that refer to John directly. We can find these quite easily with a concordance, a book that lists alphabetically all the words and names that occur in Scripture and then, under each term, presents in canonical order all the citations where that word or name occurs.[1] A quick survey in the concordance yields a list of some fifteen short stories or vignettes in the Synoptic Gospels in which John the Baptist appears as a character or as a subject of conversation. These passages or pericopes will be presented here in a kind of harmonized chronology, meaning that events around Jesus' birth will be presented first and events around the death and resurrection of Jesus and the birth of the early Church last. But notice as you read that the Gospels are not uniform; some lack certain of these stories entirely and thus frame the presentations of Jesus and John in quite different ways.

Vignette 1. The Infancy Narrative

Our first vignette is a wonderful illustration of that very principle, for it is found in only one Gospel. The Gospel of Luke presents a narrative of the infancy of Jesus in its first two chapters, and every episode in the story is mirrored by an episode from the infancy of John the Baptist. Only one other Gospel of the four in our Bibles, the Gospel of Matthew, presents an infancy narrative, and it is substantially different from Luke's, with no reference to John the Baptist at all.[2] Thus these two chapters in Luke must be attributed either to Luke's special source or to Luke himself and may therefore be taken to reflect that evangelist's particular concerns.

The Lukan infancy story is constructed like an artistic diptych, that is, a two-paneled painting in which two scenes are presented alongside each

---

[1] See Chapter 2, p. 37, note 10, for two recommended concordances.

[2] Over time, stories of the infancy and childhood of Jesus grew in popularity and therefore in number. Several of these have survived from antiquity, for example, the *Protoevangelium of James*, in which Mary is raised as a virgin from birth; the *Infancy Gospel of Thomas*, in which the divine Child has more power than any toddler should; and the *Arabic Gospel of the Infancy*, which likely influenced stories of Jesus' birth that appear in the Koran (compare *[Arab.] Gos. Inf.* 36 with Koran 3:49 and 5:110). For translations of these books, see Wilhelm Schneemelcher, ed., *New Testament Apocrypha*, 2 vols., trans. R. McL. Wilson (Louisville, Ky.: Westminster/John Knox, 1992; German original, Tübingen: J.C.B. Mohr [Paul Siebeck], 1989), or Robert J. Miller, ed., *The Complete Gospels: Annotated Scholars Version* (San Francisco: Polebridge/HarperSan Francisco, 1994). For a discussion of the canonical infancy narratives, see Raymond E. Brown, *The Birth of the Messiah: A Commentary on the Infancy Narratives in Matthew and Luke* (Garden City, N.Y.: Doubleday, 1977).

other, suggesting that they are related and should be interpreted together.[3] Unlike a static painting, however, Luke's story moves, because since a story is told in time, the author can return to the various panels of his presentation in an alternating sequence, thus governing our gaze and our interpretation of the figures.

Since the passage is the longest of our fifteen vignettes, let us take a telescopic view of the piece, beginning with the widest angle and then narrowing our focus to each individual scene. Our method of viewing these two chapters cannot be redaction criticism because there is no earlier extant source text against which to compare them. Instead, we will borrow some techniques from literary criticism to analyze the structure and content of the passage.

The structure of the two chapters as a whole alternates between John and Jesus, but not in a strict sequence. It begins in parallel fashion with a story of the annunciation of John to his father Zechariah (Luke 1:5-25), followed by the mirror account of the annunciation of Jesus to his mother Mary (1:26-38). It then overlaps the two parts of the diptych by bringing Jesus' and John's mothers physically together, both by identifying them as biological cousins and by recounting their three-month visit together (1:39-56). The author then presents the birth, circumcision, and youth of John (1:57-80), followed by a much longer account of the birth, circumcision, and youth of Jesus (2:1-52). Structurally, the author has actually given us two diptychs, one on either side of a central moment when the mothers meet (see Figure 3). Location indicates the significance of the mothers' meeting, while length indicates the relative significance of the characters; note that John and Jesus share space in the first chapter of the Gospel, while the entire second chapter is devoted to Jesus' birth and youth.

Figure 3. The Structure of the John-Jesus Diptych in Luke 1–2

Annunciation of John	Annunciation of Jesus	Mary/Jesus visit Elizabeth/John	Birth, Circumcision-Naming, Youth of John	Birth, Circumcision-Naming, Youth of Jesus (2 Temple episodes)
(1:5-25)	(1:26-38)	(1:39-56)	(1:57-80)	(2:1-52)
Annunciation Diptych		**Central Episode**	**Birth-Youth Diptych**	

[3] Brown, *Birth of the Messiah*, 248–253.

Since the overarching structure of these two chapters points to the mothers' meeting and the relative significance of John and Jesus, let us follow the literary architecture and look at these elements more carefully.

The mothers' meeting is presented as the natural result of the annunciation stories that precede it. In the first, John's father Zechariah, serving his priestly turn in the Jerusalem Temple, enters alone to burn incense, where he is visited by the angel Gabriel and told that his barren wife Elizabeth will have a son, despite their advanced age.[4] Gabriel declares that this son will be great "before the Lord," "will be filled with the Holy Spirit, even from his mother's womb," and "he will go before [the Lord God] in the spirit and power of Elijah, to turn the hearts of fathers to children, and of disobedient ones to the attitude of the just, to make ready for the Lord a people prepared" (1:16-17). The angelic promise echoes earlier prophetic promises about a future restoration of Israel, most notably Malachi 3:1, 23-24, where the messenger who will prepare the Lord's way is connected with Elijah (cf. Sir 48:10):

> See, I am sending my messenger
>   and he will prepare the way before me;
> And suddenly he will come to his temple
>   the Lord whom you seek,
> And the messenger of the covenant whom you desire.
>   See, he is coming, says the LORD of hosts.
> See, I will send you
>   Elijah the prophet,
> Before the day of the LORD comes,
>   the great and terrible day,
> To turn the heart of fathers to their sons,
>   and the hearts of sons to their fathers,
> Lest I come and strike the land with doom.

We shall explore this connection of Elijah and John more fully later; for now, simply note that Gabriel does not refer to John *as* Elijah, but rather as one who will act "in the spirit and power of Elijah," and that John's food habits ("he will drink neither wine nor strong drink," 1:15) make him sound like a Nazirite (Num 6:1-21), and thus more like Samson or Samuel

---

[4] Elizabeth's name echoes that of the wife of Aaron, Israel's first priest (Exod 6:23); the Hebrew name Elisheba (אֱלִישֶׁבַע) is translated as Elisabeth (Ἐλεισαβεθ) in the Greek translation with which Luke would have been familiar. *Gos. Eb.* 1:1-2 also mentions John's parents but probably depends on the Lukan narrative.

than Elijah (Judg 13:4; 1 Sam 1:11).[5] The fact that the angel speaks about
the fulfillment of known prophecies is all the more reason why Zechariah,
a priest educated in Jewish Scripture, should recognize and trust the word
of the messenger who comes to him in the Temple. But he does not, and his
disbelief results in his inability to speak until John's circumcision. Mean-
while, his wife Elizabeth hides herself for five months, grateful that God
has removed her reproach among her people (1:24-25).

Next the peripatetic angel visits the relative backwater of Nazareth in
Galilee, where he speaks to a young girl whose only status marker is that
she is engaged to a man descended from the line of David, the great king of
Israel's United Monarchy ten centuries earlier, long before the current
Roman occupation. Gabriel's message to Mary is different: She will conceive apart from her fiancé by the Spirit of God, her son will be called "Son
of the Most High," and God will give him David's throne. Mary's confusion
results in further explanation from the angel demonstrating rather ambigu-
ously just *how* she will conceive, but much more clearly *that* God can do
this, given the proof of the pregnancy of the aged and barren Elizabeth. In
this proof we see the first occasion on which John "prepares the way" for
Jesus, insofar as his conception demonstrates to Mary that "nothing will be
impossible for God" (1:37).

Mary, whose mysterious pregnancy gives her much greater reason to
hide than Elizabeth, instead rushes off to her cousin in Judah. There is no
hint that her three-month visit is designed to escape either small-town
tongues or her fiancé's anticipated concern; after all, she returns to
Nazareth after three months, just at the point when she would begin to
show. Rather, her haste to greet Elizabeth is entirely to give praise to God
and to animate the baby John, now five months along in his mother's
womb. Notice that it is only at the moment of Mary's greeting that the baby
John leaps in the womb, and the cloistered Elizabeth, filled suddenly with
the Holy Spirit, cries out in testimony (as her son will soon do) to the divine identity of the child in Mary's womb (she calls Mary "the mother of
my Lord," 1:43). Elizabeth's audience is not only Mary but we the readers,

---

[5] The correspondence of John with these other Nazirites goes well beyond their diet, for
if you read Judges 13 and 1 Samuel 1 you will see immediately that all three infants are born
to barren women, women who praise God for hearing their prayers and then consecrate their
sons to God's service. Samson's case is even more similar to the Lukan account, for his birth
is announced first to the mother and then to both parents by an angel. In addition, Mary's
Magnificat in Luke 1:46-55 is clearly based on the song of praise voiced by Samuel's mother
Hannah (1 Sam 2:1-10). The *Protoevangelium of James*, an infancy gospel that tells of the
birth and youth of Mary as well as Jesus, continues this dependence on the Samuel story
when it names Mary's mother "Anna."

so her exclamatory witness effectively ends her self-enclosure, though Zechariah's isolation will have to await John's circumcision for its remedy. If we recall Gabriel's promise that John would be filled with the Holy Spirit, we will recognize that the promise is fulfilled in this scene. The Spirit has come to John through Elizabeth's ears, to there from Mary's mouth, to there from the Spirit of God which has overshadowed Mary and created the child in her womb. It is thus the Spirit of God present in the fetal Jesus that animates the fetal John. Elizabeth's testimony makes sense of this invisible appointment: "Blessed is the fruit of your womb! . . . For see, when the voice of your greeting came to my ears, the child in my womb leaped in exultation" (1:42, 44). John may have preceded Jesus, but in Luke's account he is nevertheless the lesser and dependent character; his father doubts where Mary believes, his mother hides while Mary travels, his life itself is animated by his younger cousin.

The priority of Jesus over John is demonstrated in the next moment of the visitation scene as well. Elizabeth praises her cousin for believing that God's word would be fulfilled in her—precisely what her husband Zechariah did not do—and this acknowledgment prompts Mary to praise God in a famous hymn often referred to as the *Magnificat* (after the opening phrase, "My soul magnifies the Lord," 1:46-55). John's priestly father will also utter a canticle of praise once his voice returns (the *Benedictus*, 1:68-79), but it is important to notice that Mary's hymn comes first. A woman of no consequence from a rural backwater upstages a priest of Israel from the geographic heartland of Judea; she is allowed by our author to give first voice to the work that God is accomplishing in the world. And the work God is praised for doing mirrors our author's choice in privileging Mary:

> . . . he has scattered the proud in the understanding of their hearts,
> he has knocked down the powerful from thrones, and has raised up the lowly;
> the hungry he has filled with good things, and the rich he has sent away
> empty (1:51-53).

The woman of low degree has been exalted by God, and our author has followed suit.[6] But Zechariah is also redeemed when he ultimately obeys Gabriel's statement that his son should be named John. And we should

---

[6] This does not mean that Luke privileges women's voices *per se*; they are simply one of many marginalized groups whom Luke employs to illustrate his theme of inclusion and reversal. See Mary Rose D'Angelo, "(Re)Presentations of Women in the Gospel of Matthew and Luke-Acts," in *Women and Christian Origins*, ed. Ross Shepard Kraemer and Mary Rose D'Angelo (New York: Oxford University Press, 1999) 180–195; and Turid Karlsen Seim, *The Double Message: Patterns of Gender in Luke-Acts* (Nashville, Tenn.: Abingdon, 1994).

note that the two characters who give voice to hymns of praise are the same two characters to whom the message of God's saving acts had been given by Gabriel; thus God ultimately is the source of their special knowledge and their resulting proclamation.

The birth and infancy accounts of John and Jesus follow in Luke 1:57–2:52 and represent the concluding diptych of the infancy narrative. As mentioned before, the account of John's birth and youth is much shorter, comprising a mere twenty-four verses compared with the fifty-two allocated to Jesus. As if this were not enough to indicate their relative importance, there are also narrative differences between the two that are interesting. John's birth is merely surprising because of the age of his parents; Jesus' birth is the greater miracle. John's birth is met with human joy (1:58), Jesus' with angelic joy and human praise of God (2:8-20). John's circumcision seems to take place in his hometown and is accompanied by the restoration of Zechariah's Spirit-filled speech and the consequent fear and uncertainty of the townsfolk (1:59-79), while Jesus' circumcision story is augmented with an account of "their" purification in the Jerusalem Temple, during which Jesus is warmly welcomed by prophetic figures (2:21-39).[7] The two individuals who greet Jesus in the Temple are the righteous, Spirit-filled Simeon and the ascetic prophetess Anna; their prophetic identification indicates that they speak for God. The report of John's childhood is simply that he grew up, became strong in Spirit, and lived in the wilderness (1:80), while Jesus likewise grows and becomes strong, but also enjoys divine favor and is filled with wisdom, a wisdom manifested at age twelve when he is found teaching the teachers in the Temple (2:40-52). John's birth takes place in the midst of neighbors and relatives (1:58) and is talked about throughout the hill country of Judea (1:65), whereas Jesus' birth is not among kin but is set instead in the context of a worldwide imperial census, thus indicating a wider scope to his eventual influence (2:1-4). John's birth is apparently at home, while Jesus' is not; instead, Jesus is born in the city of his forebear King David, thus connecting him to the messiah promised at Israel's founding (2:4; cf. 3:31-32).[8] Given that Jesus is explicitly associated with the great King David and the Roman *imperium*, his birth is astonishingly humble: it takes place in an animal stall rather than

---

[7] Jewish law only required the *mother* to be purified after the birth of a child. The process of purification involved a period of time—forty days for a boy and eighty days for a girl—and a concluding sacrifice (Lev 12:2-8). The presentation of Jesus also fulfills a law in Exodus 13:2, 12, although the event need not have occurred in the Temple; Luke may be echoing the story of Hannah's presentation of Samuel to the sanctuary in 1 Samuel 1:24-28 (see p. 45, note 5, for other Lukan allusions to this story).

[8] In 2 Samuel 7:11-17, God had promised David that his house (monarchy) would endure forever (cf. Pss 2, 89, 132; Isa 8:23–9:6); but during the Babylonian Exile (593–539

in human accommodations, and is witnessed by shepherds rather than courtiers and kings (2:7-20). Our author has already indicated in both the *Magnificat* and the *Benedictus* that this is precisely how God acts, eschewing and even upending human constructions of power and honor. The narrative of Jesus' birth confirms this divine *modus operandi*, thus ascribing a kind of reverse honor to Jesus in the upended value system of the Lukan Gospel.

The astute reader will notice that with the birth of Jesus the narrative has become more complex. Jesus is no longer simply being contrasted with John as the greater of two figures divinely appointed for a similar mission. From this point on, a new diptych is being painted, and it is a darker one, for it portrays the contest that will ultimately lead to Jesus' execution. Here the contrasting panels are the kingdom Jesus restores as a baby in an animal stall in David's city and the Roman Empire that summoned him there in the first place to tighten its presumed hold on the world. The Lukan birth narrative is thus not the benign and peaceful story it has become in contemporary Christmas carols and cards, for while its angels sing of peace, it is a peace that will confront an empire and cost both John and Jesus their lives. In Luke's infancy narrative, the contest between the kingdoms of God and this world is not yet explicit, as in the bloody Matthean infancy narrative when King Herod tries to exterminate his unknown rival in a slaughter from which Jesus barely escapes (Matt 2:1-21; cf. Exod 1:15–2:10). Luke's scene is more irenic but no less assertive that the kingdom of God and the kingdom of this world are at odds.

It is important to note that two entities *not* at odds in Luke's infancy narrative are Israel and Jesus. John is born of a priestly family, Jesus fulfills the Davidic promise, and both families observe the Jewish law (Zechariah fulfills his priestly duties, both boys are circumcised, Mary and Joseph present Jesus in the Temple after his birth and return there every year for Passover). Moreover, those who describe God's purposes in John and Jesus are figures from Jewish tradition (the angel Gabriel, the ancestors and prophets alluded to by

---

B.C.E.), the kingly line was destroyed by the Babylonians. The Jews did return to Jerusalem from exile, but they no longer governed themselves; instead, they had to endure a succession of foreign empires (Persians, Greeks, and Romans). In this context they began to hope for a leader descended from David who would fulfill the biblical promise and be anointed to expel the foreigners and to rule them by God's law (the word for "anointed one" in Hebrew is *moshiah,* or "messiah," translated into Greek as *christos*). Old biblical texts were reinterpreted to point to this future king (Num 24:15-19 [Balaam's oracle]), while new texts were written predicting his advent (Amos 9:11; Mic 5:2-5; Jer 33:14-22; Ezek 17:3-4, 22-23; 34:23-24; Zech 3:8; 4:12, and possibly Isa 11:1-9; Jer 23:5-6). In some texts the savior is clearly a descendant of David, but in other texts he is not (e.g., Isa 45:1; Dan 7). On messianic speculation in Second Temple Judaism, see John J. Collins, *The Scepter and the Star: The Messiahs of the Dead Sea Scrolls and Other Ancient Literature*, ABRL (New York: Doubleday, 1995).

Mary, Zechariah, Simeon, and Anna), and some of them act in God's Temple and in God's Holy Spirit (Zechariah, Gabriel, Simeon, and Anna). There is only one prophetic reference that the redemption of Israel which Jesus will inaugurate will not be received by all (2:34-35), but unlike Matthew's infancy story, there are no actual Jewish characters in Luke 1–2 who oppose or fear Jesus' birth (cf. Matt 2:3). Jesus and the Jews are not at odds in Luke's infancy narrative, and the diptych of John and Jesus is employed to demonstrate this: Jesus is the messiah whose way will be prepared as prophesied in Jewish Scripture (Isa 40:3-5 + Mal 3:1; cf. Luke 1:16-17, 76-79; 3:4-5), and he is the king who will redeem Israel from the powers of this world.

We do not have any of Luke's sources against which to compare his account, but there is another way in which we can use redaction criticism to identify his characteristic teachings. After all, to the extent that Luke's infancy narrative is uncorroborated in any other source, it may be that he took great freedom in constructing it, and so reveals his redactional interests throughout. Thus the portrait of the Baptist in Luke 1, drawn through characters, dialogue, setting, and structural arrangement, reveals Luke's central themes about the man. The double diptych arranged on either side of the meeting of the mothers of John and Jesus conveys both the integral relationship of John and Jesus and the superiority of Jesus, as well as other motifs and themes important to Luke, such as joy, prayer, the role of the Spirit, and the centrality of the Jerusalem Temple. Another technique we can use to discern Luke's themes is his selection and adaptation of Old Testament references. Emphasis on prophetic and priestly characters past and present confirms the theme that Jesus is part of God's long-promised salvation, while the narrative introductions locating Jesus in Roman imperial history assert his significance for a wider audience as well. The one element of the story that some scholars take to be historical is the priestly lineage of John, because it is central to the narrative and coheres with John's future ministry of purification and separation from structures of authority.[9] The highly structured character of the narrative, the discrepancies between it and Matthew's account, and the lack of corroborating external evidence render the historicity of the story unlikely, but it is nevertheless an excellent gauge for assessing Luke's view of Jesus' significance.

Luke's account of John's birth is unparalleled in the other Gospels. Almost all the remaining references to John in the Gospels, however, are attested by at least two textual witnesses, and so allow exploration through the exegetical method of redaction criticism.

---

[9] John P. Meier is representative; see *A Marginal Jew: Rethinking the Historical Jesus*, vol. 2, *Mentor, Message, and Miracles*, ABRL (New York: Doubleday, 1994) 24–25.

Vignette 2. The Appearance of John

The first scene about John the Baptist that occurs in all three Gospels is the account of his appearance in the wilderness. The witnesses are reproduced below in a synopsis so that we can examine and mark their similarities and differences more easily, as we did in Chapter 2.

Mark 1:2-4	Matthew 3:1-3	Luke 3:1-6
Just as it is written in Isaiah the prophet, "See, I send my messenger before your face, who will prepare your way; a voice of one crying out in the wilderness: 'Make ready the way of the Lord, make straight his paths,'"	[cf. 11:10; Vignette 8]	[cf. 7:27; Vignette 8]
	[cf. v. 3 below]	[cf. v. 4 below]
	In those days	In the fifteenth year of the reign of Tiberias Caesar, during the rule of Pontius Pilate over Judea and Herod's tetrarchy of Galilee, while Philip his brother was tetrarch of the region of Iturea and Trachonitis, and Lysanias was tetrarch of Abilene, in the high priesthood of Annas and Caiaphas, the word of God came to
John the Baptizer came in the wilderness and	John the Baptist appeared	John the son of Zechariah in the wilderness. And he went in all the region around the
proclaiming	proclaiming in the wilderness of	Jordan proclaiming a
a baptism of conversion for the release of sins.	Judea and saying, "Convert, for the kingdom of the heavens is near!" For this is the one spoken of by Isaiah the prophet,	baptism of conversion for the release of sins. As it is written in the book of the words of Isaiah the prophet,
[cf. vv. 2-3 above]	saying, "A voice of one	"A voice of one crying

crying out in the wilder-
ness: 'Make ready the
way of the Lord, make
straight his paths.'"

out in the wilderness:
'Make ready the way of
the Lord, make straight
his paths. Every valley
shall be filled, and every
mountain and hill shall
be brought low, and the
crooked places shall be
made straight, and the
rough ways shall be
made smooth, and all
flesh shall see the salvation of God.'"

The first task is to identify the basic literary relationship between the witnesses in terms of the Two-Source Hypothesis. In this case it is a simple task: We have three witnesses, after all, which means that we have a case of dependence on Mark. But there are a few interesting differences. First, both Matthew and Luke choose to place the prophecy from Isaiah 40:3 after the appearance of John, whereas Mark had placed it before John's manifestation in the desert. Mark's narrative placement conveys the sense of speed with which events unfold in the first chapters of his Gospel: Something is said, and immediately it occurs (though this word had actually been said many centuries before). In contrast, the relocation of the ancient prophecy after the present event has a more reflective quality, as if the evangelists were teaching the deeper meaning of, and divine plan behind, present events to their audiences.

Of greater interest are the adaptations that Luke makes. He provides a more precise temporal setting by locating John's work in a particular period designated by the reigns of the Roman emperor and prefect, the Jewish tetrarchs, and the high priests. Moreover, John is said to travel in all the region around the Jordan, which hints at a wider spread to his activity than Mark or Matthew allow. Finally, Luke extends the words of Isaiah the prophet to include not only verse 3 but also verses 4-5 of chapter 40. The themes present in this added material are familiar to us from the infancy narrative, where John and Jesus are both placed within a larger geopolitical framework, and their births portend a new moment in the salvation of the whole world. It is no accident that the longer passage of Isaiah that Luke quotes ends with precisely the same theme that Zechariah prophesied about John (1:76-79) and that Simeon and Anna prophesied about Jesus in the Temple after his birth (2:29, 32).

The Fourth Gospel frames the moment quite differently from the Synoptics:

> There was a man sent from God, whose name was John; he came for testimony, so that he might testify concerning the light, so that all might believe through him. That one was not the light, but (came) so that he might testify concerning the light. The true light that enlightens every man was coming into the world.
>
> . . . He said, "I am the voice of one crying in the wilderness: 'Make straight the way of the Lord,' just as Isaiah the prophet said" (John 1:6-9, 23).

John's primary role in this passage is not as a baptizer but as a witness who testifies to Jesus. In fact, we never *see* John baptizing anyone, and the epithet "Baptist" is never attached to him in this Gospel. Despite these rather dramatic differences, the Fourth Gospel shares some features with the Synoptics. John is baptizing, he is in the wilderness (1:25, 28), his baptism is linked to "making straight the way of the Lord," which implies behavioral conversion, and this activity is understood in light of Isaiah 40:3.[10]

On all of these points save the Isaiah reference, Josephus agrees. Thus by the criterion of multiple attestation, we can say that these core elements—John baptizes in the wilderness and this is connected to behavioral change—are historically reliable. In addition, Mark and the Fourth Gospel independently attest that John awaited an eschatological judgment, and we will see that Q adds further credibility to the historicity of this tradition.

The scene continues in Mark and Matthew:

Mark 1:5-6	**Matthew 3:4-6**
And the whole Judean region and all the Jerusalemites were going out to him, and they were being baptized by him in the Jordan river, confessing their sins in full. And John was clothed with camel's hair and a leather belt around his loins, and he ate locusts and wild honey.	[cf. vv. 5-6 below]
[cf. v. 5 above]	Now this John had his garment of camel's hair and a leather belt around his loins, while his food was locusts and wild honey. Then Jerusalem and all of Judea and all the surrounding region of the Jordan were going out to him, and they were being baptized in the Jordan River by him, confessing their sins in full.

[10] For later gospel parallels, see *Gos. Eb.* 1:3; *Gos. Heb.* 2:1; *Gos. Naz.* 2:1.

In this passage Mark comments on the number of people coming out to John for baptism and on John's appearance. The description of John's clothing is an explicit allusion to the prophet Elijah, who is described wearing exactly these garments in 2 Kings 1:8. Elijah was one of two or three figures in Jewish tradition who did not die but ascended to heaven (2 Kgs 2:1-14), and it was thought that his return would usher in the day of the Lord in a future time (Mal 3:23-24).[11] The continuation of the story is excluded by Luke, but that is not surprising. We have seen that Luke emphasizes the universal significance of John and Jesus, something he would be more likely to do if his own audience included Gentile Christians as well as Jewish Christians. The reference to Elijah might be unfamiliar to such an audience or might have too parochial a flavor, and so Luke omits it. Luke may also be distancing himself from some of the apocalyptic traditions that saw in Elijah's return the advent of the endtimes, since, as we saw in Chapter 2, he writes after the destruction of the First Jewish Revolt and has probably lived through disappointed messianic expectations.

One historically reliable datum in this account is the popularity of John, corroborated by Josephus. The singling out of Jerusalemites is not found in Josephus but is present in all Gospel sources. This may be a function of John's location near Jerusalem in the wilderness, but it also seems to suggest a correlation of some kind with the Temple and/or national identity. This would cohere both with the purifying nature of John's activity and with the eschatological claims he was making about the coming judgment of Israel.[12] It is interesting that Josephus uses sacrificial language to speak of John's baptism (it was important that the baptism "be acceptable [to God]"), thus drawing his own connection between John's activity and the Temple. Josephus also attests to the national scope of John's activity by his report of Herod Antipas's action and of the popular reaction to Herod's subsequent military defeat.

---

[11] There is no biblical tradition that predicts Elijah's return in advance of the messiah, but only in advance of the Lord. See J.A.T. Robinson, "The Baptism of John and the Qumran Community" and "Elijah, John and Jesus," *Twelve New Testament Studies* (London: SCM, 1962) 28–52; Morris M. Faierstein, "Why Do the Scribes Say That Elijah Must Come First?" *Journal of Biblical Literature* 100 (1981) 75–86; Dale C. Allison, "'Elijah Must Come First,'" *Journal of Biblical Literature* 103 (1984) 256–258; Joseph A. Fitzmyer, "More about Elijah Coming First," *Journal of Biblical Literature* 104 (1985) 295–296.

[12] John's wild diet would have precluded dietary transgressions, thus maintaining his purity in another way. See *Gos. Eb.* 3:2, where John is said to eat "raw honey that tastes like manna, like a pancake cooked with oil." This change transforms John into a vegetarian.

Vignette 3. The Preaching of John

Josephus does not tell us anything about John's preaching, apart from the rather banal summary that he "urged the Jews to practice virtue and justice toward one another and piety toward God." Contrast this to the fire-and-brimstone preaching we hear in the Synoptic Gospels:

Mark 1:7-8	Matthew 3:7-12	Luke 3:7-18
	But when he saw many of the Pharisees and Sadducees coming to his baptism, he said to them, "Spawn of snakes, who warned you to flee from the coming wrath? So produce fruit worthy of conversion and don't even think about saying to yourselves, 'We have as father Abraham.' For I say to you that God is able from these stones to raise up children to Abraham. Even now the ax is laid against the root of the trees; therefore every tree that does not produce good fruit is cut down and thrown into fire.	So he said to the crowds that were coming out to be baptized by him, "Spawn of snakes, who warned you to flee from the coming wrath? So produce fruits worthy of conversion and don't start saying to yourselves, 'We have as father Abraham.' For I say to you that God is able from these stones to raise up children to Abraham. And even now the ax is laid against the root of the trees; therefore every tree that does not produce good fruit is cut down and thrown into fire. And the crowds were asking him, saying, "What then shall we do?" And answering he said to them, "The one who has two cloaks, let him share with the one who has not, and the one who has food, let him do the same." And tax collectors also came to be baptized and they said to him, "Teacher, what must we do?" And he said to them, "Collect no

He proclaimed, saying,

"The one stronger than me is coming after me, of whom I am not worthy to stoop down and untie the thong of his sandals. I baptized you with water; he will baptize you in the Holy Spirit."

I baptize you in water for conversion, but he who comes after me is stronger than me, of whom I am not worthy to   carry the sandals;
   he will baptize you in the Holy Spirit and fire. His winnowing fork is in his hand and he will purge his threshing floor and gather his grain in the barn, while the chaff he will burn in an inextinguishable fire."

more than what has been assigned to you." Soldiers also were questioning him saying, "And we, what shall we do?" And he said to them, "Don't extort or shake down anyone and be satisfied with your pay." Now the people were in expectation and they were all considering in their hearts concerning John, whether perhaps he were the Christ; John answered saying to all, "I baptize you with water; but the one stronger than me is coming,
      of whom I am not worthy to   untie the thong of his sandals;
   he will baptize you in the Holy Spirit and fire; his winnowing fork is in his hand to purge his threshing floor and to gather the grain in his barn, while the chaff he will burn in an inextinguishable fire." So with many other exhortations, he preached the good news to the people.

The relationship of the three Gospels is a bit more complex than it was in Vignette 2. Here we have evidence of the double tradition in the first and last parts of the passage and of the triple tradition toward the end. You'll remember that the double tradition is explained in the Two-Source Hypothesis as a case of Matthean and Lukan reliance on Q, while the triple tradition is evidence of dependence on Mark. In addition, we have an expansion on John's preaching that is found only in Luke.

Let's begin with the Q material, since it dominates the passage. This is in fact the first of two large "Baptist blocks" of material in Q, with the other at Q 7:18-35 (Vignettes 7-9). In this passage the correspondences between Matthew and Luke are among some of the tightest in Q, suggesting that this material was fixed early on and is therefore relatively reliable.[13] Matthew and Luke differ in their designation of John's audience, but the words John preaches are identical.[14] The people are called "spawn of snakes," are told of a wrath so imminent that the ax has already been laid to the root of the trees (cf. Isa 10:33-34; 32:19), and are told that their ethnic identity as Jews alone is utterly irrelevant to their salvation. Harsh words indeed! The same harsh words continue in the Q material at the end of the passage: The one yet to come has a winnowing fork that he will use to separate good grain from chaff, and he will burn the chaff in an inextinguishable fire. It's hard to imagine how Luke could conclude with a summary that refers to these exhortations as "good news"!

If we look at the special material that Luke alone inserts between these raging critiques, however, we may find part of our answer. In Luke alone, three types of individuals approach John and ask for his advice about what they should do. John tells them to share their extra cloak and food, to collect only the required taxes, not to extort or shake down people, and to be content with their pay. These aren't entirely easy commands, but they're certainly not impossible, and by inserting them here Luke moderates the harsh eschatological message of John into a realizable ethical program. That is not to say that John never offered moral advice; in fact, it is likely that he did, for we have evidence that he had disciples and taught them at least how to fast and pray. But is this economic exhortation the kind of advice he offered? It is probably impossible to know.[15] We should also notice the diversity of the crowds that approach John: They include children of Abraham, tax collectors collaborating with the Roman government, and Roman (or possibly Herodian) soldiers themselves.

Another reason why Luke could call John's message good news is that those drawn to his message may by and large be identified as the good grain he is gathering to the threshing floor in preparation for the final winnowing. Granted, the harvester also gathers the chaff, but John's activity of preaching and baptizing is preparing the good grain for its reward.[16]

---

[13] Meier, *A Marginal Jew*, 2.28.

[14] The Fourth Gospel mentions that "the Jews from Jerusalem sent to him priests and Levites" (John 1:19; in *Gos. Eb.* 3:1 it is "the Pharisees and all Jerusalem").

[15] Thus Meier, *A Marginal Jew*, 2.42.

[16] Thus Robert L. Webb, *John the Baptizer and Prophet: A Socio-Historical Study*, JSNTSup 62 (Sheffield: JSOT Press, 1991) 277.

There is one passage in the vignette that is shared by all three Synoptic Gospels, and that is John's prophecy of his own status relative to that of the coming one. All three Gospels share the basic assertions that the coming one will be stronger than John, that John will be unworthy to carry or untie his sandals, and that both will baptize, but in different ways. However, Luke sets this up differently from the others, in that John professes these claims in response to the misperception that he himself might be the messiah.[17] Regardless of the narrative frame, the function of all these assertions is to deal with the awkward relationship of John and Jesus: John is first and popular, but Jesus is stronger and more significant. It is highly likely that John preached of a coming figure; we have only to note the presence of this theme in Mark, Q, and John and the kind of expectation Josephus attributes to the crowds around him. But whether that coming figure was to be identified with Jesus was the contested point, and, as we shall see, the Gospels themselves will later admit that John was not so sure. We see the evangelists trying to deal with the relative significance of the two figures here in Vignette 3, in the employment of Isaiah 40:3 in Vignette 2, and in the Lukan infancy narrative (Vignette 1). The very awkwardness of the problem recommends the historicity of John's claim that a greater figure had yet to come.[18]

Matthew and Luke make some modest alterations of their Markan source in this part of the vignette. They both speak of the baptism to come as one in "Holy Spirit and fire" rather than simply the "Holy Spirit," as in their source Mark; the additional term ties the passage in with the eschatological

---

[17] The Fourth Gospel provides an even more open-ended discussion of who John is in 1:19-28:

> And this is the testimony of John, when the Jews from Jerusalem sent to him priests and Levites so that they could ask him, "Who are you?" And he confessed and did not deny, but confessed, "I myself am not the Christ." And they asked him, "What then? Are you Elijah?" And he said, "I am not." "Are you the prophet?" And he answered, "No." They said then to him, "Who are you, so that we may have an answer for those who sent us. What do you say concerning yourself?" He said, "I am the voice of one crying in the wilderness: 'Make straight the way of the Lord,' just as Isaiah the prophet said." Now they had been sent from the Pharisees. And they questioned him and said to him, "So why are you baptizing if you are neither the Christ nor Elijah nor the prophet?" John answered them saying, "I baptize in water; among you stands one whom you do not know, the one who comes after me, of whom I am not worthy to untie the thong of his sandal." This happened in Bethany beyond the Jordan, where John was baptizing.

Note the correspondence of this passage with the Synoptic "sandal saying"; cf. Acts 13:25.

[18] The Fourth Gospel tries in its own way to explain the relationship of the two: "John testifies concerning him and cries out saying, 'This was he of whom I said, "The one who comes after me is ahead of me, because he was before me"'" (1:15; cf. 1:30, Vignette 4).

fire that will consume the chaff in the next verse. Matthew adds one phrase about John's baptism that reiterates the purpose of it ("water for conversion").

Vignette 4. The Baptism of Jesus

We discussed the next vignette back in Chapter 2 (pages 24–28), and there is no need to repeat the analysis here. It will be useful for us, though, to review the material and compare it with the Fourth Gospel.[19]

Mark 1:9-11	Matthew 3:13-17	Luke 3:21-23
And it was in those days that Jesus came from Nazareth of the Galilee	Then Jesus arrived from the Galilee to the Jordan, to John to be baptized by him. But John prevented him saying, "I need to be baptized by you, and you would come to me?" But Jesus answered and said to him, "Permit it now, for in this way it is fitting for us to fulfill all righteousness." Then he	Now it was when all the people had been baptized
and was baptized in the Jordan by John. And immediately as he was coming up from the water, he saw the heavens tearing and the Spirit	permitted him. And when Jesus was baptized immediately he came up from the water; and see, the heavens were opened [to him] and he saw the Spirit of God descend	and Jesus had been baptized, and was praying, the heaven was opened and the Holy Spirit descended on him in
like a dove coming down to him. And a voice was from the heavens, "You are my Son, the beloved; in you I am well pleased."	like a dove and come on him; and see, a voice from the heavens saying, "This is my son, the beloved, in whom I am well pleased."	bodily form like a dove, and a voice came from heaven, "You are my son the beloved, in you I am well pleased."

---

[19] See also Acts 1:21-22; 10:36-39; *Gos. Eb.* 4:1-8; *Gos. Heb.* 3.

Recall that Jesus is baptized by John without comment in Mark, while there is a lot of comment in Matthew trying to explain why this is necessary, and in Luke John is in prison when Jesus is baptized. In this progression we are watching as the early Church deals with the awkwardness of Jesus' relationship to John. The Fourth Gospel completes the trajectory. Like Luke's scene, John will not baptize Jesus, but unlike Luke's scene (or the other Synoptics, for that matter), John will be absolutely certain who Jesus is:

> On the next day he sees Jesus coming to him and says, "See, the Lamb of God who takes away the sin of the world. This is the one about whom I said, 'After me comes a man who is ahead of me, because he was before me. I myself did not know him, but so that he might be revealed to Israel—on account of this I came baptizing in water. And John testified, saying, "I saw the Spirit descending as a dove from heaven and it remained on him. I myself did not know him, but the one who sent me to baptize in water, that one said to me, 'The one on whom you see the Spirit descending and remaining, this one is the one baptizing in the Holy Spirit.' I myself have seen and have testified that this one is the son of God" (1:29-34).[20]

We probably need not reiterate how awkward it was for the early Church to admit that John baptized Jesus; simply witness the anxiety displayed in the emendations of the tradition. The fact that Jesus' first followers are former disciples of John in the Fourth Gospel reinforces the growing claim that Jesus was the greater figure (John 1:35-42). Yet none of the evangelists erases the story from the tradition, and so by the criteria of awkwardness and multiple attestation it seems likely that John did indeed baptize Jesus and that Jesus was a follower of John for a time.

---

[20] This passage is followed by an unparalleled account in which John's witness leads two of his followers to follow Jesus:

> The next day John was standing with two of his disciples and he looked at Jesus as he walked and says, "See, the lamb of God." And his two disciples heard him speaking and followed Jesus. Jesus turned around and, seeing them following says to them, "What do you seek?" They said to him, "Rabbi," which, when translated, means teacher, "where are you staying?" He says to them, "Come and see." They came, therefore, and saw where he was staying and stayed with him that day; for it was about the tenth hour. Andrew, the brother of Simon Peter, was one of the two who heard from John and followed him; this one found first his brother Simon and says to him, "We have found the Messiah," which is translated Christ. He led him to Jesus. Looking at him, Jesus said, "You are Simon the son of John, you shall be called Kephas," which is translated Peter/Rock (1:35-42).

Another criterion of historicity bears upon the baptism account, and that is the criterion of dissimilarity. Nowhere in Jewish tradition was baptism associated with the messiah or the endtimes, notwithstanding the interrogation of John by priests and Levites in the Fourth Gospel (1:19-28).[21] This is discontinuous with Jewish tradition and therefore more likely to be a historical innovation, at least of the evangelists' and perhaps of John's.

Vignette 5. John's Arrest

Jesus' ministry begins after the arrest of John in the Synoptic Gospels, yet in Mark and Matthew the story of his arrest and execution is postponed to a later point in the narrative, with just a passing reference to it before Jesus begins his work. Luke restores order to the narrative by recounting the arrest and its cause before Jesus' ministry begins, but he never returns to John to recount the story of his execution. For the sake of coherence, the two passages that treat the arrest in Mark and the two in Matthew are presented together below:

[21] There is also a tradition preserved in the Fourth Gospel that Jesus baptized, but since this is not corroborated in the Synoptics, we cannot analyze it with redaction criticism. The text itself indicates that Jesus likely did baptize, for a final redactor added the unusual phrase in 4:2 that contradicts the prior material (the denial is italicized below)! The passage anticipates material we will see in Vignette 6, namely, Jesus' use of the bridegroom metaphor when his disciples are compared unfavorably to John's:

> After this Jesus came and his disciples into Judean territory and he spent time with them there and baptized. And John was baptizing in Aenon near Salim, because there was much water there, and they came and were baptized; for John had not yet been thrown into the prison. So a debate happened between the disciples of John and a Jew concerning purification. And they came to John and said to him, "Rabbi, the one who was with you beyond the Jordan, to whom you testified, see this one baptizes and all are coming to him." John answered and said, "A man is not able to receive anything unless it has been given to him from heaven. You yourselves testify to me that I said that I am not the Christ, but that I have been sent before that one. The one who has the bride is the bridegroom; the friend of the bridegroom, who stands and hears him, rejoices with joy because of the voice of the bridegroom. Therefore this joy of mine has been made full. That one must increase, while I must diminish. The one who comes from above is above all; the one from the earth is from the earth and from the earth speaks. The one who comes from heaven is above all; he testifies to the things that he has seen and heard, yet no one receives his testimony. The one who receives his testimony has certified that God is true. For the one whom God sent speaks the words of God, for it is not by measure that he gives the Spirit. The father loves the son and has given everything into his hand (cf. *Gos. Thom.* 61:3). The one who believes in the son has eternal life; while the one who does not believe in the son will not see life, but the wrath of God rests with him." So when Jesus knew that the Pharisees heard that Jesus was making and baptizing more disciples than John—*although Jesus himself was not baptizing but his disciples*—he left Judea and departed again to the Galilee (John 3:22–4:3).

Mark 1:14-15 + 6:17-18	Matthew 4:12-17 + 14:3-4	Luke 3:19-20
After the handing over of John,　Jesus came into the Galilee,	Now when he heard that John had been handed over, he withdrew into the Galilee. And leaving Nazareth he went and dwelt in Capernaum by the sea, in the region of Zebulun and Naphtali; so the word spoken by Isaiah the prophet could be fulfilled, saying, "Land of Zebulun and land of Naphtali, the road to the sea, beyond the Jordan, Galilee of the Gentiles. The people sitting in darkness have seen a great light, and for those sitting in the region and shadow of death, light has dawned on them." From then	
proclaiming the good news of God and saying, "The time has been completed and the kingdom of God is at hand; convert and believe in the good news." For he, that is Herod, sent forth and seized John and bound him　　　in prison on account of Herodias, the wife of Philip his brother, because he had married her. For John had said to Herod, "It is not permitted for you to have the wife of your brother."	Jesus began to proclaim 　　　　　and to say, "Convert; for the kingdom of the heavens is near." For　　Herod　　had seized John and bound [him] and put him away in prison on account of Herodias, the wife of Philip his brother, 　　　for John had said to him, "It is not permitted for you to have her."	But Herod the tetrarch, who had been reproved by him concerning Herodias the wife of his brother and concerning all of the evil things Herod had done, added even this to them all and locked up John in prison.

The material on the arrest is present in the triple tradition, but in this case Matthew and especially Luke have altered the tradition quite a bit. Note that Mark presents John's arrest and Jesus' appearance as a simple sequence, whereas Matthew introduces a note of causality or intention; Jesus heard that John had been handed over, so he withdraws to the Galilee and then to the seaside town of Capernaum. This move is presented as the fulfillment of prophecy, much as we saw in Vignette 2 (Isa 8:23; LXX 9:1). When Jesus does appear, his message is abbreviated in Matthew and made to cohere precisely with the message of the Baptist in Matthew 3:2. The arrest scene itself is cleaned up; Matthew adds a verb for the actual imprisonment, deletes the unnecessary phrase "because he had married her," and drops the redundant reference to "the wife of your brother" at the end of the passage. Matthew clearly wants to improve on the story, but beyond that and his emphasis on the fulfillment of prophecy it is difficult to discern any further redactional interests. Luke also cleans up the story by summarizing it and thereby eliminating the redundancies. He also moves the narrative of the arrest up, placing it before Jesus' baptism, genealogy, temptation, and public manifestation. Thus all that is public about Jesus' adult life takes place while John is bound in prison. This has the effect of giving Jesus the entire stage, thus manifesting his superiority. Luke has afforded himself this luxury because of the diptych in the infancy narrative. There stories of John and Jesus were presented in tandem, but the message was ultimately the same: these men are related, but Jesus is superior.

The passage is partly historical, but much of it is likely legendary (and we will encounter this in the completion of the story in Vignette 11 as well). Herod Antipas certainly arrested John; Josephus provides the corroborating witness. But the reason given by the Synoptic evangelists is not as plausible. To begin with, Herod did marry Herodias, and she had been married to one of Herod's half brothers, but it was not Philip but a sibling named Herod. This Herod and Herodias had a daughter Salome, who married Philip, the half-brother of Antipas (see Josephus, *Ant.* 18 §136). So Mark has gotten his facts confused. We will save the other errors for Vignette 11; suffice it to say for now that the details of Mark's account are unreliable, and the other Synoptic authors followed Mark into some or all of that error (note that Luke does not specify the brother's name).

Vignette 6. Comparison of the Disciples' Practices

The next vignette occurs while John is still in prison. This is not an irrelevant detail, for when the disciples of John approach Jesus to question his practice, he can afford to symbolize himself as the bridegroom because he is still a free man:

Mark 2:18-22	**Matthew 9:14-17**	**Luke 5:33-39**
And John's disciples and the Pharisees were fasting; and they come and say to him, "Why do John's disciples and the disciples of the Pharisees fast, but your disciples do not fast?" And Jesus said to them, "The sons of the bridal chamber cannot fast while the bridegroom is with them, can they? As long as they have the bridegroom with them, they cannot fast. The days will come when the bridegroom is taken away from them, and then they will fast in that day.	Then the disciples of John come to him, saying, "Why do we and the Pharisees fast [much], but your disciples do not fast?" And Jesus said to them, "The sons of the bridal chamber cannot mourn as long as the bridegroom is with them, can they?	*[Scribes and Pharisees speaking]* So they said to him, "The disciples of John fast often and pray, likewise those of the Pharisees as well. Yet yours eat and drink." And Jesus said to them, "You cannot make the sons of the bridal chamber fast as long as the bridegroom is with them, can you?
	The days will come when the bridegroom is taken away from them, and then they will fast.	The days will come when the bridegroom is taken away from them, then they will fast in those days.
No one sews a patch of unshrunken cloth on an old garment;	Now no one puts a patch of unshrunken cloth on an old garment;	And he told them a parable also: "No one tears a patch from a new garment and puts it on an old garment; otherwise,
otherwise, the fullness takes up from it, the new from the old, and a worse tear occurs. And no one puts new wine into old wineskins; otherwise, the wine will burst the skins, and the wine is lost and the wineskins, but new wine into new wineskins."	for the fullness of it takes up from the garment and a worse tear occurs. Neither do they put new wine into old wineskins; otherwise, the skins burst, and the wine is spilled and the wineskins are lost; but they put new wine into new wineskins, and both are protected."	he will tear the new, and the patch from the new will not match the old. And no one puts new wine into old wineskins; otherwise, the new wine will burst the skins, and it will be spilled and the wineskins lost; but new wine must be put into new wineskins. And no one who drinks the old wishes the new; for he says, 'The old is good.'"

This vignette is a case of the triple tradition. The bridegroom saying is set up differently in each Gospel, although in each case the disciples of John and the Pharisees are paired by virtue of their fasting practice and are contrasted (unfavorably?) with Jesus' followers.[22] In Mark and Matthew, the disciples of John and the Pharisees are further linked because together they question Jesus, while in Luke the disciples of John are referenced but do not question Jesus.

We need not spend time on the bridegroom sayings, interesting as they are, for they have more to do with Jesus than with John, and they serve to warrant a change in Christian practice after Jesus' death.[23] These issues don't necessarily render the entire passage anachronistic, however. It is quite possible that the story first circulated as a legitimate point of contrast or debate between Jesus' disciples and those of the Baptist. After all, fasting was a time-honored act of piety, and so anyone breaking from the practice would have some explaining to do. The fact that the passage authorizes a change of practice after Jesus' death indicates that Jesus' disciples did not fast before, which makes the controversy plausible. The phrase "disciples of the Pharisees" is an odd phrase, unattested in Josephus until the end of the first century c.e., when the power of the group was increasing. The original event was therefore more likely a simple contrast between the celebratory ministry of Jesus and the ascetic ministry of John (see also Vignette 9).

Luke alone says that the contrast in practice is about prayer as well as fasting, and so we are not surprised that Luke picks up the prayer contrast a bit later in his Gospel. In this case, however, there is no opposition between John and Jesus. Jesus' disciples would like to learn to pray, and ask Jesus to teach them as John has taught his disciples (Luke 11:1-4):

> And it happened that when he was praying in a certain place, as he ceased, one of his disciples said to him, "Lord, teach us to pray, as John also taught his disciples." He said to them, "When you pray, say: 'Father, hallowed be your name, may your kingdom come, give us for today our daily bread, and release us from our sins, for we ourselves release all who are indebted to us; and do not bring us into temptation.'"

Matthew, of course, shares the prayer in 6:5-8 but not the narrative set-up.[24] Only in Luke is the prayer prompted by a comparison with the Baptist.

---

[22] John is not mentioned in reference to the fasting question in the *Gospel of Thomas*; see *logia* 6, 14 (cf. Matt 6:16-18).

[23] It is interesting that the independent Fourth Gospel also refers to Jesus as the bridegroom but places this analogy on the lips of John himself. See John 3:29-30, translated in Vignette 4 above; see also *Gos. Thom.* 47, 104.

[24] Cf. *Gos. Thom.* 6, 14.

This unique Lukan introduction is interesting; it shows Jesus at prayer—a common motif in this Gospel—and thus whatever he teaches his disciples will not be John's prayer but his own.

In terms of the historicity of the passage, the introduction is only found in one Gospel, so it fails the criterion of multiple attestation. We do have evidence from multiple sources *that* John had disciples, and they certainly prayed. A prayer practice would cohere with John's message of purity, conversion, and the coming of God. Furthermore, the motifs in the prayer Jesus teaches provide another point of coherence, insofar as they include themes found in the Baptist's preaching (the coming of God's kingdom, the just distribution of resources, the release from sin).

Vignette 7. Messengers from the Imprisoned John

This vignette and the next two form the second major "Baptist block" of material in Q. If the first block dealt with traditions of John's own preaching (Vignette 3), this block deals with Jesus' preaching about John. As in the earlier block, the narrative framing is unique to each redactor, but the shared Q material is remarkably similar:

Matthew 11:1-6	Luke 7:18-23
And when Jesus had finished instructing his twelve disciples, he passed over from there to teach and proclaim in their cities. Now when John heard in the jail about the deeds of the Christ, he sent (word) through his disciples and said to him, "Are you he who is coming or shall we wait for someone else?"	And John's disciples reported to him about all these things. And John called two of his disciples to him and sent them to the Lord saying, "Are you he who is coming or shall we wait for another?" And when the men had come to him, they said, "John the Baptist sent us to you saying, 'Are you he who is coming or shall we wait for another?'" In that hour he cured many from diseases and sufferings and unclean spirits, and to the blind he granted to see.
And answering, Jesus said to them, "Go and report to John what you hear and see; the blind regain sight and the lame walk, lepers are cleansed and the deaf hear, and the dead are	And answering, he said to them, "Go and report to John what you have seen and heard; the blind regain sight, the lame walk, lepers are cleansed and the deaf hear, the dead are

raised and the poor have the good news proclaimed to them; and blessed is the one who is not scandalized by me."

raised, the poor have the good news proclaimed to them; and blessed is the one who is not scandalized by me."

Matthew explicitly mentions that John is in jail when he hears about Jesus' deeds; Luke does not repeat this, but since John was imprisoned before Jesus' baptism, there is nowhere else he could be (Luke 3:19-20).[25] Both passages point to the role of John's disciples in transmitting messages between Jesus and the prison where John is held. The core of the passage is the Q saying of Jesus, in which he defends the assertion that he is the one who is coming by virtue of his deeds. Those deeds are portrayed as consistent with Jewish prophecy, though in Jewish Scripture they are not associated with the messiah (Isa 35:4; 29:20; 61:1-2). The major addition to Luke simply renders the deeds visible to John's disciples at that very moment, so that their report can be firsthand.

This story is a bit awkward from a Christian vantage point—of *course* Jesus is the coming one in the eyes of the evangelists. But John's prophecy of fire and brimstone is not exactly fulfilled in the cure of disease and the spread of good news, so his question is apropos. Moreover, John never responds to Jesus.[26] The evangelists probably wish he would have, for then they would have incontrovertible proof to present to John's disciples and the rest of their audience. These awkward elements, and the apparently early Q tradition (early by virtue of its lack of divergence between Matthew and Luke), point toward the historicity of the inquiry, even acknowledging the lack of multiple attestation.

---

[25] There is a passage in the Fourth Gospel that mentions John in proximity to Jesus' signs or healings: "And he went again across the Jordan to the place where John was first baptizing and remained there. And many came to him and said, 'John performed no sign, but everything that John said concerning this man is true.' And many believed in him there" (John 10:40-42). In another passage Jesus castigates the audience for failing to recognize him either by John's testimony or by his own signs:

"If I testify concerning myself, my witness is not true; there is another person who testifies concerning me, and I know that the testimony that he testifies concerning me is true. You sent (people) to John, and he testified to the truth; though I do not accept the testimony according to man, but I say these things so that you may be saved. That man was the burning and shining lamp, and you were willing for a time to rejoice in his light. I have the testimony greater than that of John; for the works that the father has given me so that I might complete them, these works which I do, testify concerning me that the father has sent me. And the father who has sent me has himself testified concerning me. You have never heard his voice nor seen his form, nor do you have his word remaining in you, because you do not believe in the one whom he sent" (John 5:31-38).

[26] Meier, *A Marginal Jew*, 2.130–136.

Vignette 8. Jesus' Testimony About John

Q continues seamlessly in both Matthew and Luke as Jesus goes on to describe John the Baptist to his audience. There are at least three components to this testimony: who John is (cf. *Gos. Thom.* 78), a teaching on the kingdom of God (cf. *Gos. Thom.* 46), and a description of those who accepted and rejected John. We follow Matthew's order below, which treats the first two elements in chapter 11 and the last in chapter 21 (Vignette 15).

Matthew 11:7-15	**Luke 7:24-30 + 16:16**
As they were going away Jesus began to speak to the crowds about John: "What did you go out into the desert to look at? A reed shaken by the wind? But what did you go out to see—a man clothed in soft (things)? See, those wearing soft things are in the houses of kings. But what did you go out to see? A prophet? Yes, I tell you, and one even greater than a prophet. This is the one about whom it is written, 'See, I send my messenger before you, who will prepare your way before you.' Truly, I tell you: There has not arisen from those born of women one greater than John the Baptist; but the least one in the kingdom of the heavens is greater than he. From the days of John the Baptist until now the kingdom of the heavens has been constrained and violent people take it by force. For all the prophets and the law prophesied until John; and if you wish to accept it, this man is Elijah, the one who is to come. He who has ears, let him hear."	When the messengers of John had left, he began to speak to the crowds about John; "What did you go out into the desert to look at? A reed shaken by the wind? But what did you go out to see—a man clothed in soft garments? See, those who are in glorious clothing and luxury are in palaces. But what did you go out to see? A prophet? Yes, I tell you, and one even greater than a prophet. This is the one about whom it is written, 'See, I send my messenger before you, who will prepare your way before you. I tell you: There is no one greater of those born of women than John. But the least one in the kingdom of God is greater than he.
[cf. 21:31-32, Vignette 15]	[cf. 16:16, below]
	[7:29] And when all the people and the tax collectors heard this, they justified God, having been baptized with the baptism of John; but the Pharisees and the lawyers rejected the purpose of God for themselves, not having been baptized by him.

16:16: "The law and the prophets were
until John; from then, the good news of
the kingdom of God is proclaimed and
everyone takes it by force."

Even within the first two units identified above, the component sayings of
Jesus likely circulated separately before being threaded together in this
passage. Insofar as both Matthew and Luke follow the Q order, both contrast John favorably with those who wear soft things, namely, the very king
who has imprisoned John. Jesus affirms John without reserve. The association of John with the guiding angel of Exodus 23:20 and the messenger of
Malachi 3:1 (cf. Mark 1:2), along with the elaborate formula "This is the
one about whom it is written" and the transformation of scriptural citations
to point to "you" (that is, Jesus), indicates a process of reflection in the
early Church rather than Jesus' likely reflection on the Baptist. But the af-
firmations of John contained before and after the scriptural quotations do
not betray such reflection, and so are likely historical.[27] As we have seen, it
is the later Church that nuances this favorable portrayal so that Jesus' superior status is clear.

The material in Q 16:16 is treated here because this is where Matthew
locates it. John Meier believes it does not belong to the second major
Baptist block of Q, and that differences in wording between Matthew's
and Luke's versions raise the possibility that it is not a Q saying at all.[28]
Matthew has the unique and clear statement that John *is* Elijah (see his
similar statement in 17:13); this is found in no other Gospel and under-
scores Matthew's interest in demonstrating that prophecy has been fulfilled. Moreover, Matthew's placement of this passage here in the Q block
demonstrates his concern to collate similar material. Both Gospels (and
therefore Q?) agree that John stands at the fulcrum point between the law
and the prophets on one hand and the kingdom of God on the other, and
that the kingdom of God has generated violent opposition. Beyond that,
there is great debate among redaction critics about this brief and obscure
teaching.

Vignette 9. Jesus and John vs. This Generation

Vignette 9 represents the third section of a coherent Q Baptist block in
Matthew and Luke.

---

[27] Meier, *A Marginal Jew*, 2.137–144.
[28] Meier, *A Marginal Jew*, 2.156–157.

Matthew 11:16-19	Luke 7:31-35
"But to what shall I compare this generation? It is like children sitting in the marketplaces calling out to others saying, "We played the flute for you and you did not dance, we sang a dirge and you did not mourn. For John came neither eating nor drinking, and they say: 'He has a demon.' The son of man came eating and drinking, and they say, 'See, a glutton and wine-drinker, a friend of tax collectors and sinners.' But wisdom is justified by her deeds."	"Therefore to what shall I compare the men of this generation, and what are they like? They are like children sitting in a marketplace and calling out to each other who say, "We played the flute for you and you did not dance, we sang a dirge and you did not weep. For John the Baptist has come neither eating bread nor drinking wine, and you say: 'He has a demon.' The son of man has come eating and drinking, and you say, 'See, a glutton and wine-drinker, a friend of tax collectors and sinners.' But wisdom is justified by all her children."

Redaction criticism will again not get us very far, because our redactors have not adapted the Q material on John very much. Luke adds greater specificity to Jesus' initial rhetorical question and also specifies the exact food and drink from which John abstained. The final saying about wisdom bears signs of redaction in Matthew, who may choose the term "deeds" to close off the Q Baptist block (see Vignette 7). Luke by this logic follows Q in letting the "children" form a kind of inclusion just for this vignette.[29]

Once again, the criterion of awkwardness helps to establish, even in the absence of multiple attestation, that this saying is historical. Why in the world would the early Church preserve a saying that equates John and Jesus, and worse yet calls John a demoniac and their own leader a glutton and drunkard, unless the saying had a strong claim to authenticity?[30] Josephus attests that John's martyrdom gave him added popularity, so it is unlikely that the demoniac charge circulated after he had been hallowed by execution.

Vignette 10. Herod Confuses Jesus and John

The next vignette introduces the story of John's execution. In Mark and Matthew, a longer account of the execution follows the introduction (Vignette 11), whereas Luke allows this brief passage to carry the full weight of the execution report.

[29] Meier, *A Marginal Jew*, 2.153.
[30] Meier, *A Marginal Jew*, 2.144–151.

Mark 6:14-16	**Matthew 14:1-2**	**Luke 9:7-9**
King Herod heard of it, for his name had become known, and they were saying, "John the Baptizer has been raised from the dead, and because of this the powers are at work in him." But others were saying, "It is Elijah"; and others were saying, "It is a prophet, like one of the prophets." But when Herod heard, he said,	At that time Herod the tetrarch heard the report about Jesus,	Herod the tetrarch heard about everything that had been done and was perplexed because it was said by some that John had been raised from the dead,
		by some that Elijah had appeared, by others that some prophet of old had arisen. But
"The one whom I beheaded, John, this one has been raised."	and said to his courtiers, "This one is John the Baptist, he is raised from the dead and because of this the powers are at work in him."	Herod said, "John I beheaded; who is this one about whom I hear these things?" And he sought to see him.

The account of Herod's confusion is part of the triple tradition; Matthew and Luke depend on Mark and abbreviate his account each in their own way. Matthew attaches the correct title to Herod, deletes any reported confusion about Jesus' identity, and puts on Herod's lips rather than the crowd's the attribution of power to resurrection. Luke likewise corrects Herod's title, but he also deletes any correlation of resurrection with Jesus' powers and smoothes the narrative by telling us that Herod heard the rumors that were circulating (Mark juxtaposes the rumors with Herod's thoughts but doesn't connect them). The nature of the changes recommends the thesis that Matthew and Luke cleaned up Mark. Note also that Luke refrains from using the epithet "the Baptist," which seems to be a redactional preference of his (see Vignette 8; in Vignette 7 the epithet appears, but on the lips of John's disciples, and he is "John the son of Zechariah" rather than John the Baptist in Luke's column of Vignette 2).

The historicity of this passage is questionable, as is the account of Herod's execution. To begin with, we have only one source reporting the story, namely Mark; the others merely depend on him. The plausibility of an accurate report is unlikely on the basis of the eyewitness criterion; how might any of the evangelists have discovered what Herod was thinking? In addition, the passage plays a rather obvious role in the literary structure of the Gospels, though that role differs somewhat from Gospel to Gospel. In Mark and Matthew, it sets up the account of the execution of John and anticipates the disciples' report of rumors about Jesus' identity (Mark 8:27-30; Matt 16:13-16). In Mark, the entire Baptist interlude (Vignettes 10-11) interrupts the sending and return of the Twelve, thus "buying time" at the level of the story for the disciples to be out and about; Luke uses Vignette 10 in the same way.

Vignette 11. Herod's Execution of John

Mark and Matthew continue directly to recount a story of the execution of John.

Mark 6:19-29	Matthew 14:5-12
And Herodias had a grudge against him, and wanted to kill him, but she was unable; for Herod feared John, knowing him to be a righteous and holy man, and he protected him, and when he heard him, he was very much at a loss, and yet he listened to him gladly. And a suitable time came when Herod on his birthday gave a banquet for his courtiers and commanders and for the leaders of Galilee. When his daughter Herodias came in and danced, she pleased Herod and those reclining at the table. The king said to the girl, "Ask me for whatever you wish, and I will give it to you." And he swore to her much, "Whatever you ask me, I will give you, even half of my kingdom." And she went out and said to her mother, "What should I ask for?" She replied, "The head of John the Baptizer." And immediately she came in with haste to the king and asked, saying, "I want at once for you to give me on a platter the head of John the Baptist." Though deeply grieved, the king did not want to refuse her because of the oaths and the recliners. And immediately the king	And [Herod] wanted to kill him, but feared the crowd, because they held him to be a prophet.

But when the birthday of Herod came,

the daughter of Herodias danced in their midst and pleased Herod,   so that he promised with oaths to give her whatever she might ask.

But she was prompted by her mother;

"Give me," she says, "here on a platter the head of John the Baptist." Though   grieved, the king commanded it be given, because of his oaths and those reclining with (him), and he   sent |

sent forth a soldier, commanding him to bring his head. And he went and beheaded him in the prison and brought his head on a platter, and gave it to the girl, and the girl brought it to her mother. And when his disciples heard, they came and took his body and laid it in a tomb.	and beheaded John in the prison. And his head was brought on a platter and given to the girl, and she brought (it) to her mother. And his disciples approached and took his body and buried it and came and reported (it) to Jesus.

A quick visual survey illustrates the literary dependence of Matthew on Mark. But it is interesting to note how much Matthew deletes. Gone are the redundancies (Herod's confusion at the beginning of Mark was already apparent in Vignette 10) and the additional details and color (for example, the list of party guests, the dialogue between Herodias and her daughter). Matthew also corrects the major historical inaccuracy in the Markan story: Herod married a Herodias and had a daughter Salome with her, but Mark presents the *daughter* as "Herodias." Now it is often the case that stories grow over time, so we might expect the longer account to be later. It is important, though, to look not only at length but also at the direction of changes to determine which came first. It is easier to explain why Matthew dropped these pieces of Mark than to explain why Mark introduced certain errors into his account. The redactional interest of Matthew in this passage seems to be simply to clean it up. Luke drops it entirely, though we cannot know whether he did that to sweep out the legendary material or to de-emphasize the Baptist.

This story does not stand up well to the criteria of historicity, apart from the core tradition that Herod executed the Baptist, a fact confirmed in all our sources. The dance of Herod's daughter is in only one independent witness, Mark. The names of the characters are confused if compared against Josephus's account of Herod's family. Mark implies that John was executed in Galilee, while Josephus reports that the event took place at the fortress of Machaerus, east of the Dead Sea. The story suffers from the eyewitness criterion as Vignette 10 did: Who would have seen this event to report it to the Baptist's disciples and thence to Jesus? Matthew's account even seems to acknowledge the transmission problem by adding the phrase that John's disciples reported the event to Jesus, as if to claim that there is indeed a chain of tradition here. We might also mention the criterion of discontinuity, which, like the criterion of eyewitness testimony, is relevant for its absence. That is, this story is so similar to other accounts in the Jewish Scriptures that it appears to have been crafted out of them. The most likely analogue is the story in 1 Kings, where the prophet Elijah goes head to head with King Ahab and his notorious wife Jezebel (19:1-2; 21:17-26). Is it any surprise at this point that a story about Elijah the prophet might provide a model for a story about the Baptist? The two interface constantly in the Gospel texts—and we are not yet done with the allusions! There are also literary criteria within the Gospels that make the historicity of the story unlikely: there is some logic to the placement of the tale, but by and large it interrupts the forward progress of the story with a flashback and is not well integrated into the surrounding plot apart from serving both as a literary foil to Jesus' style of leadership and as a foreshadowing of Jesus' own death.

Given all of this skepticism about the historicity of the story, there is one interesting coincidence that should be mentioned. Josephus reports that Herodias was responsible, in a very indirect way, for John's death. When Herod Antipas decided to marry her, he had to divorce his first wife, who was the daughter of the Nabatean king Aretas IV. This affront, combined with territorial disputes, led to the battle in which Aretas wiped out Herod's army, and this catastrophe, Josephus reports, was attributed in some people's eyes to divine vengeance for Herod's execution of the Baptist (see Chapter 1). It is a much more circuitous chain of causation than Mark's simple account of jealousy and revenge!

Vignette 12. Jesus Mistaken for John

The next Baptist vignette takes up a question about Jesus' identity that we first saw in Vignette 10:

Mark 8:27-30	Matthew 16:13-20	Luke 9:18-21
And Jesus went out and his disciples into the villages of Caesarea Philippi; and on the way he asked his disciples, saying to them, "Who do men say that I am?" And they spoke to him saying, "John the Baptist, and others Elijah, and others that (you are) one of the prophets."	And when Jesus came into the region of Caesarea Philippi, he asked his disciples, saying, "Who do men say that the son of man is?" And they spoke: "Some John the Baptist, and others Elijah, and others Jeremiah or one of the prophets."	And it happened that as he was praying alone, the disciples were with him, and he asked them, saying, "Who do the crowds say that I am?" And they answered saying, "John the Baptist, and others Elijah, and others that some prophet from of old has been raised."

And he asked them, "And you, who do you say that I am?" Peter answered and says to him, "You are the Christ."	He says to them, "And you, who do you say that I am?" And Simon Peter answered and said to him, "You are the Christ, the son of the living God." And Jesus replied, saying to him, "Blessed are you, Simon Bar-Jonah, for flesh and blood have not revealed to you but my father who is in the heavens. And so I say to you that you are Peter, and on this rock I will build my church and the gates of Hades will not overpower it. I will give you the keys of the king-dom of the heavens, and whatever you bind on earth will be bound in the heavens, and what-ever you untie on earth will be untied in the heavens."	And he spoke to them, "And you, who do you say that I am?" Peter answered and said, "the Christ of God."
And he rebuked them to speak about him to no one.	Then he ordered the disciples to tell no one that he was the Christ.	And he rebuked them and in-structed (them) to tell this to no one.

Vignette 10 introduced us to the speculation about Jesus' identity. In that earlier account, the association of Jesus with a resurrected Baptist is made by anonymous people and Herod in Mark, by Herod alone in Matthew, and by the anonymous people alone in Luke. Here Jesus asks his disciples to tell him what people are saying, and once again we hear about the ru-mors and speculation. All three of our accounts this time concur on the proposed identifications of Jesus: he is John the Baptist, he is Elijah, or he is one of the other prophets. The interfaces abound! But the purpose of this passage is not to emphasize the confusion of an unworthy leader, as we saw in Vignette 10; rather, it is to underscore the clear insight of a worthy disciple. Peter confesses that Jesus is more than these other figures, that he is in fact the messiah/Christ (Mark), the Christ, the son of the living God (Matthew), or the Christ of God (Luke), after which Jesus commands the disciples not to report this.[31] This is a clear case of the triple tradition—Matthew and Luke depend on Mark.

The redactors' fingerprints can be lifted fairly easily. The narrative set-ups differ across the board, as we have come to expect. Note that Matthew and Luke clean up the rather confused syntax of Mark ("And Jesus went out *and his disciples* into the villages of Caesarea Philippi"). Luke goes a step beyond grammatical grooming: he drops the geographic notation and sets the passage instead in a framework of prayer, a motif that dominates many of his editorial changes (recall Vignettes 1 [the infancy narrative] and 4 [the baptism]). Matthew's characteristic tendency to emphasize the fulfillment of the law and the prophets is borne out here by the additional reference to Jeremiah (recall Vignettes 4 [the baptism] and 5 [the arrest]). Matthew also adds a long section that singles out Peter as the "rock of the church"; note also that he alone combines the Hebrew name Simon with the Greek name Peter.

What we are left with is a single witness to the tradition that Jesus was confused with John. But the criterion of multiple attestation in this case must take us further afield because Vignette 12 is not the only passage in which this confusion occurs. We have already seen that Herod heard similar rumors, and while we have every reason to doubt the authenticity of that particular claim, we need not discard the datum that rumors were circulating. Many of our vignettes betray some confusion about the relative status and expected roles of John and Jesus, and together these witness to the awkward problem that Jesus' identity was confused and contested by strangers, enemies, *and* friends. Moreover, we can advance the thesis that this confusion continued into the evangelists' day on the basis of one of our criteria of historicity: hortatory passages indicate behaviors. If our evangelists must spill a lot of ink to tell us that Jesus is greater than and not equal to John, then it is likely they are still countering rumors to the contrary. To some extent, the Gospels themselves contribute to the confusion, for they seek to link these very different charismatic figures.

---

[31] Peter confesses Jesus to be the Holy One of God in the Fourth Gospel (John 6:67-71). See also John 1:19-28, where John himself refutes that he is the messiah, Elijah, or a prophet.

Vignette 13. John and Elijah

Just after Peter's climactic confession, Jesus takes Peter and two other disciples up a mountain and is transfigured before their eyes (Mark 9:2-10 *par.* Matt 17:1-9 *par.* Luke 9:28-36). Moses and Elijah appear with him, but they do not gleam as he does. As Jesus and his followers are coming back down the mountain, Mark and Matthew report the following dialogue:

Mark 9:11-13	Matthew 17:10-13
And they asked him, saying, "Why do the scribes say that 'Elijah must come first?'" And he said to them, "Indeed, Elijah is coming first to restore all things. And how then is it written that the son of man will suffer many things and be treated with contempt? But I say to you that Elijah has come, and they did to him whatever they wished, just as it is written about him."	And the disciples asked him, saying, "Why, then, do the scribes say that 'Elijah must come first?" And he answered, saying, "Indeed, Elijah comes and will restore all things; but I say to you that Elijah has already come, and they did not know him but did to him whatever they wished; and in this way also the son of man is about to suffer at their hands." Then the disciples understood that he was speaking to them about John the Baptist.

Matthew depends on Mark in this passage, but he has made some changes. To begin with, he cleans up what appears to be an illogical sequence in Mark: Elijah is coming / son of man will suffer / Elijah has come and has suffered. Matthew's version moves the prophecy of the suffering son of man to the end, thus removing the interruption. It is now clear that Elijah's fate anticipates the fate of the son of man. It is not only grammatical obscurity that Matthew clears, but he also takes away any question about the identity of this "Elijah." He clearly states that the Baptist is Elijah *redivivus*, an equation he also made baldly in Vignette 8. In Mark, a messiah who tries to hide himself witnesses to his Elijah-precursor obliquely; in Matthew, a more open messiah identifies his Elijah-precursor by name. Matthew's redactional interest in this passage is to present Jesus more clearly as Messiah and to defend that identification by making John the messianic forerunner.

The criteria of historicity will not get us very far with this passage. Only one independent source attests it. Although we have multiple sources that tie John to Elijah, this association has no necessary connection to the relationship between John and Jesus. After all, it was not part of Jewish speculation that Elijah would return before the messiah; Elijah was simply supposed to return before the day of the Lord (Mal 3:23-24).[32] Our vignette actually solves a few problems. To the concern that the day of the Lord could not occur unless Elijah came first, the passage answers that Elijah has come. As for the belief that Elijah was not expected to appear in conjunction with the messiah, the disciples' innocent question offers the opposite reading of Jewish Scripture. To the concern that Jesus might not be the messiah because no prophecy in Jewish Scripture said the messiah would suffer, this passage predicts that Elijah and the messiah will share precisely that fate. There is so much theological explanation in this passage, in fact, that it appears to be more the product of the early Church than of a historical event. It is so continuous with later Church teaching that it fails the criterion of discontinuity.

Vignette 14. Jesus' Authority and John's Authority

If the last vignette tried to establish Jesus' superiority over John through the theological reflection of the early Church, the present vignette seems to place them on an equal plane:

Mark 11:27-33	Matthew 21:23-27	Luke 20:1-8
And they came again into Jerusalem. And as he was walking around in the Temple,	And when he came into the Temple,	And it happened one day that he was teaching the people in the Temple and proclaiming the good news,
the chief priests and the scribes and the elders came to him and said to him, "By what authority do you do these things? Or who has given you this power so that you can do these things?" And Jesus said to them, "I will ask you one question, and answer me,	the chief priests and the elders of the people approached him while he was teaching, saying, "By what authority do you do these things? And who has given you this power?" And answering, Jesus said to them, "And I will ask you one question, and if you tell me	the chief priests and the scribes together with the elders stood near and spoke saying to him, "Tell us by what authority you do these things, or who it is who gave you this power." And answering, he said to them, "And I will ask you a question, and you tell me:

[32] See the Bibliography at note 11, page 53.

and I will tell you by what authority I do these things. The baptism of John— was it from heaven or from men?" And they reasoned among themselves saying, "If we say, 'from heaven,' he will say 'Why then did you not believe him?' But shall we say, 'from men?'"—they feared the crowd; for all held John to be truly a prophet. And answering to Jesus they say, "We do not know."

And Jesus says to them, "Neither do I tell you by what authority I do these things."

I will tell you by what authority I do these things. The baptism of John, where was it from—from heaven or from men?" And they reasoned with one another saying, "If we say, 'from heaven,' he will say, to us, 'Why then did you not believe him?' If we say, 'from men' we fear the crowd; for all hold John to be a prophet." And answering to Jesus they said, "We do not know."

And he said to them, "Neither do I tell you by what authority I do these things."

The baptism of John, was it from heaven or from men?" And they discussed among themselves, saying, "If we say, 'from heaven,' he will say, 'Why did you not believe him?' But if we say, 'from men,' all the people will stone us, for they believe that John is a prophet." And they answered, "We do not know where from." And Jesus said to them, "Neither do I tell you by what authority I do these things."

This is our final case of the triple tradition, and our accounts are remarkably consistent. In fact, apart from the narrative set-up (Jesus is teaching in Matthew-Luke rather than simply walking around) and Luke's specification that the fear of Jesus' opponents was that the crowd would stone them, the other differences are mere redundancies of phrasing. Our redactors Matthew and Luke have done little to alter the Markan story line.

How historical is this passage? It would appear on the surface that we have only one source for it, but some have made the claim that the Fourth Gospel has a similar account.[33] In that Gospel Jesus upsets the tables in the Jerusalem Temple at the beginning of his ministry, an act that occasions a challenge from the Jerusalem authorities, much like what Jesus is facing here. Jesus' response differs, in that he makes a Christological claim to authority in John 2:18-22, whereas he poses the riddle about the Baptist in the Synoptics. The Synoptic passage equates the authority of Jesus and John, which is discontinuous with later Church belief that Jesus is manifestly superior, as in the Christological claim of the Fourth Gospel and as we saw in development of the baptism scene (Vignette 4). Thus this teaching about the Baptist is coherent with some of the earliest Q and Markan material that

[33] See Meier, *A Marginal Jew*, 2.167.

places the Baptist and Jesus on a relatively equal footing. This coherence cannot demonstrate that this entire passage as reported is historical, but it can point to an early stage of reflection on the relationship of Jesus and John.

Vignette 15. Who Responded to John

Matthew continues the defense of Jesus' authority with a parable and "moral" that contrast his interlocutors with the followers of John. The material about John's followers appears in a different location in Luke's Gospel that corresponds to Vignette 8, but its content will be discussed here:

Matthew 21:28-32	Luke 7:29-30
"How does it seem to you? A man had two children. And he approached the first and said, 'Child, go work in the vineyard today.' But he replies, saying, 'I don't want to,' but later changed his mind and went. He approached the other and said the same. And he replied, saying, 'Here I am, Lord,' but he did not go. Which of the two did the will of his father?" They say, "The first." Jesus says to them,	
"Truly I tell you that the tax collectors and the prostitutes precede you into the kingdom of God. For John came to you in the way of righteousness, and you did not believe him, but the tax collectors and the prostitutes believed him; you saw, but did not change your minds later so as to believe in him."	And when all the people and the tax collectors heard this, they justified God, having been baptized with the baptism of John; but the Pharisees and the lawyers rejected the purpose of God for themselves, not having been baptized by him.
	[cf. Vignette 8]

Matthew's parable is clearly unique to him, but the final saying about John is shared with Luke. In this case, however, there is not the kind of verbal similarity that we have seen in other cases of the double tradition. For example, the Jewish leaders and those who believed in John differ— all characters who are central to the episode. In addition, Matthew emphasizes John's message of repentance and righteousness, while Luke emphasizes the baptism. These and other differences have led many scholars to dispute that this is a Q saying.[34] But if it is not a Q saying, then we have two

---

[34] For bibliography, see John S. Kloppenborg, *Q Parallels: Synopsis, Critical Notes and Concordance* (Sonoma, Calif.: Polebridge, 1988) 58.

independent sources (special Matthean material and special Lukan material) that attest to the same phenomenon: John attracted some socially marginal types, the very kind of people who would need to be purified, and who would *know* that they needed to be purified. This openness to the impure was not discontinuous with Jewish tradition; as we will see in Chapter 5, the Pharisees and the Jesus movement also sought to "clean up" the population, and even the Essenes, with their dualistic ethics, would accept anyone willing to abide by their new standard of purity. Moreover, this final notice about John is coherent with the evidence that large masses of people came out to John, a fact attested not only in Christian sources but in Josephus as well.

Some Redaction-Critical Results

We are now in a position to step back from our detailed redaction-critical analysis of individual passages and to theorize about the theological interests and social location of our redactors Matthew and Luke. For this exercise, it is the differences between the accounts that will be most important, whereas in our final reconstruction of the historical Baptist the criteria of historicity will be our guides.

The Baptist in Matthew

Matthew relies heavily on Mark and Q for his portrait of the Baptist. He does, however, have some unique material on John that betrays his editorial interests. In the baptism scene Matthew adds a dialogue between John and Jesus that ameliorates the awkwardness of their relative status by subordinating John more clearly to Jesus (Vignette 4). Like Mark, Matthew ties John's arrest to the beginning of Jesus' public ministry, but he goes on to ground Jesus' actions in Jewish prophecy (Vignette 5). This interest in the prophets is also apparent in Vignette 12, where Matthew adds the prophet Jeremiah to the list of figures with whom Jesus has been confused.

Matthew makes some minor alterations of Mark and Q that emphasize his particular themes and possible social location. For example, when John appears in the wilderness, Matthew shifts John's preaching into direct discourse and replaces the purpose of the conversion ("for the release of sins") with a more openly eschatological message ("the kingdom of the heavens is near"). This conforms John to Jesus, whose words are identical when he begins his public preaching (Matt 4:17). Matthew augments the Markan identification of John as Elijah; but whereas Mark is somewhat cryptic and allusive about the relationship (Vignettes 2, 13), Matthew bluntly equates the two figures in Vignettes 8 and 13.[35] There are many other occasions where Matthew cleans up grammatical rough spots and redundancies of content in the Markan narrative (for example, Vignettes 11 and 12). The emphasis on the fulfillment of the law and the prophets, the added reference to Jeremiah, the emphasis on Elijah, and even the minor detail of joining Peter's Hebrew name Simon to his Greek name point to the social location of the author: he was writing from a Jewish context to an audience that included many Jewish Christians, who would understand these references to Jewish terminology and traditions. This is further supported by a minor difference between Matthew and Luke in Vignette 15: Matthew emphasizes the "way of righteousness" that John preached—that is, a deeply Jewish tradition—whereas Luke emphasizes the baptism of John, a practice that in Luke already extends to the Gentile world.

The Baptist in Luke

Like Matthew, Luke relies on Mark and Q for his treatment of the Baptist. But unlike Matthew, he employs a great deal of unique material about John. For example, Luke alone provides us with an infancy narrative of John that carries the weight of establishing the relative status of Jesus and John in the absence of a direct meeting of the two adult men in Luke 3. In addition, he sets John's ministry at a precise moment in history by mentioning the political and religious rulers at the time John appeared (Vignettes 1 and 2), much as he does for Jesus at his birth (Luke 2:1-2). Another major addition in Luke is the preaching of John, which is expanded well beyond the eschatological message of Q to include ethical advice about economic obligations to the neighbor (Vignette 3). This interruption of the vision of eschatological judgment has the effect of tempering that judgment and its sense of immediacy. To these major additions to the Gospel we should add the traditions found only in Acts of the Apostles, the second volume of Luke's work. There we discover that Jesus' ministry is rooted in John's baptism in an integral way, but that the baptism Jesus offers in the Holy Spirit is superior by virtue of its divine origin, universal range, and resulting gifts.

Luke also adds shorter elements to the Markan and Q records that augment the existing narrative in the direction of his own interests. To the citation of Isaiah 40:3 he adds Isaiah 40:4-5, thus emphasizing that "all flesh shall see the salvation of God" (Vignette 2). This universalizes the significance of John

---

[35] Matthew deletes the correlation of John and Elijah in Herod's mind (Vignette 10) but keeps it in Vignette 12.

and Jesus and coheres with the prophecies of Zechariah, Simeon, and Anna that introduced the theme of universal salvation in the infancy narrative (Luke 1:76-79 and 2:29, 32). It is also coherent with the strategy of locating John and Jesus in the historical reigns of Roman emperors; Luke thus proposes that John and Jesus are significant figures on the world stage. In the scene depicting John's preaching (Vignette 3), the same motif is present in Luke's unique designation of the people who approach John. They include the (Jewish) crowds, Jewish tax collectors, who collaborate regularly with Gentiles, and Gentile (or possibly Herodian) soldiers, indicating that John's message has significance for the whole world.

Another minor alteration is made to indicate John's status in relation to Jesus, a theme that had been introduced in the infancy narrative through the literary diptych. In the baptism scene, Luke erases John entirely; he is imprisoned when Jesus is baptized. This eliminates the problem of their relative status posed by Jesus' subservience in the Markan version (Vignette 4).

Yet another Lukan concern is to create a more orderly narrative, as he admits in 1:3. This is carried out in the Baptist material in several episodes. Luke deals with John's arrest entirely at the outset rather than flashing back to it later in Jesus' ministry, as Mark and Matthew do, thus creating a story sequence that mirrors the historical order of events. In Vignette 7, John's disciples are not simply told to report the healings they have seen but are actually allowed to see those healings first. The theme is present in another way in Vignette 11, the story of John's execution; Luke does not present it at all, perhaps because he was aware of its historical problems.

Another important theme that Luke emphasizes is prayer. We saw the long prayers in the infancy narrative that frame the births of John and Jesus, but the theme appears in smaller passages as well. For example, Luke alone contrasts (or rather compares) the practice of prayer among John's and Jesus' disciples (Vignette 6). He alone sets up the question of Jesus' identity and Peter's confession by portraying Jesus at prayer (Vignette 12).

What Luke deletes is as important as what he adds. We have already discussed the effect of his innovation that John did not actually baptize Jesus. Luke also erases Mark's allusion to Elijah in the account of John's appearance (Vignette 2) and in the Q saying that the kingdom comes by violence (Vignette 8), and he does away entirely with Jesus' post-transfiguration commentary on the sequence of Elijah and messiah (Vignette 13). Why he does this is open to speculation, but some likely hypotheses are (1) that the reference may be less familiar to his Gentile audience; (2) that there was no prophecy that Elijah *would* precede the messiah, and so Luke chooses not to perpetuate the inaccuracy; or (3) that the Elijah tradition may associate John with apocalyptic traditions that Luke would rather downplay. Luke does allow in the infancy narrative that John will go before God "in the spirit and power of Elijah to turn the hearts of fathers toward children" (Mal 3:23-24), but this is not as bald an assertion as Matthew's *equation* of John with Elijah. More often, when Luke does allow mention of Elijah, it is in passages about *Jesus'* identity. This suggests a third hypothesis for Luke's dissociation of John and Elijah, which is that it allows Jesus alone to be compared at that level. This strategy is consistent with Luke's attempts elsewhere to enhance Jesus' status vis-à-vis John.

The Historical Baptist

Our redaction-critical analysis has highlighted those portions of the Gospel record that were altered by later editors. In the process, it has revealed core elements of the tradition that have a greater claim to historicity. Those elements became visible as we applied the criteria of historicity to each vignette above. From the results we can form the following picture of the historical Baptist.[36]

To begin with, the criteria indicate that there *was* a historical Baptist, and he did baptize Jesus.[37] The criteria of multiple attestation and awkwardness were particularly useful in establishing this. The infancy narrative of John yielded the possible datum that he was born into a priestly family. Regarding his preaching activity, we can be certain that he worked in the region governed by Herod Antipas, and more specifically that he baptized in the wilderness around the Jordan River, since Mark and the Fourth Gospel converge on this point, though precisely *where* along the Jordan is disputed. In his preaching he emphasized the importance of behavioral conversion subsequently marked in the flesh by his purifying baptism. The

---

[36] The most important recent reconstructions of the historical Baptist are Josef Ernst, *Johannes der Täufer: Interpretation-Geschichte-Wirkungsgeschichte* (Berlin: Walter de Gruyter, 1989); Robert L. Webb, *John the Baptizer and Prophet: A Socio-Historical Study*, JSNTSup 62 (Sheffield: JSOT Press, 1991); John P. Meier, *A Marginal Jew: Rethinking the Historical Jesus*, vol. 2, *Mentor, Message, and Miracles*, ABRL (New York: Doubleday, 1994) 19–233; W. Barnes Tatum, *John the Baptist and Jesus: A Report of the Jesus Seminar* (Sonoma, Calif.: Polebridge, 1994); Joan E. Taylor, *The Immerser: John the Baptist Within Second Temple Judaism* (Grand Rapids, Mich.: Wm. B. Eerdmans, 1997). See also John H. Reumann, "The Quest for the Historical Baptist," in *Understanding the Sacred Text: Essays in Honor of Morton S. Enslin on the Hebrew Bible and Christian Beginnings*, ed. John H. Reumann (Valley Forge, Pa.: Judson, 1972) 181–199.

[37] Rudolf Bultmann, *The History of the Synoptic Tradition* (Oxford: Blackwell, 1963) 47. Robert L. Webb summarizes the consensus in "John the Baptist and His Relationship to Jesus," *Studying the Historical Jesus: Evaluations of the State of Current Research*, ed. Bruce D. Chilton and Craig A. Evans, NTTS 19 (Leiden: Brill, 1994) 179–229.

stability of the Q tradition and the discontinuity of the understanding of his baptismal role as a preparatory gesture allowed us to conclude that he also preached of one coming after him who would complete the eschatological judgment for which he was preparing the people. We could not say with equal certainty, on the basis of the criteria of historicity, that he understood Jesus to be that person. He had disciples who practiced his charismatic acts of fasting and baptism, and Jesus and some of his adherents were likely numbered among them. John taught his disciples to pray as well, but beyond this we cannot know for certain what he taught them. John was certainly executed by Herod Antipas, but the reasons given in the Synoptics present certain anachronisms that render them unlikely.

The ministry of Jesus shares many features with John's: an openness to outcasts, a requirement of conversion, a promise that God's kingdom was near, the opposition of Jewish religious leaders, the fact of execution. But Jesus' ministry also differs from John's in its lack of ascetic rigor and in the growing stature attributed to Jesus as the Gospel tradition develops. These differences, initially of practice and gradually of belief, create tension between John and Jesus in the narrative that has its historical kernel in John's questions about whether Jesus was the coming one. Finally, the Gospels and Acts testify to the ongoing baptizing activity both of Jesus' disciples and of John's and to some competition between the movements, not only in Israel but in the larger eastern Mediterranean basin. This is explicit in Acts but implicit in the evangelists' various attempts to work out Jesus' relationship to John in a manner that respects the Baptist tradition.

CHAPTER FOUR

Another Angle on the Baptist Movement: Social-Scientific Criticism

Redaction criticism and our quest for the historical Baptist have proven to be rich veins to mine. It is clear by now that narrative texts tell more than a story; they also reveal the circumstances and theological interests of their authors and the historical and literary sources those editors had at their disposal. Redaction criticism is a powerful tool for refining the editors' motives from the raw material of so many parallel texts. But it is not the only way to assess the original catalysts and contexts of the story's production. And it provides no way of reconstructing that context and thought world apart from the text itself. What if we wanted to know, for example, just why John was cleaning people or why his baptizing movement was so popular? The Gospels, with their interest to augment Jesus' reputation at John's expense, will not likely answer this question for us. Neither will Josephus, who so wants to mitigate the impression of rebellious Jews for his Roman audience that he portrays John as a self-controlled philosopher. If there were more of an edge to the man, we would never hear it from Josephus.

There is another reason in addition to an author's motives why texts cannot tell us everything we might want to know, and it has to do with the cultural void that lies between a modern reader and the original audience. An author can assume that he and his contemporary audience share certain perspectives and assumptions. For example, if an author today mentioned the two words "nine-eleven," it would immediately evoke powerful visual images of destruction in New York, Washington, Pennsylvania, and Afghanistan, along with various constructions of meaning readers would have created for themselves regarding terrorism, U.S. global policies, patriotism, homeland security, the "other" (whoever they might be), the

Israeli-Palestinian conflict, and perhaps other issues as well. An author would not have to supply and identify what she *means* by "nine-eleven" if she knows that the audience shares the same point of view. Sociologists refer to this as a high-context reading situation, which simply means that the author and audience share a lot of context, so that little has to be explained or defended.

The Gospels, and indeed most of the biblical books, are high-context documents. Their authors presumed that they shared with their audiences a lot of assumptions, social institutions, and cultural values and behaviors, and so they did not explain or defend those fundamental elements of their world and worldview.[1] But of course, a modern reader is not part of that context, and where we might need explanation we simply don't get it. Worse yet, we might think we *do* get it simply because of the way the Bible is read. Many people read the Bible as if it were timeless, and understand that to mean that the text can speak directly to the reader without the mediation of either the ancient or the present culture. They would not accept the premise of this book, namely, that texts, however inspired, are nevertheless written and interpreted within (limited) human frameworks of meaning. The result is a kind of naïve or resolute literalism that equates the meaning I determine with *the* meaning of the text, a choice that, ironically, demonstrates the point that humans are implicated in the construction of meaning. For those readers who accept the human dimension of scriptural production, there is a cultural void between the original and the modern context with which every beginning student of Scripture is uncomfortably familiar. We often just don't "get" the biblical text because the verses are obscure and the metaphors unfamiliar. For us, the description of John the Baptist wearing camel's hair and little else and eating locusts and wild honey in a desert makes him sound either extremely bizarre or like a recent contestant on the TV series *Survivor*, but it does *not* immediately make us think of Elijah, as the author intended it to.

Social-scientific criticism helps us disregard *Survivor* and discover Elijah. It is a method, or rather a group of methods, that helps us to reconstruct the world that the original audience inhabited. It utilizes methods, theories, and models from the social sciences (anthropology, sociology, archaeology, political science, economics) and applies these to biblical texts and to the ancient Mediterranean world in order to enhance our sense of

---

[1] Josephus would be an exception, to some extent, because he is trying to explain the Jews to a different and sometimes hostile audience. The difficulty with an apologetic or defensive construction like Josephus's opus is that he frames the Jews in terms of the *Roman* context so that the Romans will understand them, which makes him a transparent source for the Roman perspectives, but an opaque source for the emic or native Jewish worldview.

that other world. Social-scientific criticism helps us to travel across the void of two thousand years and imagine more effectively the social relationships, values, and customary behaviors of another time.

Definition, Scope, and Methods

Social-scientific criticism analyzes the social and cultural dimensions of the text and of the environment that produced the text through the lens of the social sciences.[2] Social-scientific criticism is "social" because of its focus and "scientific" because of its method. The social focus is understood here in its broadest sense to include not only all manner of social relationships and institutions (familial, political, economic, religious) but also the cultural scripts that regulated values and behaviors within those relationships and institutions. The scientific methods, drawn from any and all of the social sciences, always involve an empirical phase and an interpretive phase. In the empirical phase the researcher gathers data from the text or (more often) from a broad *array* of literary texts, archaeological records, and epigraphic data.[3] The researcher organizes and classifies the data according to a particular research design, which in turn is shaped by the hypothesis with which he approaches the material. In the interpretive or explanatory phase of the research, the critic makes explicit the working hypothesis and method, analyzes the data in relation to the model, and finally evaluates the adequacy of both the model and the working hypothesis. One of the critic's ultimate goals, no matter what her specific method or focus, is to understand what the authors of our texts said and meant within the contours of their original environment.

An analogy may be helpful at this point. The 1999 movie *The Matrix* imagines the world in 2199 as controlled by artificial-intelligence machines that feed off human beings while programming them to believe that they are living in a "normal" if nondescript world (the artificial "matrix").[4] A group of mysterious rebels draws a computer hacker named Thomas A. Anderson (a.k.a. "Neo") out of the cyberdream and into their number, and together they launch a war against the mechanical manipulators of the matrix. The

---

[2] John H. Elliott, *What Is Social-Scientific Criticism?* GBSNTS (Minneapolis: Fortress, 1993) 7. This introductory section depends on Elliott's comprehensive presentation of the method.

[3] Epigraphic data are inscriptions. The term does not refer to literary works (such as the biblical books) or documentary texts (such as contracts or deeds of sale), but rather to inscribed statements memorializing a person (such as a funerary epitaph) or a benefaction (say of a suppliant to a temple or a benefactor to the construction of a public edifice).

[4] Directed by Andy Wachowski and Larry Wachowski, Warner Brothers Studio.

concept of a matrix, an alternative world created by someone, is analogous to the complex ancient worlds that social-scientific critics attempt to construct, except without the sinister component. These critics are not simply trying to reconstruct the theological motives of a particular author, as in redaction criticism, but rather the values, behavioral codes, and institutions of the ancient world with all its diversity of peoples and cultures. They are trying to (re-)build a world for us. And far from trying to manipulate their readers into an all too easy positivism about their results, as if saying, "this *is exactly* how the ancient world operated and this is what you must think as a result," the social-scientific critic is concerned to tell you just how she came to these results (her method) so that you may test the results yourself. It's as if she exposes not only the world but the fact that this is her construction of it, and then she provides you with the blueprints to explore it yourself. Your role is not simply to read and replicate the blueprints but to rewrite them. As in a biology lab or a sociology internship, you learn the theory, you test it in the world, you discover your own results, and you adjust the theory to fit your results.

The goal of re-creating an entire world is ambitious, and in fact most social-scientific projects are more modest in scope. Some do explore the dynamics and institutions of the culture on the macro-level, examining systemic social or cultural features such as the behavioral honor-shame code in the circum-Mediterranean region or the impact of Roman imperial political organization and propaganda on Christian concepts of the divine man. Many other social-scientific projects, however, focus more narrowly on the micro-social level, examining one text or one aspect of culture or society and slowly building a larger matrix of the ancient world by combining the results of these smaller studies.

The aim of this chapter is to introduce you to the diversity of scope, foci, and exploratory strategies of the social-scientific method. We will begin with a general map of the choices one must make when designing a social-scientific research project. We will then embark on a sample project so that you have a hands-on sense of how social-scientific criticism can be applied.

The relationship of this chapter to the next is not as organic as the relationship of Chapters 2 and 3. You will recall that Chapter 2 provided a method that was then applied to a sequence of vignettes in Chapter 3. With social-scientific criticism, we do not have one method that can be applied to multiple texts; instead, we have many methods that can be applied to many texts, or alternatively we can begin with texts and see what social-scientific questions and models they stimulate. This diversity suggests that the best introduction will be one that provides several different examples. Therefore, this chapter and the next will incorporate four very different exercises. For the sake of continuity, they will all be grouped around the character of John, and those in Chapter 5 will cluster around his baptizing activity and its related cultural script, "purity and pollution."

An Initial Exercise:
A Map for Designing a Social-Scientific Inquiry

There are a variety of issues that a social-scientific critic must address at the initial stage of the research project. These can be broadly classified along several axes.[5] Each of these axes will be introduced individually below and then combined into an image of social-scientific analysis. We will then take these axes together and imagine some lines of inquiry they could generate for our study of John the Baptist. In this way you will get a sense of the breadth of this critical method and of the many windows it can open onto the ancient world.

The first axis is the *focus* to be explored: Will it be a social system or a cultural system? The social system includes social relations, groups, organizations, institutions, events, and political organization, while the cultural system includes the less tangible codes of behavior and patterns of meaning that often govern the social relations and institutions. Each of these systems is itself quite complex and presents a variety of options, which are charted in Figure 4 below.

---

[5] These axes are based on the topics elucidated by Elliott, *What Is Social-Scientific Criticism?* 60–70.

Figure 4. Some Elements of Social and Cultural Systems in the Ancient Mediterranean Region

Social System		Cultural System

Family[6]
   marriage patterns and
     terms
   kinship networks
   gender definitions and
     roles
 Politics
   institutions
   processes
   culture
   legal and military
     mechanisms
 Economics
   land tenure, crafts,
     industry
   occupational patterns
   commerce, trade, finance
   classes, social relations
   property
	Religion
	   organization
	   mythology/
	     ideologies
	   ritual behavior
	 Group formation and
	   maintenance
	   education and
	     socialization
	   patron-client
	     relations
	   social conditions
	     of group
	     formation
	   processes of
	     cooperation,
	     competition,
	     conflict
	   symbols and
	     strategies used
	     to establish
	     group
	     identity
	   constituency
	   organization
	   geographic
	     location
	   ideology
		Values
		   honor and shame
		   personality structure
		   hospitality
		   perception of access
		     to goods
		   purity and pollution

For example, we could explore the controverted relationship between John and Jesus in Matthew's baptism scene as a case of patron-client confusion, with John in the position of patron recognizing that he should be Jesus' client (social system), or we could examine Mark's account of Herod's concession to Herodias at his birthday party as a decision dictated by the values of honor and shame (cultural system).

---

[6] The arenas of the social system listed here are based on the more elaborate lists created by Thomas F. Carney, *The Shape of the Past: Models and Antiquity* (Lawrence, Kan.: Coronado, 1975), and Elliott's rendering of them in *What Is Social-Scientific Criticism?* 64–65.

A second axis is the *scope* of the study: will it be at the macro-level or the micro-level? Once the first axis has been selected, the researcher must decide how broad the scope of inquiry will be. For example, a macro-level analysis of the economic system in first-century C.E. Palestine would place that study in the context of the Roman imperial system of production and commerce, while a micro-level economic analysis might focus on the role of tax collectors in that system and consequently the significance of John's advice to them in Luke 3:13.

The third axis is the *entry point*: Will it be a text or the context? All social-scientific methods rely on texts—literary, archaeological, epigraphic—as the raw data that can be processed through interpretation into a meaningful construct of the ancient world. That construct, in turn, is the context, the social and cultural patterns that shaped life and thought in that world (axis no. 1). Critics can begin with a text, exploring its form, content, and rhetoric (how it communicates and persuades) to discern the assumptions, dynamics, social constructs, and cultural scripts that the author and audience shared. For example, we could start from Josephus's portrait of the Baptist and explore just what he is trying to tell his Roman audience through his characterization of John. Alternately, a critic can begin with some element of the social or cultural system and then select a text or group of texts within which that element may be profitably explored. Thus we could begin with a model of conflict management and test whether it helps to explain Josephus's apologetic techniques or the relationship of the Jesus movement to the Baptist movement. A materialist assumption is implicit in this axis and in the social-scientific method in general: We are presuming that there is a relationship between the ideology communicated in the themes of the text and the material conditions under which the text was written. That is, the text was generated in a particular time and place by a particular author who used the literary genres, cultural scripts, and rhetorical options of his time to communicate his particular message. The author had reasons for writing his text, reasons that were generated by his context or circumstances. Once again, this assumption will be problematic for people who understand the texts to be divinely revealed *if* they understand that revelation to be unmediated by the material world and human imagination.

The fourth axis is related to the third, since it involves the *direction of the inquiry* after the starting point is chosen. The issue here is whether the logical path of the inquiry will be inductive or deductive. An inductive approach begins with data and builds a hypothesis from the data. These data may be drawn from a variety of sources or from a single text. We will do an inductive exercise in this chapter in which we will begin with a single text and move toward a hypothesis about the rhetorical strategy of the author. A deductive approach, on the other hand, begins with a hypothesis, theory, or model and applies it to the data. This is a very common approach in the social-scientific study of biblical texts. This approach, too, will be illustrated by an exercise in Chapter 5 in which we will examine the cultural script of purity and pollution in light of our sources on the Baptist and Jesus. In reality, critics do not choose either an inductive approach or a deductive one but rather fall somewhere on the axis between the two. The reason for this is that even the most inductive approach begins with some operational definitions, however unconscious, that organize and shape the data that the researcher is collecting. Likewise, even the most deductive approach is formulated on the basis of the researcher's familiarity with some measure of data. Therefore, social-scientific critics of biblical texts sometimes speak of their method as one of *abduction*, understanding this term to describe a process that is both inductive and deductive, constantly alternating between theory and data.[7]

The fifth and final axis is the *temporal range of the inquiry*. The issue is whether you will examine the development of a particular social group or phenomenon across a period of time or whether you will freeze-frame time and examine the phenomenon at one particular historical moment in relation to other social phenomena of the same moment. The former approach, which moves through time, is called "diachronic," while the latter, which looks at several phenomena together in one temporal moment, is called "synchronic."

These axes represent the initial decisions that researchers must make in order to define the scope, nature, and path of their inquiry. They are presented as axes to indicate that they each represent further choices that must be made and that together they combine to shape the inquiry. The point at which they intersect is the social-scientific exercise they define. And that exercise is only one of many that might be chosen. Figure 5 illustrates the point.

---

[7] Elliott, *What Is Social-Scientific Criticism?* 48–49.

Figure 5. The Axes of Social-Scientific Inquiry

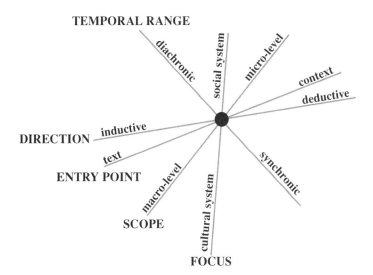

Now that you have a sense of the initial issues that must be addressed, we can reframe them as the first steps of the research process. The first axis is the choice to examine an aspect of either the social system or the cultural system. This is the most complex of the choices you will need to make because the options are so numerous. At this point it is useful to consult a list of the options, such as Figure 4 on page 90. Consider which of the listed topics interests you the most. As you select an option, you will need to decide about axes 2 and 3—how wide your scope will be and whether it will begin with context or text. These first three axes are interrelated; the choice of one will limit your choices on the others. Once you have selected the focus, topic, scope, and entry point, you have two further decisions to make: you must decide whether you would like to begin with data and build a hypothesis to explain the evidence or whether you would like to begin with a theory or model and apply this to the data. Your final decision is whether you want to examine the phenomenon over a period of time or at one moment in time.

Now let's apply this image of social-scientific analysis to John the Baptist. All we want to do at this point is to generate lines of inquiry along the combined axes. This will not be an exhaustive exercise but merely exemplary, as we will simply be generating projects that could be pursued. Later we will explore three specific projects in greater depth; for now, we just want to get a sense of the breadth of the field and the manner in which social-scientific inquiry begins. In this exercise John will return as our guide and object of study.

John is imprisoned in the Synoptic Gospels because he spoke against Herod's marriage to his own brother's wife. What was wrong with this practice? Because our authors never provide an answer to this question, we can safely assume that the authors and their original audiences shared the same definitions about which degrees of relation were sanctioned as legitimate for marriage. But we do not share that context, and so we have to do a little digging to rediscover it. A social-scientific inquiry can provide us with the heuristic tools we need. Our first decision will be to select as our focus either the social system or the cultural system. Since our inquiry involves legal customs related to marriage, the social system is the most suitable focus because it encompasses social institutions like marriage, as well as legal and religious mechanisms for maintaining those institutions. Our second decision is the scope of the study: do we want to do a cultural comparison of marriage practices in pre-industrial agrarian societies (the macro-level), or should we reduce the scope to first-century C.E. Judean customs regarding marriage to a brother's wife (the micro-level)? The third decision we will have to make is whether to focus on a text, which in our case would likely be the source-text Mark, or the context, which in this case would be the marriage custom(s). As I generate these options for the first three axes, I realize that I am most interested in the first-century C.E. Judean norms regarding permitted degrees of marriage. In terms of the first three axes, I have chosen to explore the social system (and particularly the marriage institution), the micro-level, and context. The final two decisions are now easier to make because my inquiry is beginning to take shape. I don't know anything about the permitted degrees of relationship, so it would be impossible for me to generate a hypothesis yet about this social phenomenon. Because of this, I will select an inductive approach to the data, which will allow me to survey the data first and then draft a hypothesis to explain it. And I will not likely find a lot of material on this topic for the first century alone, so I will have to expand the temporal range of my inquiry to include data from surrounding centuries (the diachronic approach).

This first attempt to generate a project is not yet a social-scientific inquiry, because it has not yet gathered data and attempted to interpret that data. It is, however, a necessary preliminary stage, in which the researcher defines the "axes" of focus, scope, entry point, direction, and temporal range.

Two further examples will help to illustrate the breadth of this method. The first has already been suggested. While reading Mark's account of John's execution, I am puzzled by the fact that King Herod is powerless to deny his wife's daughter her wish. I have a hunch, based on

Mark's narrative, that this uncharacteristic impotence is due to the public nature of his promise that he would give her anything she wished. He cannot risk the shame of violating his public oath. I am curious about how the value of honor is more powerful than the king himself, and so this feature of the cultural system will be the focus of my study. This time I want to explore the mechanics of the honor-shame value system as it operates in the Markan text. But because I need to learn first about the value system, my entry point will be this contextual value rather than the text, and my method will be deductive, which means that I will begin by defining for myself what the honor-shame value system is, and then I will apply that model to the data to test whether it explains the Markan passage adequately. I am not examining the honor-shame value system over time but rather in the freeze-frame moment of the Markan pericope, so the temporal range of my study will be synchronic.

Our final example is drawn from the several passages in Acts that mention Apollos, who was traveling around Asia Minor and Greece preaching the good news of Jesus but baptizing in the name of John. I recognize that the act of baptizing represents initiation into a group, and I am curious about the formation of groups baptized in John's rather than Jesus' name. The passages in Acts narrate that Priscilla and Aquila, and then Paul himself, have to "correct" Apollos or his initiates, and that seems to indicate some level of conflict between the followers of Jesus and those of John. I will use a model drawn from the analysis of social systems, namely, internal conflict management, to analyze the Acts material and other references to Apollos in Paul's own letters. The focus on the relation between the disciples of John and those of Jesus makes this a micro-level analysis, and the use of a sociological model suggests that my entry point should be the model, and thus the context, which I will then use to interpret the texts. This represents a deductive approach (from theory to data). Since the passages from Paul and Acts were likely written some thirty years apart, they allow a modest diachronic study of the relationship between these two (competing?) Jewish groups.

As you can see, the axes generate scores of possibilities for social-scientific projects. Once the project has been defined, the actual inquiry may begin. As mentioned earlier, it includes two steps: the collection and classification of the data and the interpretation or explanation of that data. The data is the raw material mined from the texts and archaeological remnants of antiquity. The interpretation, already implied to some extent in the process of collection and classification, is the refining process that uses contemporary tools and techniques to view the data in suggestive new ways.

The final exercise in this chapter will introduce you to the steps of the social-scientific method. It takes an inductive approach, moving from data to theory, and illustrates how the critic moves beyond the initial generation of an inquiry to the inquiry itself.

An Inductive Exercise: From Text to Hypothesis

One of the ways of proceeding with a social-scientific inquiry is to begin with a text (our third axis) and to examine the social information it yields about its author, audience, and the social and cultural situation they share. This is an inductive approach (our fourth axis) because it moves from the data to a theory or model that explains the data. This kind of research usually begins with a particular text that the critic has selected rather than with a particular feature of the social or cultural system (our first axis). The critic has to become familiar with the text so that the other research decisions can flow naturally from the data.

The process of becoming familiar with the text is more than a matter of reading it a few times. It is best if the researcher can first examine it carefully through the traditional methods of textual and historical criticism so that manifold textual clues can yield their evidence of the most likely shape of the original text,[8] the author, the time of composition, the themes of the work, and the historical circumstances that shaped those themes. You are already able to do much of this because of your redaction-critical skills, which yield some sense of the author, the audience, the themes, and the social circumstances of the work. But you can also save yourself some time by securing a good commentary on your text and reading the intro-

---

[8] Textual criticism is a method of analysis that attempts to establish the earliest form of the biblical text. This is a tall order, when you consider that the evidence includes over 5,300 Greek manuscripts of the New Testament (some quite fragmentary), translations into other ancient languages, lectionaries for liturgical use, and citations in early Church documents. The text critic must utilize every witness to a given passage in order to ascertain the most likely original reading where the readings vary (and they often do in hand-copied manuscripts). Text critics produce a composite text of the New Testament based on all such decisions, and then translation committees prepare vernacular translations for contemporary readers from this composite text. It is important to remember that the composite text you are reading in translation did not exist in antiquity; instead, ancient listeners and readers had some version of the biblical book with its own unique constellation of variant readings. See Kurt Aland and Barbara Aland, *The Text of the New Testament: An Introduction to the Critical Editions and to the Theory and Practice of Modern Textual Criticism*, 2nd rev. ed. (Grand Rapids, Mich.: Wm. B. Eerdmans, 1995) and Bruce M. Metzger, *The Text of the New Testament: Its Transmission, Corruption, and Restoration*, 3rd ed. (New York: Oxford University Press, 1992).

duction.[9] Your goal in this preliminary research is to establish the geographic and temporal location of the author and audience and some basic information about the social situation. This will lay a foundation for you as you examine the situation and rhetorical strategy of your focal text.

Our focal text will be the scene in Luke 3:7-18, where John castigates and advises the crowds that come out to him (from Vignette 3, "The Preaching of John," p. 54). We begin by rereading the text and then refreshing our sense of the author, audience, geographic location, and social circumstances of the Gospel.

> So he said to the crowds that were coming out to be baptized by him, "Spawn of snakes, who warned you to flee from the coming wrath? So produce fruits worthy of conversion and don't start saying to yourselves, 'We have Abraham as father.' For I say to you that God is able from these stones to raise up children to Abraham. And even now the ax is laid against the root of the trees; therefore every tree that does not produce good fruit is cut down and thrown into fire." And the crowds were asking him, saying, "What then shall we do?" And answering he said to them, "The one who has two cloaks, let him share with the one who has not, and the one who has food, let him do the same." And tax collectors also came to be baptized and they said to him, "Teacher, what must we do?" And he said to them, "Collect no more than what has been assigned to you." Soldiers also were questioning him saying, "And we, what shall we do?" And he said to them, "Don't extort or shake down anyone and be satisfied with your pay." Now the people were in expectation and they were all considering in their hearts concerning John, whether perhaps he were the Christ; John answered saying to all, "I baptize you with water; but the one stronger than me is coming, of whom I am not worthy to untie the thong of his sandals; he will baptize you in Holy Spirit and fire; his winnowing fork is in his hand to purge his threshing floor and to gather the grain in his barn, while the chaff he will burn in an inextinguishable fire." So with many other exhortations, he preached the good news to the people.

Our first task is to review the results of redaction-critical examination of this passage before we embark on a social-scientific reading. You will recall from Chapter 3 that this passage in Luke attests to all three of Luke's sources. To help refresh your memory, those verses shared with a single source, Matthew, are underlined with a single line above. According to the

[9] See Chapter 2, p. 36, note 9, for some recommended commentaries.

Two-Source Hypothesis, these verses were part of Q, the sayings source. The next section of material on Luke's advice to the crowd is unique to Luke and therefore derives from him or from his special Lukan source (plain text in the excerpt above). The next group of verses, underlined with two lines, is shared with two other texts, Mark and Matthew. According to the Two-Source Hypothesis, Luke borrowed from Mark for this part of the narrative on John's preaching. The concluding summary is unique to Luke (plain text).

If we are interested in identifying the author's themes and interests, the unique material is the clearest indicator of his perspective. The unique material in the above passage emphasizes that John's baptism was open not only to Jews but also to Jews who collaborated with Romans (the tax collectors) and to Romans themselves (the soldiers). This message of the inclusive baptism is one that Jesus picks up as well. The inclusivity of the message is also present at other critical junctures of Luke-Acts: in the infancy narrative "overture" to the Gospel (recall Mary's *Magnificat*), in Luke's careful location of Jesus' birth and baptism in the context of Roman history, and in the narrative of Acts in which the message is brought to Gentiles as well as Jews through a new baptism of Spirit as well as water. The repetition and locations of this teaching indicate that it is a central theme, a teaching that the work is designed to emphasize. Another theme that is present in the unique material above is the special attention the author pays to economic issues. In fact, each of the three groups that approach John to ask his advice receive counsel about how to deal with goods and money. This is a special interest of Luke's Gospel, although it is explicitly integrated with the Baptist traditions only here.

Historical-critical examination of the Gospel of Luke and the Acts of the Apostles has produced a portrait of the author, audience, and social situation that goes beyond these two themes.[10] The author is only called Luke by convention; the original Gospel was anonymous, as were all the Gospels. While we don't know the author's name, we know something about him from his books. He admits that he was not an eyewitness to the events he reports (Luke 1:1-3), so he was likely a second- or third-generation Christian. He writes well by Synoptic standards and alludes frequently to the Greek Septuagint and Greek literature, indicating that he was well-read and that his social status was fairly high. But he was not very familiar with Palestinian geography, suggesting that he lived and wrote elsewhere. Redaction-critical examination of the entire Gospel indicates that he omits some of the controversies between Jesus and the Jewish leaders over purity

---

[10] The following summary depends upon Joseph A. Fitzmyer's two-volume commentary, *The Gospel according to Luke*, AB (New York: Doubleday, 1979), especially 1.35–62.

concerns as well as certain Aramaic words preserved in Mark and Matthew. These clues accord well with his interest in a Christianity inclusive of both Jew and Gentile and suggest that he was not Jewish himself, or at least that his intended audience was neither Palestinian nor predominantly Jewish. In fact, the style of the prologues is evocative of Greek historiographic works, and this indicates that Luke was well educated. He addresses both volumes to "most excellent Theophilus"; the epithet "most excellent" indicates that Theophilus had high social status and was well respected.[11]

As to the author's geographic origins, Joseph Fitzmyer suggests Antioch, one of the great cities of the Roman Empire because of its strategic location on the route to the East.[12] Internal evidence in the Acts of the Apostles suggests that the author was familiar with early Christian history in this city, and some early Christian traditions external to Luke-Acts recommend that the "Luke" who was a companion of Paul was an Antiochene (Col 4:14; 2 Tim 4:11; Phlm 24). We cannot identify the author or his geographic origins with any greater certitude, and we have no evidence whatsoever of where he or his audience was when he composed his two-volume work. The most we can say is that it was not Palestine and was likely a Gentile place.

Our "working draft" of author, audience, and social situation is severely limited by the nature of our evidence; but it nevertheless gives us something on which to base our social-scientific inquiry. From this base, the next step we must take is to decide what kind of social-scientific inquiry we would like to conduct. We could, for example, explore the social circumstances of the author more carefully using a social-science model of social location to determine the arenas of the social system shared by the parties in the narrative enterprise.[13] But this model requires data from the entire text,

---

[11] Luke addresses both works to Theophilus, though he only uses the honorific *kratiste* in the Gospel (Luke 1:3 and Acts 1:1). Jews often had Greek names, so the name alone will not help us discern Theophilus's ethnic origin. The fact that Luke addresses the works to a single individual makes these books public documents and suggests that they were intended for the benefit of larger audiences (Fitzmyer, *The Gospel according to Luke*, 1.299–300).

[12] *The Gospel according to Luke*, 1.41–47.

[13] For an example of this kind of study, see Vernon K. Robbins, "The Social Location of the Implied Author of Luke-Acts," in *The Social World of Luke-Acts: Models for Interpretation*, ed. Jerome H. Neyrey (Peabody, Mass.: Hendrickson, 1991) 305–332. Robbins offers nine "arenas" of the social system: previous events, natural environment and resources, population structure, technology, socialization and personality, culture, foreign affairs, belief systems and ideologies, and the political-military-legal system. The parties to the narrative enterprise are the characters and audiences *in* the story, the narrator and the one to whom he is speaking, the inscribed author and inscribed reader mentioned in the text, and the implied author and implied reader that you the reader imagine as you read.

and we want a type of inquiry that will allow us to examine this single pericope. Therefore I will use a method developed by John Elliott in his study
of 1 Peter.[14] Elliott poses nine questions to the biblical text and attempts to
answer them.[15] The answers generate a sense of the strategy employed by
the author and consequently suggest a range of social circumstances that
might have given rise to this strategy. The nine questions are:

1. Who is the intended audience of the text? What can we know
   about them?
2. Who is the author of the work, and what is the author's relationship to the audience?
3. How is the social situation described in the text?
4. How does the author diagnose and evaluate the situation?
5. How is the strategy of the text evident in its genre, content, and
   organization?
6. What response does the author seek from the intended audience?
7. How does the author attempt to motivate and persuade the
   audience?
8. How would the situation and strategy of the piece be identified
   using a contemporary social-scientific *etic* perspective?[16]
9. What self-interests or group interests motivated the author to
   produce the text?

As Elliott demonstrates, these questions work particularly well with rhetorical texts, that is, books or passages that explicitly exhort people to certain courses of action (for example, epistles, speeches). The Lukan
Baptist's advice exhorting the crowds to a behavioral conversion is a good
example of a rhetorical text and so would seem to lend itself to this method
of analysis. So let us take each question in turn.

1. Who is the intended audience of the text? We have already dealt
with this question in the context of the general historical-critical background of the passage, although we can amplify it a bit more at this point.
The geographic location of the audience is somewhere in the Gentile
world. Their social location is varied; the Gospel is open to both high-

---

[14] *A Home for the Homeless: A Social-Scientific Criticism of 1 Peter, Its Situation and Strategy*, rev. ed. (Minneapolis: Fortress, 1990; original 1981).

[15] Elliott provides an abbreviated version of his method in *What Is Social-Scientific Criticism?* 70–86.

[16] Social scientists distinguish between the *emic* and *etic* perspectives. The *emic* perspective is that of the subject or native population being studied. The *etic* perspective is the
interpretation of the outsider or researcher.

status and low-status individuals (for example, Theophilus and Mary), to Jew and Gentile and those in between (Jewish crowds who would consider Abraham to be their father, Roman soldiers, and tax collectors who served the Romans by collecting from the Jews). The frequent mention of women in the Gospel suggests that they were numbered among Luke's audience.[17]

2. Who is the author of the work, and what is the author's relationship to the audience? Again, we have already determined that the anonymous author was most likely a Gentile Christian whose relatively high status is assured by the quality of his education and writing style. Moreover, he represents his project as one of composing a more orderly account than those prepared by his predecessors, which indicates that he was not an eyewitness and companion of Jesus, that he must have been writing in at least the second generation after Jesus, and that he is sensitive to the issue of accuracy and order. The famous "we-passages" in the Acts of the Apostles lead some scholars to propose that the author might have been a companion of Paul, which in turn suggests the path through which the traditions about Jesus might have reached him (through the apostles to Paul to "Luke").[18]

3. How is the social situation described in the text? This short passage is a narrative text, and so it operates at two levels. There is a social situation described in the story, that is, in the world of the characters, and there is another social situation implied in the discourse, or the world of the author and his audience.[19] We can presume some correlation between the story and discourse worlds in the Gospels; in fact, it is this very correlation that compromises the Gospels as historical records of John and Jesus (see Chapter 1).

We begin with the story itself. The social situation is that "crowds" desire John's baptism, and he warns them what it entails. It requires a behavioral conversion that is connected to an apocalyptic judgment. In this judgment, participation in the Jewish *ethnos* will be no guarantee of protection; rather, the only criterion will be one's behavior, the "fruits worthy of conversion." Moreover, the judge who will "gather the grain" or render judgment will be Jesus, not John; John is merely the preliminary harvester

---

[17] Redaction-critical analysis indicates both that Luke introduces more women into the narrative *and* that he diminishes their public roles; see Mary Rose D'Angelo, "(Re)Presentations of Women in the Gospel of Matthew and Luke-Acts," in *Women and Christian Origins*, ed. Ross Shepard Kraemer and Mary Rose D'Angelo (New York: Oxford University Press, 1999) 171–195.

[18] The narrator switches to first-person narration at Acts 16:10-17; 20:5-15; 21:1-18; and 27:1–28:16.

[19] For the "story-discourse" distinction in narrative criticism, see Seymour Chatman, *Story and Discourse: Narrative Structure in Fiction and Film* (Ithaca, N.Y.: Cornell University Press, 1978).

of the grain.[20] This much is borrowed from Mark and repeated in Matthew. What Luke adds is further explication of what the behavioral conversion looks like and who is eligible to convert. In every case the behavioral conversion entails the redistribution of resources along lines we presume are not customarily followed. The "crowds" are told to share their own clothing and food; tax collectors are advised to collect only the tax and not the surcharge they would normally impose for their services; soldiers are told not to steal money or harass people to pay protection money. A close reading of the entire Gospel would illustrate how important the proper use of resources is to Luke and how characteristic it is of his themes.[21] Luke's placement of this passage in the midst of an apocalyptic discourse suggests that he understood economic justice to be central to the restored, redeemed world of the new age. Indeed, this theme is borne out in Acts, where our earliest summaries of the Christian community in Jerusalem describe its members as sharing all things in common, selling their property and possessions and dividing the proceeds among them according to each one's need, so that there would *be* no need among them (Acts 2:42-47; 4:32–5:11; see Deut 15:4, which Luke cites). The interruption of the apocalyptic preaching with this more prosaic advice for individuals actually diminishes the sense that the judgment is imminent by emphasizing how to behave until it occurs.

The social situation in the story suggests the social situation in the discourse. Luke is writing in the second or third generation after Jesus. The promised definitive return of the messiah has not yet happened, and the Christian movement needs both to grapple with that delay and to maintain itself according to the founding vision just at the time when the last of the founders are dying.

---

[20] Thus Robert L. Webb, *John the Baptizer and Prophet: A Socio-Historical Study*, JSNTSup 62 (Sheffield: JSOT Press, 1991) 262–278.

[21] On the subject of Luke's redactional interest in economic issues, see Luke T. Johnson, *The Literary Function of Possessions in Luke-Acts*, SBLDS 39 (Missoula, Mont.: Scholars Press, 1977), and *Sharing Possessions: Mandate and Symbol of Faith*, OBT (Philadelphia: Fortress, 1981); David Peter Seccombe, *Possessions and the Poor in Luke-Acts*, SNTSU, vol. 6 (Linz: Studien zum Neuen Testament und seiner Umwelt, 1982); Philip F. Esler, *Community and Gospel in Luke-Acts: The Social and Political Motivations of Lucan Theology*, SNTSMS 57 (Cambridge: Cambridge University Press, 1987); John Gillman, *Possessions and the Life of Faith: A Reading of Luke-Acts*, ZSNT (Collegeville, Minn.: Michael Glazier/The Liturgical Press, 1991); Halvor Moxnes, "Social Relations and Economic Interaction in Luke's Gospel: A Research Report," in *Luke-Acts: Scandinavian Perspectives*, ed. Petri Luomanen (Helsinki: Finnish Exegetical Society, 1991) 58–75; and S. Scott Bartchy, "Community of Goods in Acts: Idealization or Social Reality?" in *The Future of Early Christianity: Essays in Honor of Helmut Koester*, ed. Birger A. Pearson (Minneapolis: Fortress, 1991) 309–318.

4. How does the author diagnose and evaluate the situation? Luke's "diagnosis" and evaluation of these problems are not so apparent as these features are in an epistle, which directly addresses a particular problem or problems that have arisen in a particular community. In a narrative we have to discern the author's diagnosis through the lens of his story. But redaction criticism at least enables us to discern this author's particular interests in his editing, modification, and rearrangement of his sources. Looking chiefly, then, at the unique Lukan material, we see that the author deals with the problems in his social situation. Luke compensates for the loss of eye-witnesses by composing "an orderly account" of their testimony, thus offering the reader the best possible rendering of the tradition. He maintains the founding vision that the judgment is imminent, but he adapts this teaching by interpolating a unique passage of prosaic advice. This advice re-creates the world before the full dawning of the new age by altering the patterns of resource distribution. If Luke's advice is followed, the judgment need not come so soon, because the just relationships it promises will already be in place. John's adapted exhortation thus suits the author's strategy for dealing with both the delayed parousia and the Christian conundrum of how to behave in the meantime. Furthermore, the list of questioners confirms the legitimacy of including Gentiles in the Christian mission and challenges even Luke's Christian audience to continue to preach John's and Jesus' message to these people.

5. How is the strategy of the text evident in its genre, content, and organization? Our answer to this question is already suggested in the paragraph above. Luke's strategy is to explain the delayed return of Christ and to devise an interim Christian ethic. He does this rather artfully in one move by locating ethical advice between two apocalyptic passages, so that the physical placement parallels the temporal situation in which his audience finds itself. The difficult advice he offers likely remains difficult for the Christian audience; this is further supported by Luke's repeated emphasis on the theme throughout the Gospel and Acts. The challenge to share resources and the implication that one must do so across the social boundaries of Jew-Gentile, taxpayer-tax collector, and colonized-colonizer are difficult enough that the Christian audience might have appreciated the extra time before the judgment to measure up to the new standard.

6. What response does the author seek from the intended audience? Luke would not augment John's teaching unless he expected his audience to heed his advice. Luke consistently portrays John as a parallel figure to Jesus, albeit a lesser and prior partner. We can therefore expect that John's teaching remains in force for Luke's audience just as Jesus' teaching stands. Luke wants his audience to heed John's advice, to understand that the

Gospel is for Jew *and* Gentile, and to appreciate that much remains to be done before the eventual return of Christ.

7. How does the author attempt to motivate and persuade the audience? The techniques employed by Luke include the fire-and-brimstone, fear-inducing techniques inherited from Mark and Q. From Q we have the address to the crowd, "Spawn of snakes," a phrase not likely to endear either the characters in the story or an audience sympathetic to them to the speaker's message. The Q threat of the ax at the root of the tree, the insult that God could raise children to Abraham from stones, and the Markan warning that anyone judged chaff will burn in an inextinguishable fire— these are all calculated to induce fear and attention in an audience. But we have seen that Luke interrupts this strategy with another and opposing strategy, which is inclusive, hopeful, and quite pragmatic. John spends a great deal of time in Luke telling people *how* to produce fruits of conversion rather than simply threatening them *that* they should. If the audience had grown disillusioned that the promised destruction of evil had not yet come, this insertion would have the effect of shifting their attention from the destruction of the evil to the conduct of the good.

8. How would the situation and strategy of the piece be identified using a contemporary social-scientific etic perspective? We have identified a few strategies that appear to be operative in Luke's text. One of these strategies related to Luke's interpolation of some prosaic advice right in the middle of a blistering sermon on the coming judgment. It was suggested that the interpolation allowed Luke to deal with both the delayed parousia and the Christian conundrum of how to behave in the meantime. Luke effectively takes the fire out of the fire-and-brimstone by interrupting an apocalyptic speech with an economic exhortation and by broadening a characteristically Jewish apocalyptic perspective to generic proverbial advice that any Gentile could understand, a fact reinforced by the introduction of Gentiles and Gentile-sympathizing characters into the scene.

At this step in our analysis, we require a contemporary social-scientific perspective that will help to explain Luke's strategy. There are many models and theories that have been developed to analyze various cultural scripts and social dynamics, and it is helpful to consult a list of them to become familiar with some of the available options.[22]

---

[22] Elliott includes a list of models in Appendix 4 of his book, *What Is Social-Scientific Criticism?* 124–126, as well as his article, "Social Scientific Criticism of the New Testament: More on Methods and Models," *Semeia* 35 (1986) 1–33. You might also scan the tables of contents of some journals that specialize in the sociological or anthropological analysis of Scripture or religion, such as *Biblical Theology Bulletin, Journal for the Scientific Study of Religion, Journal of Ritual Studies, Review of Religious Research,* and *Sociology of Religion.*

For our immediate project, a theory that might prove useful is the cognitive dissonance theory originally proposed by Leon Festinger *et al.* and subsequently adapted by other scholars. In their 1956 study *When Prophecy Fails*, Festinger and his co-authors explored the responses to failed prophecy in a millenarian group.[23] Their thesis was that when strongly held beliefs are disconfirmed, the group holding those beliefs reduces the cognitive dissonance (the discrepancy between what one thinks or believes and what one experiences) by strengthening their beliefs and embarking on intensified missionary activity. This evangelizing activity yields a psychological or cognitive benefit: If others can be convinced, then this will validate the beliefs recently invalidated.[24] Indeed, some have explained the early evangelical fervor of Christianity in precisely these terms: the apostles, disappointed in the failure of their messiah, altered their beliefs (the messiah was *supposed* to suffer, Jesus was crowned and vindicated by God in his crucifixion and resurrection) and simultaneously compensated for their disappointment by successfully convincing others of their newfound faith. Luke's Gospel is part of this project, as it enables the dissemination of the Gospel message to a wider audience by virtue of both its form (an easily circulated book) and its content (a Gospel pitched to the Gentiles). In light of this model, Luke's redaction of Mark and Q and the interpolation of content into John's otherwise apocalyptic speech is part of the redefinition of belief that reduces cognitive dissonance. John predicted a definitive end, but that end is delayed, and so John now provides guidance for an interim ethic.

Other scholars of religion have found Festinger's theory of cognitive dissonance to be inadequate.[25] Studies of other groups whose central prophecies

---

[23] Leon Festinger, Henry W. Riecken, and Stanley Schachter, *When Prophecy Fails* (Minneapolis: University of Minnesota Press, 1956). See also Festinger, *A Theory of Cognitive Dissonance* (Evanston, Ill.: Row, Peterson, 1957). Millenarian groups believe that the present age will soon end, often at a prophesied point in time, and that a thousand-year "new age" will begin. The "thousand-year" belief is based on Revelation 20:1-5, which says that Christ will return and reign in this thousand-year period.

[24] Festinger *et al.* propose that this response is determined by five factors: (1) the belief must be held with deep conviction and have some relevance to one's action/behavior; (2) the believer must have made some commitment that is difficult to undo; (3) the belief must be sufficiently specific and concerned with the real world so that events may unequivocally refute it; 4) undeniable disconfirmatory evidence must occur and be recognized by the believer; and (5) the individual believer must have social support (*When Prophecy Fails*, 4).

[25] See J. Gordon Melton, "Spiritualization and Reaffirmation: What Really Happens When Prophecy Fails," *American Studies* 26 (2 1985) 82; A. B. Van Fossen, "How Do Movements Survive Failures of Prophecy?" *Research in Social Movements, Conflicts and Change* 10 (1988) 193–202; W. S. Bainbridge, *The Sociology of Religious Movements* (New York: Routledge, 1997); but see also D. Batson and L. Ventis, *The Religious Experience: A Social Psychological Perspective* (New York: Oxford University Press, 1982), who dispute that the flying-saucer group analyzed by Festinger *et al.* was influenced by the researchers.

failed have indicated that proselytization is *not* a common response after the disconfirming event, and that in fact there are multiple strategies that groups use to diminish cognitive dissonance.[26] For example, the group may reaffirm their beliefs as Festinger suggested, restating that the prophecy was accurate but that something got in the way; but it may also adapt those beliefs by admitting some error, reappraise them by asserting that the event occurred but was not visible, or collapse under the weight of its error.[27] Moreover, it is rare that a social group would be organized entirely around a single prophecy or belief; it is more often the case that its organization is a complex blend of doctrines, beliefs, political structures, relationships of members to charismatic authority, and rituals, all of which can play a role in diminishing the cognitive dissonance engendered by a single failed prophecy.[28] In fact, if the failed prophecy is just one belief among many, the failure of it is often appropriated as a positive event, a test that strengthens the group in their other beliefs. Because there are multiple variables within social groups, there are multiple responses possible to an occasion of failed prophecy. Thus cognitive dissonance is resolved not only by irrational denial, as Festinger *et al.* proposed, but also by strategies of rational explanation and "noncognitive consonance" such as ritual.[29] As John G. Gager has put it, some millenarian movements simply "reach the millennium in other, less obvious ways."[30]

[26] J. R. Stone, *Expecting Armageddon: Essential Readings in Failed Prophecy* (New York: Routledge, 2000); earlier criticisms included J. A. Hardyck and M. Braden, "Prophecy Fails Again: A Report of a Failure to Replicate," *Journal of Abnormal and Social Psychology* 65 (2 1962) 136–141; R. W. Balch, G. Farnsworth, and S. Wilkins, "When the Bombs Drop: Reactions to Disconfirmed Prophecy in a Millennial Sect," *Sociological Perspectives* 26 (2 1983) 137–158; L. Dawson, "When Prophecy Fails and Faith Persists: A Theoretical Overview," *Nova Religio* 3 (1999) 6–82; C. Bader, "When Prophecy Passes Unnoticed: New Perspectives on Failed Prophecy," *Journal for the Scientific Study of Religion* 38 (1 1999) 119–131.

[27] J. F. Zygmunt, "When Prophecies Fail," *American Behavioural Scientist* 16 (1972) 245–268.

[28] For a fascinating study of the role of ritual enactment in the reinterpretation of a predicted "end," see Susan J. Palmer and Natalie Finn, "Coping with Apocalypse in Canada: Experiences of Endtime in la Mission de l'Esprit Saint and the Institute of Applied Metaphysics," *Sociological Analysis* 53 (1992) 397–415.

[29] Simon Dein argues for the rational nature of a group's response to failed prophecy in "What Really Happens When Prophecy Fails: The Case of Lubavitch," *Sociology of Religion* 62 (3 2001) 383–401. Another interesting exercise in attributing rational choice to seemingly irrational phenomena is Rodney Stark's study *The Rise of Christianity: How the Obscure, Marginal Jesus Movement Became the Dominant Religious Force in the Western World in a Few Centuries* (San Francisco: HarperSanFrancisco, 1997; original Princeton, N.J.: Princeton University Press, 1996). The phrase "noncognitive consonance" is from Palmer and Finn, "Coping with Apocalypse in Canada," 411.

[30] "The End of Time and the Rise of Community," in *Kingdom and Community: The Social World of Early Christianity*, PHSR (Englewood Cliffs, N.J.: Prentice-Hall, 1975) 49.

Once the etic perspective has been discussed, its capacity to explain the text must be evaluated. The theory of cognitive dissonance does a better job of explaining a group's immediate response to unfulfilled prophecy than it does of explaining a single author's third-generation response as we have in the Gospel of Luke. Moreover, some of the research techniques used and information sought by contemporary sociologists cannot be applied to or found in the New Testament; in Luke's case, our subjects are dead and our Gospel is uninterested in supplying some of the data we need. So in what way is the social-science theory a helpful tool for interpreting the social situation in our text?

While it is true that Luke himself was not privy to the original disappointment, it is still likely that his second or third generation had to face it and explain it. Early Christianity had its critics, and even the most well-disposed God-fearer would have questions about following someone crucified as a common criminal.[31] Of the three Synoptic Gospels, Luke's is oriented toward a more sophisticated Gentile readership, and this audience may have needed an interpretation of the events that made sense to them. It has already been suggested that this could explain Luke's insertion of proverbial advice and Gentile characters into the baptismal preaching scene. The criticisms of the original cognitive dissonance theory are useful as well, for they demonstrate that individuals do not believe apart from social networks and that they have multiple strategies for dealing with disappointment. This suggests that we should be cautious in limiting Luke's strategy to a single factor, such as the delayed parousia. This challenge to belief may have occasioned Luke's reinterpretation of salvation history, particularly if the recent battle over Jerusalem had been invested with messianic expectations that went unfulfilled. But the delayed return of Christ is not likely the only impetus to Luke's unique addition. He may have seen the preaching episode as yet one more occasion to harmonize his portraits of Jesus and John; since Jesus preached about shared goods, so must John. This strategy, in turn, may have been conceived to draw followers of the Baptist into the Christian movement, just as we have seen Luke's interest in drawing Gentiles into the story.

Finally, cognitive dissonance theory suggests several attributes for the historical movements around John and Jesus. Both survived the death of their charismatic leaders at an early moment in their history. The fact that

---

[31] For a famous pagan critique of early Christianity, see Celsus's second-century treatise *On the True Doctrine: A Discourse Against the Christians*, trans. R. Joseph Hoffmann (New York: Oxford University Press, 1987). The text has been reconstructed from the lengthy quotations preserved by the third-century Christian Origen in his work *Contra Celsum*, trans. Henry Chadwick (Cambridge: Cambridge University Press, 1965).

both could absorb that shock and survive indicates that they share certain attributes with new religious movements in the modern world that also survive an early crisis. These include a leadership structure that can direct the movement after the founder's death (disciples), a way of routinizing the charismatic activity of the founder that was approved by the founder before his death, and a complex of beliefs and rituals (baptism, fasting/meals) that could cushion the impact of a catastrophe like the founder's death.

9. *What self-interests or group interests motivated the author to produce the text?* Luke is concerned to establish Christianity as a respectable heir of Judaism within the Roman Empire. He, like Josephus, is interested in diminishing the impression that this group of Jews threatens the social order, so he moderates the provocative apocalyptic material he inherits with more prosaic advice. He presents Christians as faithful Jews deeply connected to their ancestral heritage but also open to the Gentile world in a way that other Judaisms were not. These Christians practice piety and peace, values that would be respected in the Roman world. This portrait of Christianity creates a space for the community in the Roman world at the same time that it helps Christians understand their place in a history that will not end soon. At the same time, Luke takes yet another opportunity to harmonize the portraits of John and Jesus: Both preach that sharing one's goods is a sign of the new age. The underlying strategy may be to provide a place in the Christian community for followers of the Baptist, just as Luke created new spaces for the Gentiles.

This abbreviated exercise applied a list of exploratory questions to a particular text in order to detect the social situation and compensatory strategy of an author. Data about the social situation and rhetorical strategy in turn suggested a sociological theory that could be applied to the text. The questions were heuristic devices, that is, tools meant to help us discover aspects of the social matrix from which this text was generated. They enabled us to gather data from the text. The theory was an explanatory device, that is, a tool that interpreted the data. We presented the theory, applied it to the text, and evaluated its effectiveness for explaining Luke's unique interpolation in the episode of John's preaching.

From this first complete social-scientific exercise, we now turn to two related exercises in Chapter 5. Both cluster around John and around his purifying ministry, but each does this with its own unique configuration of the axes of social-scientific inquiry.

CHAPTER FIVE

*Purification Movements
in First-Century C.E. Judea*

The aim of social-scientific criticism is to explore the meaning of the biblical text in the context of the ancient world. Our study of Luke 3:7-18 in Chapter 4 accomplished this by beginning with the text and moving toward an explanatory theory that helped us to come up with new questions, if not new answers. In this chapter our approach will be somewhat different. We will embark on two related inquiries, each with a discrete focus, scope, entry point, direction, and temporal range. While the inquiries will be different, their subject will be similar; both will focus not only on the figure of the Baptist but also on some aspect of his characteristic activity of cleansing people.

Cleanliness and dirtiness are culturally defined. Of course, it is true that there is an objective thing called dirt, and presumably the more of it on a thing, the dirtier it is. But if you've ever lived with other people in a house or a dorm or traveled to another country, you know that there are sometimes very different definitions of permissible dirtiness or ideal cleanliness operative. To some extent, "clean" and "dirty" are defined differently by different people.

It is with this insight that two exercises will begin in this chapter. We won't exactly be focusing on physical hygiene, but rather on an intangible notion related to it, that of "purity and pollution." Every culture defines a map for itself of appropriate human behaviors performed at appropriate times in appropriate places by the appropriate people. Following the groundbreaking work of Mary Douglas, anthropologists have understood the cultural categories of purity and pollution in these terms.[1] Purity refers

---

[1] *Purity and Danger: An Analysis of Concepts of Pollution and Taboo,* 2nd ed. (New York: Routledge, 2000; original 1966).

to a state in which the map is intact; pollution refers to a state in which the map has been compromised. John's baptizing activity cleansed the bodies of people who had already cleansed their behavior—all our sources agree about this. And this suggests that we cannot understand what John was up to without analyzing the cultural notions of purity and pollution within which he and our sources were operating.

Our second social-scientific exercise expands our focus beyond John's movement to others like his. There were *several* purification movements in first-century C.E. Palestine, including the Pharisees, various revolutionary and prophetic groups, the Jesus movement, the Qumran Essenes, and the Baptist movement. The turn to examine these group phenomena shifts our attention from the cultural system to the social system and from a deductive to a comparative method. While four groups will be introduced, only two will be compared closely: the Qumran Essenes and the Baptist movement. The selection of these two groups is warranted because the parallels between them are numerous—so numerous that some scholars believe John to have been an Essene initiate before launching a ministry of his own. The Essenes and the Baptist groups will be analyzed with a multivariate matrix model that will help us to compare the range of activities the groups sought to purify.

The two following exercises are freestanding investigations, each with its own configuration of axes, but together they will help to create a social and cultural matrix within which we might better understand the worlds of John the Baptist and of the authors who wrote about him. The multiplicity of approaches has the added advantage of illustrating yet again how many options can be generated and insights gathered by using social-scientific criticism.

A Deductive Exercise:
From Model (Purity and Pollution) to Text

We begin this exercise at the macro-level of the cultural system. Our focus is one value in that cultural system, purity and pollution, and therefore the entry point of our inquiry is context rather than a text. Our initial presentation of the purity/pollution phenomenon will be synchronic, examining the model in an atemporal fashion before applying it to our texts about the Baptist.

Definitions of Terms

The reference to purity and pollution as a "value" requires some explanation. A value is simply a notion that is invested with significance by a group of people. When a group identifies a person, place, or event as pure and another as polluted, they are investing that person, place, or thing with positive or negative significance, as the case may be. We speak of honor and shame as values in the ancient world as well.[2] In this case, a group identifies an attribute or behavior of an individual as having positive or negative significance. Likewise, we can speak of the ancient value of the collective over the individual: here the relation of the individual to the larger group is at stake, and what is evaluated positively is group inter-action over individual self-reliance. In the individualistic culture of the United States today, the evaluation is reversed; self-reliance is evaluated positively, while group cohesion or conformity is not. This illustrates that values are socially constructed and reveals just one of the many cultural discrepancies that can impede a modern interpretation of ancient texts. The values of purity and pollution, honor and shame, and the collective over the individual are just some of the values of the ancient world. Each of these values represents a social investment of significance.

Now as we have already determined in the case of dirt, one society's investment may differ considerably from that of another society. We see this in every social situation where diverse cultures are represented and their values contested, just as we saw it in the reading situation above with its different views of the individual. Divergences such as these confirm the claim that values are socially constructed; they are not a result of biology or genetics or natural law or any other unalterable cause we may at any given moment assign. And their construction is more complex than the simple attribution of positive or negative value. The values are applied to situations in life—to persons (self and others), to objects, to time, to place, to nature, to the divine. These applications that order life are frequently re-ferred to in social-scientific exegesis as "maps." The metaphor is apt, since maps provide a symbolic replication, not of the real world, but of our or-dering of it (consider, for a moment, whether state boundaries always cor-respond to something you can see on the ground or why north must always be at the top of a map). A map is the patterning we do that classifies aspects of the world according to our ideas and values.

---

[2] Bruce J. Malina, "Honor and Shame: Pivotal Values of the First-Century Mediter-ranean World," in *The New Testament World: Insights from Cultural Anthropology* (Atlanta: John Knox Press, 1981; 3rd ed., Louisville, Ky.: Westminster John Knox, 2001) 25–50; with Jerome H. Neyrey, "Honor and Shame in Luke-Acts: Pivotal Values of the Mediterranean World," in *The Social World of Luke-Acts: Models for Interpretation,* ed. Jerome H. Neyrey (Peabody, Mass.: Hendrickson, 1991) 25–65; and Halvor Moxnes, "Honor and Shame," in *The Social Sciences and New Testament Interpretation,* ed. Richard Rohrbaugh (Peabody, Mass.: Hendrickson, 1996) 19–40.

The complementary values of honor and shame, for example, are mapped onto facets of our daily lives. An individual in our culture might be viewed as honorable if she blew the whistle on corporate fraud, risking her position in the company to act with integrity. In another culture, such a lack of conformity might be considered shameful. In the United States, persons who regularly risk their lives to help others are honored, but killing oneself in order to kill others, as in homicide bombings, is considered shameful. There are certain locations in our country that are invested with significance due to their association with honor, such as the Tomb of the Unknown Soldier at Arlington National Cemetery, while other places are synonymous with national shame, such as the Japanese-American internment camps at Manzanar and Tule Lake, California. And for many the image of the divine realm includes a god who acts honorably and an evil power that does not.

The terms "value" and "map" have been defined, but there is yet another term that requires explanation. Social-scientific critics of biblical texts often mention cultural "scripts" that guide behavior within a given society. A script is the behavioral code that accompanies and complements the value maps. The example of the Tomb of the Unknown Soldier will demonstrate the interrelationship of value, map, and script. The value of honor is mapped onto the place of the tomb because the remains buried there represent all those who died deaths consonant with the script of honor in our nation. The script is the behavioral code of how to act honorably, and this has included at most moments in our nation's history the willingness to fight and die in the nation's wars. At times there may be competing versions of the script, as there was during the American Civil War, while at other times the script may be more fundamentally challenged, as by pacifists or anti-war protestors; but even rival claimants attest to the power of the script of honor insofar as they would reclaim or redefine it.

It is easy enough to recognize the values, maps, and scripts in our own culture. But when we turn to antiquity, the task is more difficult, and therefore even more interesting. The methodological problem confronts us: *how* are we supposed to discern values, maps, and scripts in the archaeological detritus and literary fragments that remain of this lost world?

The task is not so difficult as it might at first appear. The reason is that the values and their associated maps and scripts were embedded in the social institutions of those lost cultures, and therefore leave their imprint like so many fossils on the archaeological and literary record. The scripts in particular are visible in traces of repeated behavior and in the institutionalizations of this behavior in things like law codes, calendars, educational curricula, judgments, and rituals (social rituals like meals, for example, or religious rituals like prayer, fasting, and sacrifice). They are also visible in narratives about transgressive behavior and in comedy and satire, which lampoon characters or individuals on the basis of expectations that the audience and author share (which is why comedy rarely translates well from one society to the next).[3] Finally, scripts are visible in historical clashes between cultures if we have an accompanying record of the causes of those conflicts and if some of those causes involve incompatible cultural expectations and norms. All of these provide hints of pivotal values around which social life was organized, as well as traces of the maps and behavioral scripts that governed daily life.

A final phrase that requires definition is "plausibility structure." This term refers to the overarching framework of meaning within which values, maps, and scripts operate and achieve their legitimacy. We have already seen that each society patterns behavior and assigns value; it is also the burden of each society to "make sense of it all" by creating and replicating a kind of superstructure within which those values fit and appear valid. Returning to our example of the Tomb of the Unknowns, the plausibility structure goes beyond the single value of honor mapped onto this place because of the social script embodied by the persons buried there, and includes related values such as patriotism and sacrifice, a narrative of the nation's history within which such sacrifices can be understood, an educational system that teaches that history, institutions that enforce those values, national rituals that reiterate commitment (the Pledge of Allegiance, elections, the singing of the national anthem at athletic events), and so on. Upon reflection, one could easily add more of the elements that buttress the system. Together they function to reinforce each other and thus maintain the patterns deemed valuable in a given society.

The goal of social-scientific criticism is to reproduce as much of that plausibility structure as possible. To do this, at least when reproducing cultural values, the critic must examine as much evidence from a given social unit as possible so as to identify the typical. It would not do to identify the unusual, since values, maps, and scripts are meant to put everything in its place. So what we want to try to find is the place where everything was supposed to be, not where it really was or, alas, where it ventured in moments of creativity and innovation.

"The Typical" Then vs. "The Typical" Now

Before turning to the specific cultural value of purity and pollution and how that was mapped and scripted in first-century Judea and Galilee, it

[3] For laughter and comedy as social mechanisms that reveal cultural assumptions, see Blake Leyerle, "Ridiculous Men," in *Theatrical Shows and Ascetic Lives: John Chrysostom's Attack on Spiritual Marriage* (Berkeley: University of California Press, 2001) 100–142.

will be useful to have a general sense of the type of society we are talking about. Bruce J. Malina and Richard Rohrbaugh have provided a comparative model of the agrarian society of antiquity and the industrial-technological society in which we live (see Figure 6):[4]

Figure 6. A Comparative Model of Agrarian and Industrial-Technological Societies

	Agrarian Society	Industrial-Technological Society
Demographics	90+% of population live in rural areas	90+% of population live in urban areas
	Birth rate: 40 per 1000 per year	Birth rate: less than 20 per 1000 per year + dramatically lower death rates yield rapidly rising population
	Life expectancy: 40 years for those who survive infancy, 20 years if infancy is included	Life expectancy: 74.6 men, 80.4 women (U.S.);[5] though statistics for inner city poor, rural African Americans and Native Americans are closer to agrarian society
	Largest city in Judea/Galilee: Jerusalem, at 35,000	Largest city in U.S.: New York, at 8,008,278 (2000 census)[6]

figure 6 continued

[4] Adapted from Malina and Rohrbaugh, *Social-Science Commentary on the Synoptic Gospels* (Minneapolis: Fortress, 1972) 7–8. For further information about models of agrarian societies, see Conrad M. Arensburg, "The Old World Peoples: The Place of European Cultures in World Ethnography," *Anthropological Quarterly* 36 (1963) 75–99; Bruce J. Malina, "Dealing with Biblical (Mediterranean) Characters: A Guide for U. S. Consumers," *Biblical Theology Bulletin* 19 (1989) 127–141; John J. Pilch, *Hear the Word*, vol. 2, *Introducing the Cultural Context of the New Testament* (New York and Mahwah, N.J.: Paulist Press, 1991).

[5] United Nations, "Indicators on Health," *United Nations Department of Economic and Social Affairs Statistics Division.* Cited 27 October 2002. Online: http://unstats.un.org/unsd/demographic/social/health.htm. The statistic indicates life expectancy at birth in years for the period 2000–2005.

[6] "Population," *New York City Department of City Planning.* Cited 27 October 2002. Online: http://www.nyc.gov/html/dcp/html/census/pop2000.html.

Literacy	2-4% literate	2-4% illiterate
Family	More than half of families broken during childbearing and childrearing years by death of parent; many widows and orphans (an orphan is a child who has lost a father)	Life expectancy rates make it more likely that a family will be split by divorce than by death; 43% of new marriages end in divorce[7]
	Main unit of production and consumption (see economics)	Family production has largely ended; family is only one unit of consumption
	Children provide both labor for family production and support for parents in old age	Children use more of family income, produce less of it; parents may support selves in old age (with some government support)
Economics	90-95% engage in primary industries (agriculture, extraction of raw materials)	4-9% engage in primary industries (U.S.)
	1-3% own 33-66% of arable land; thus the 90% of society that are peasants are subsistence farmers	
	Less occupational diversity	
	Family is the chief unit of production and consumption	Family production has largely ended; family is only one unit of consumption
	Goods and services mediated by patrons	Goods and services mediated by markets, businesses, and government
		Productive capacity exceeds agrarian society by over a hundredfold
Politics	Tremendous political instability	In democratic societies, balance of power and transfer of power moderate instability

[7] E. Mavis Hetherington and John Kelly, *For Better or for Worse: Divorce Reconsidered* (New York: W. W. Norton, 2002).

This is a model, an abstract, selective representation of the relationships of social phenomena used to conceptualize, analyze, and interpret patterns of social relations and to compare and contrast one system of social relations with another.[8] You have already used a model in Chapter 4; there we analyzed the text of John's baptismal preaching in Luke 3 with the aid of an implied model of the communication process (author, text [form, content, rhetoric], audience, and the socio-cultural context within which these interact). The model was not identified at the time because it would have complicated our work unnecessarily. But at this point in our study we need to make our operational models more specific to provide ourselves greater access to the thought-world of the first century (although we should always remember that these models are *our* construct of what that world looked like). This model indicates the cultural void that lies between the modern and ancient worlds. It suggests how different day-to-day life must have been and gives some sense of the institutions within which purity and pollution were inscribed.

Purity and Pollution: Value, Maps, and Scripts

We are now at a point where we can apply our initial definitions to the value we have targeted for attention—purity and pollution. To reiterate, purity and pollution are not "things" that are always and everywhere the same; rather, they are significances—investments of value that people make—and so they are applied to "things" (persons, objects, time, place, nature, deity) differently by different cultures. These things, from our perspective, point to the values a society has given them, and thus the parts of the map are the symbols in the symbolic universe of the culture. A symbol is something that points to and participates in another reality; thus a "pure person" like a Christian saint would point to and reinforce the symbolic universe of Christianity, where purity is defined in certain ways the saint is thought to embody.

Anthropologist Mary Douglas developed definitions of purity and pollution that have been widely accepted in the field of biblical studies, in part because she took the first step in applying her insights from comparative analysis of contemporary social groups to the Levitical purity system in the Jewish Scriptures. Interested as she was in discerning the "maps" of the societies she studied, Douglas found that it was a society's map of *order* that determined its definitions of purity and pollution. Purity thus

---

[8] John H. Elliott, *What Is Social-Scientific Criticism?*, GBSNTS (Minneapolis: Fortress, 1993) 132.

refers to any person, thing, time, place, part of nature, aspect of the divine that is in its proper place on the map of order that the society has drawn. Now in fact these elements rarely behave in the way a given society would like, because, after all, the map is an artificial ordering of a more random reality. Pollution describes the condition of the thing when it transgresses the boundaries designed by the society. Pollution, or "dirt," as Douglas put it, is "matter out of place."[9] Purity and pollution are fluid rather than static categories. Something may not be pure or need not be polluted for very long. All one needs to do is transgress a boundary to become polluted; and all one needs to do to remedy pollution is to put the matter back "in place."

At this point it may be tempting to think that purity and pollution are religious categories, since this is a book about John the Baptist, and he is a figure in the Christian New Testament. But that would be a misconception. It is true that religious systems have rich vocabularies for classifying what is pure and polluted ("holy/unholy" "sinless/sinful," "blameless/defiled," "clean/unclean," spotless/stained," "pure/impure"[10]), and many of their rituals, political structures, and Scriptures are predicated on and organized around these notions. But the values of purity and pollution can be mapped across society in multiple institutions and situations. For example, there is some tension in U.S. society, or at least there was in the "dot.com" culture of Silicon Valley in the late 1990s, over the long hours and weekends required to get a company off the ground. The phrase "24/7" described the lifestyle of many tech workers hoping to "strike it rich" in the new California silicon rush. A boundary that had mapped our society—the forty-hour workweek and weekends for personal time—was changing, and though there were many people willing to live this way, others questioned the shifting priorities of money over time. Some people felt that a 24/7 lifestyle was the new order ("time *in* place"), while others felt that the pace was completely insane ("time *out of* place"). Why is it that we laugh at the commercial in which an ordinary guy standing in an endless line in a bank wanders into the next room, where the preferred customers are treated to champagne in a sumptuous, gilded lobby, and is summarily escorted out as soon as his true status is discovered? Person out of place. Gamers spend hours destroying beasts, machines, weapons, and evil enemies—the more matter "out of place," the better. In some cases we can't quite decide whether matter is in place or not, as with gays in the military or new skyscrapers on the site of the World Trade Center towers. The definitions may

[9] *Purity and Danger,* 35.

[10] Neyrey presents a comprehensive semantic word-field for purity and pollution in "The Symbolic Universe of Luke-Acts: 'They Turn the World Upside Down,'" in *The Social World of Luke-Acts,* 275–276.

change and the conditions themselves may be fluid, but there is no doubting that the values of purity and pollution themselves are present across institutions and in our society as well as in the ancient ones.

You could probably now generate a fairly complex map of the purity/pollution value in our culture. If you tried to produce a script as well, you would simply consider the behavioral codes that we have designed to create, maintain, and reinforce the values. Our government has law codes, our schools socialize us into social scripts, our family teaches its preferred behaviors, the residence halls have their policies, and your social group creates its own implicit rules to define how to behave. Sometimes these scripts are all at odds with each other; consider simply the different scripts related to alcohol. "Matter in place" according to the government is responsible drinking by people twenty-one and older, usually inside a building. Your family, dorm, and social group may impose very different maps and expect you to behave by very different scripts, and you have to make frequent decisions for yourself in the face of these competing expectations. Because you are familiar with these scripts, you could sketch them out fairly easily.

It is more difficult to sketch the scripts of the ancient world because we are not members of that culture and our own cultural perspectives can cloud our vision. The only remedy is to absorb as much of that culture as possible through its artifacts, namely, literature and the archaeological record. It is not expedient, though, for the average student to spend years mastering this vast body of material, let alone the many languages in which it survives. Therefore we rely on the work of social scientists who have studied a great deal of the evidence and have organized the results of their data collection for us. In particular, we are interested in what social scientists can tell us about how purity and pollution were mapped onto persons, objects, time, place, nature, and deity in first-century C.E. Judea and Galilee.[11] This will provide a basis against which we can assess the work of John the Baptist. While our focus will be Jewish conventions, it should be mentioned that the pagan cultures of antiquity also inscribed the value of purity in many of the same ways.

Persons. There are several maps of persons in a culture, including those that organize the social body and those that organize the individual body. One of the maps of the social body was the hierarchy of purity thought to inhere in the ritual system. According to this map, the most pure people were priests, followed by Levites, who provided support services in the Temple, then Israelite men, Israelite women (more often impure than

---

[11] See, for example, Malina, *The New Testament World*, 131–137.

men because of menstruation and childbirth), converts, and, at the bottom of the list, sojourners and Gentiles (see Exod 12:43-49; 20:10; Deut 14:21). The fundamental distinction between Jew and Gentile was mapped on the Jewish man's body by circumcision. Persons were also mapped in terms of their physical condition, with intact people on top and amputees and the disabled at the bottom (see Lev 21:17-21).[12] Both of these maps are visible in the arrangement of space and personnel in the Jewish Temple; for example, only priests were allowed into the innermost court, and all the priests and the animals they sacrificed there had to be physically whole and unblemished (see Lev 21:21-23; 22:21-25).

As for the individual's body, there is a hierarchy of its parts, with the head or reason usually accorded value, and the feet, sexual organs, and emotions at the bottom of the list (see 1 Cor 12 and John 13:1-20). All the orifices of the body are potentially dangerous because they provide entrance and egress for impurity (see Gen 3:7). Clothing is a kind of social skin that maps many social categories on top of the body. Tattoos, branding, and piercing likewise plot the skin with socially significant maps; in antiquity, these inscriptions were primarily used to mark slaves. The maps of physical body and social body are not unrelated; one of Douglas's greatest contributions was the correlation she drew between how the body and society are organized and understood in a given social group.[13]

The circumstances of life would alter the average person's purity, but only for a time. For example, sexual intercourse was considered polluting because of the transfer of bodily fluids, but this condition was easily remedied by purification rituals.[14] Likewise, skin diseases and other illnesses, the preparation of a corpse for burial, and childbirth all rendered one impure until the required ablutions could be made. Other daily activities, such as economic intercourse, food preparation, and shared meals, had the potential to defile a person if done in the "wrong" way but were not in and of themselves polluting. For example, foods and liquids could transfer impurity to

[12] See tractate *Megillah* 2.7 in the Talmud for one such Jewish ranking (the Talmuds are codifications of Jewish case law generated by Jewish rabbis as a reflection on the Torah and Mishnah around the years 400–600 C.E.).

[13] *Natural Symbols: Explorations in Cosmology* (New York: Pantheon, 1982; original 1970) 65–81. One example of the application of this insight to the world maps of antiquity is Peter R. L. Brown's *The Body and Society: Men, Women, and Sexual Renunciation in Early Christianity* (New York: Columbia University Press, 1988).

[14] See the summary of purifications mandated in the Jewish literature of the biblical and Second Temple period in Robert L. Webb, *John the Baptizer and Prophet: A Socio-Historical Study,* JSNTSup 62 (Sheffield: Sheffield Academic Press, 1991) 95–162; for the Qumran material and rabbinic material, see also Hannah K. Harrington, *The Impurity Systems of Qumran and the Rabbis: Biblical Foundations,* SBLDS 143 (Atlanta: Scholars Press, 1993).

containers and to people under certain conditions. Economic interactions could be defiling as well: tax collectors were viewed as polluted because they regularly trafficked with the Gentile Romans (and gouged the Jews in the process, which was against the Jewish law). It is important to note that impurity in these cases is not the same as sinfulness, with the exception of our tax collector, who also committed usury. Sin is a subset of impurity and refers only to those acts that violate God's laws. Impurity in general simply violated boundaries, and these kinds of "transgressions" could easily be undone. Paula Fredriksen refers to the restoration rituals as a system of "wash and wait"—a purification followed by a transitional period was all that was needed to restore the person to human society.[15]

Objects. We have already seen that certain things could convey impurity, either because of their nature or condition. Corpses, bodily fluids, anything that came into contact with an unclean person or thing—all these transmitted impurity to other things and to people. There were also things that could purify or sanctify a person, such as immersion in a ritual bath (*miqveh*), fasting and other ascetic behaviors, acts of charity and justice, and of course donations and sacrifices offered in the Temple. In addition, things could be made pure by sanctifying them to God's use; in some cases this made the property off-limits to others who might want it, such as a parent in need of support (see Matt 15:1-6; 23:16-22 and parallels).

Time. Time was mapped in the ancient world through the scripts of liturgical calendars maintained by priests and political leaders. These calendars were, in turn, tied to the agricultural cycle, since many religious festivals were intended to celebrate agricultural events and maintain the productive cycle of the earth. There were competing Jewish calendars during the first century C.E. The Qumran Essenes, for example, followed a luni-solar calendar, while the Jerusalem Temple followed a lunar calendar. This meant that the festivals of these groups would fall on different days. Of course, the calendars of Jews and Gentiles differed; only Jews rested on the Sabbath, and the festival cycles were completely different. These differences made the Jewish communities in the Diaspora very visible to the surrounding peoples and were often the source of great friction. Time was also mapped in apocalyptic literature. Whether through an elaborate periodization of history or through a simple sense that the end was approaching, scribes distinguished between the present time of evil and a future time when evil would be destroyed.

---

[15] *Jesus of Nazareth, King of the Jews: A Jewish Life and the Emergence of Christianity* (New York: Vintage, 1999) 53.

Place. The holiest or purest place in Israel was the Temple in Jerusalem. The arrangement of physical space within the Temple was a microcosm of the map of purity and pollution obtaining without. Just as Jerusalem had its Temple, so too within the Temple there was a holy center, the "sanctuary," within which was the Holy of Holies, where the invisible God was thought to dwell. Surrounding this center was the Court of the Priests, sanctified for the service of God, just as Jerusalem was considered a holy city where special scripts or laws were imposed. Beyond the Court of the Priests was the Court of Israel (for Jewish men), and outside that was the Court of Women (for Jewish women), just as beyond Jerusalem was the Holy Land where Mosaic Law ordered daily life. Outside all these courts was the Court of the Gentiles, just as the Gentile world lay outside the bounds of Israel.

Figure 7. Schematic Maps of Temple and World: A First-Century Jewish Perspective

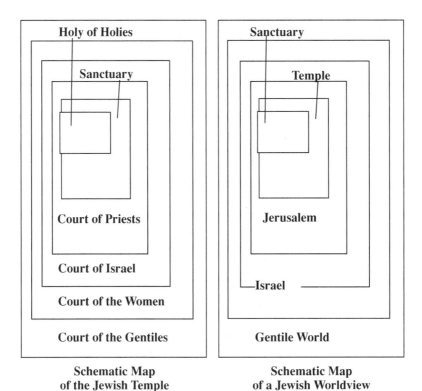

Schematic Map	Schematic Map
of the Jewish Temple	of a Jewish Worldview

The map of sanctified space in the Temple replicates the map of sanctified space in the cosmos, reinforces that map by its physical arrangement and the rituals that occurred there, and maintains the Jewish sense of order through architecture and worship.[16] Violate that place and you challenge the entire worldview, which is why the destruction of the Jewish Temple, first by the Babylonians in 587 B.C.E. and then by the Romans in 70 C.E., was such a devastating blow to Jewish culture, and was calculated to be such by Israel's enemies.[17] Persons who entered the Temple were approaching the deity, and therefore they themselves and everything they brought to God had to be in a pure state.

Nature. The division of nature into hierarchies is visible in the order of creation in Genesis 1: the dome of the heavens was created before/above the land and sea; the heavens were populated with luminaries (stars) before the sky and water were populated with creatures before the earth was populated with animals and creeping things. Finally, the Creation was capped off with the introduction of human beings, and Genesis 2–3 makes clear the priority of humans over all other creatures, and then the domination of male over female. Hierarchies or maps of nature are also visible in dietary codes, which designate certain foods and combinations of foods pure and impure in some correlation to the map of creatures. Even animals were put on a diet in Genesis (1:29-30), and the humans, who were told to observe a vegan dietary script in paradise, were allowed to eat bloodless meat after the Flood (Gen 9:3), before the more complex script of *kashrut* was introduced in Leviticus 11.[18] It should not surprise us that much of this material in Genesis and Leviticus was written by priests, for their role was to maintain the order of the cosmos by their ritual performances and physical sanctity.[19] The map of nature is also visible in the sacrificial system.

---

[16] See Mishnah tractate *Kelim* 1.6-9 for third-century C.E. evidence of these maps, published and discussed even though by that point the Temple had been destroyed for over a century. The Temple was so central to Jewish life that it still dominated the Jewish worldview despite its physical absence.

[17] The destruction of temples in antiquity was not undertaken lightly, especially by polytheistic nations that might find it more politically advantageous, vis-à-vis both the subject peoples and their god(s), to maintain the vanquished cults. The central place of the Temple in the Jewish worldview explains why lesser acts, like Antiochus IV's sacrifice of an unclean animal in the Jewish Temple sanctuary and his insertion of a statue of an unclean pagan god there, would spark riots and revolts. Antiochus's acts led to the Maccabean Revolt (ca. 167 B.C.E.).

[18] See Douglas, *Purity and Danger*, 41–57.

[19] The "Priestly author(s)" is the name given to one of four hypothetical sources of the Torah, or Pentateuch—the first five books of Jewish Scripture (Genesis, Exodus, Leviticus, Numbers, and Deuteronomy). This author or authors are identified as priests because of the

When Jews brought gifts to God's altar to be burned, or consumed by priests, or sanctified and then consumed by the offerers, the gifts of produce and animals had to be the "firstfruits" and "unblemished" creatures. Here we see several maps coalesce: maps of nature (the offering), of time (birth of a child or animal, firstfruits of the harvest), of place (from the land of Israel to its Temple), and of the deity.

Divine. Perhaps *the* central principle in Jewish society regarding the deity was the purity or holiness of a single God (Lev 19:2; Deut 6:4-5). In fact, the singleness of God, so unusual in the midst of polytheistic cultures, enhanced the perception of God's uniqueness, separateness, and purity. God was understood as that power which created order in the first place and which revealed the "map" of the created order to humans through the script of the Mosaic Law. Because God was understood as the ordering power of the universe, it was assumed that God could intervene in that created order in any place and at any time. In fact, the narrative of Jewish Scriptures was a record of those interventions, beginning (it should not surprise us) with an account of God's creation of order and the revelation of the Mosaic Law in the Torah (the first five books of Jewish Scripture). God's relationship with humanity is often portrayed in these Scriptures as either blessing or curse (for example, Deut 30:15-20). In the covenant system, both of these divine acts maintain order: blessing is the reward for behavior that coheres with the law, while curse is the punishment for behavior that transgresses the law.

Applying the Model to the Synoptic Baptist

Now that we have a sense of how the value of purity was mapped onto persons, objects, time, place, nature, and the divine realm, we are ready to apply the model to the Synoptic texts we examined in Chapter 3. It would, of course, be extremely interesting to apply the model to the other divergent witnesses, namely, Josephus and the Fourth Gospel, but one must draw the

---

interests and vocabulary manifested in their compositions. These compositions include the first Genesis creation story, one of the Flood accounts, and the book of Leviticus. The priestly authors are thought to have written during the period of the restoration after the Babylonian Exile, when Judaism had to rebuild its cultural system without benefit of a native political establishment. Their orderly account of creation and their attempt to maintain cosmic order in the ritual system manifest the kind of mapping we are discussing. For the Documentary Hypothesis of the authorship of Torah, see Joseph Blenkinsopp, *The Pentateuch: An Introduction to the First Five Books of the Bible,* ABRL (New York: Doubleday, 1992), and Richard Elliott Friedman, *Who Wrote the Bible?* (San Francisco: HarperSanFrancisco, 1997; original 1987).

line somewhere, and the Synoptic texts are the ones with which we are most familiar. The technique in this section is to use the categories and understandings we have developed from the model to discern evidence of the map in the Synoptic texts. Therefore, we will follow the same order of topics in this section as we did in the last, which seems fitting given our topic.

Persons. Luke's diptych of John the Baptist and Jesus immediately inscribes both men in the purity hierarchy of Jewish society. John's father is not only a priest of the division of Abijah but is serving in the Temple when the annunciation of John's birth comes to him (1:8-23). John's mother is likewise identified as "from the daughters of Aaron" (1:5), which we would expect, because priests had to marry women from priestly families in order to maintain a pure bloodline. The Gospel recognizes not only their genealogy but also their behavior as pure: "Both were *righteous* before God, following all the commandments and laws of the Lord *blamelessly*" (1:6; italics identify the purity language). John's own purity is assured by the manner of Gabriel's announcement: Zechariah is in the sanctuary of the Temple; he is burning incense in the daily ("Tamid") service (burning is understood as a purifying act); the "whole assembly of the people" is praying outside; and a divine being appears at the right side of the altar of incense. We also hear *how* John will be pure: he will avoid wine and strong drink, he will be filled with the Holy Spirit, he will prepare a people fit (read "pure") for the Lord (1:15-17). The divine good news is too much for Zechariah, and his inability to believe results in his inability to speak until the promise is fulfilled. It is a kind of temporary pollution resulting from the transgression of disbelief. Note how both he and his wife are separated from human society for a period of time—he until he can speak at John's circumcision (1:57-79), she for the first five months of her pregnancy (1:26). Separation functions differently in each case; in Zechariah's case, he is quarantined for his disbelief, while Elizabeth's seclusion helps to establish the purity of her child and anticipates John's initial seclusion in the wilderness (1:80).

Of course, if Elizabeth is pure, Mary is more pure; if John is pure, Jesus will be more so. This is the function of Luke's diptych and its central episode, the meeting of Elizabeth and Mary: it establishes not just the purity of individual bodies but the hierarchy of those persons. There the purity of the two babies is marked by the presence of the Holy Spirit, who animates the leaping baby John, Elizabeth in her greeting, Mary in her *Magnificat,* and most importantly Jesus himself. Eventually Zechariah will also be filled with the Holy Spirit and make a more public acclamation (1:67-79). These possessions by the pure Spirit all have the effect of inspiring speech, which is an inherently public event.

The baptism scenes in the Synoptic Gospels also map purity onto the social body. This is perhaps clearest in the memorable moment when John denounces as "spawn of snakes" the crowds (Luke 3:7) or Pharisees and Sadducees (Matt 3:7). Snakes, thanks to Genesis 3, pagan cultic practice, and human experience, were a part of nature mapped impure in Jewish tradition (see below). Matthew's specification that it is Pharisees and Sadducees who are so designated is highly ironic, because the Pharisees were a lay purification movement and the Sadducees were part of the priestly aristocracy that lived in Jerusalem (see below). If these people from the top of the purity map could be called "spawn of snakes," then the entire purity map assumed by most Jews could be called into question. This is also the import of John's subsequent teaching about the spawn or children of Abraham. In both Matthew and Luke, John nullifies the prior purity map that placed sons of Abraham over the Gentiles (Matt 3:9-10; Luke 3:8-14). In the purifying fire of the new age, the "chaff" will be anyone who does not live by the new purity script, a script that begins with behavioral conversion, proceeds to John's baptism in water, and is completed in Jesus' baptism in the Spirit (Mark 1:7-8 and parallels).[20] Those who do not follow this path will be separated from the good grain and burned in an inextinguishable fire (Q 3:17).

As we have seen, Luke adds a few speaking characters to the scene in the crowds, tax collectors, and soldiers. These groups, who have all been called "spawn of snakes" in this Gospel, seem to become snakier as we move down the list. On a Jewish purity map, we move from your average Jew (the crowds) to Jews with one foot in the Gentile world who enforced Roman economic exploitation (tax collectors) to the nadir of the social hierarchy, the Gentile Roman occupying force itself. It is all the more interesting, given the expected purity map, that all seem eligible for John's baptism in Luke's Gospel. This reversal is visible in Q as well, when, later in the Gospel narrative, all the people and the tax collectors (Luke) or the tax collectors and prostitutes (Matthew) justify God for redeeming them, but the Pharisees and lawyers (Luke) or the chief priests and elders (Matthew) reject God's purpose for themselves (Q 7:29-30). By refusing to receive John's baptism or to accept Jesus, these individuals have spurned God's grace and have thus polluted themselves.

The one person who should not be eligible for baptism is Jesus, not because he is mapped with the impure, but rather because of his close

---

[20] See also the Acts material in Chapter 1. Given our portrait of the historical Baptist at the end of Chapter 3, it is likely that the historical John preached only the behavioral conversion and water baptism.

association to God. Mark's Gospel, which has no infancy narrative, takes little notice of the anomaly of Jesus' purification by John. But Matthew and Luke, who have mapped Jesus as pure by this point in their narratives, are at greater pains to address the unusual nature of Jesus' baptism. As we saw in both Chapters 2 and 3, each evangelist uses a different strategy: Matthew inserts a conversation in which John declares his lower status and greater need for purification, while Luke removes John from the scene entirely and thus diminishes the problem. Even though Jesus is still baptized, Luke rephrases this as a past action, focusing attention on the descent of the Holy Spirit and the divine voice, both of which function in all the narratives to separate and mark Jesus as God's special agent. The divine voice expresses pleasure with Jesus, as if Jesus were an acceptable offering at the Temple.

The account of John's arrest offers us a new locus on the map of purity and pollution. John is arrested because he declares Herod's marriage impure. The marriage to one's brother's wife was not permitted while that brother was alive; in the view of Leviticus, it would disgrace the brother and was classified as incest (Lev 18:16; 20:21). The only exception was if the brother died childless; since that was a greater disgrace, because the brother's name would not be perpetuated, his widow was required to marry one of his brothers (Deut 25:5-10).[21]

There are many maps implied in this passage, visible to us because the notions seem unfamiliar. We would not classify the marriage of a man and his sister-in-law as incest, although under certain circumstances it might be frowned upon. Nor would our cultural system map childlessness as a disgrace, and we certainly would not require a woman to marry for the sake of her dead husband's children (of course, we wouldn't consider them "his" children either, as if the woman who bore them was dispensable). While these implied maps are fascinating in their own right and suggest all kinds of lines of inquiry into kinship systems and gender roles, our focus must remain on purity. The Synoptics agree that Herod is impure because of a marital irregularity; Luke adds that John had also reproved him for "all the evil things [he] had done" (Mark 6:17-18 *par.* Matt 14:3-4; cf. Luke 3:19-20). From the Synoptics' vantage point, Herod had John arrested for enforcing the traditional Jewish law. The new age John preached is in many ways a call back to the old purity map, a symbolic universe that had been compromised by transgressive crowds and a corrupt Jewish king.

The contrast between Herod and John is sharpened in John's execution scene (Mark 6:19-29 *par.* Matt 14:5-12). There we hear that Herod (Matthew)

---

[21] This custom, referred to as "Levirate marriage," may also be found in Genesis 38:8 and Ruth 2:20.

or his wife Herodias (Mark) want to kill John (an impure act). Herod does not do this in Mark's Gospel because he considers John a "righteous and holy man," terms we recognize now as part of the purity script. In the midst of a banquet, Herod is duped into killing John and serving up his head. An ironic end indeed for the man who never ate or drank! The execution fulfills Herod's oath, but in Mark at least it is a tremendous violation of the protection he had earlier accorded the prophet, and the gratuitousness of serving the head on a platter is a profound violation of hospitality. Apart from the crucifixion, it is hard to imagine a scene in the Gospels where matter is more offensively out of place (the scenes are of course related; see Matt 17:12-13). The affront here is tempered somewhat by the careful ministrations of John's disciples, whose acts are narrated with an economy that permits the audience to grieve ("And when his disciples heard, they came and took his body and laid it in a tomb," Mark 6:29). Nevertheless, the story leaves one angry with Herod, who has elevated pleasure, indiscretion, and his own honor above the righteousness of this man. This scene is ironic because the king should maintain the order of the kingdom, and in a Jewish kingdom that order should be consonant with God's rule.

Jesus' disciples ask him to teach them to pray "as John also taught his disciples" (Luke 11:1-4). While the subsequent prayer Jesus teaches is present in Matthew 6:9-13, the comparison with the Baptist's practices is not. We cannot know whether this prayer is like those the Baptist might have taught, but many of its themes are consistent with John's baptismal preaching.[22] The individual prays for the advent of God's reign, just as John preached the coming judgment. The prayer for release from sins as the sinner releases others from their debts recalls John's exhortation to receive his baptism only after a behavioral conversion (share your cloaks and food, do not gouge, do not extort). These prayers for restoration and release are pleas for the triumph of purity over pollution couched in the language of God's reign.

The final two vignettes present the clash between John/Jesus and the Temple establishment (Mark 11:27-33 and *par.;* Matt 21:28-32 and *par.*). The location is the Temple. Jesus has just entered the holy city, where he will soon be executed. From the account of John's execution, we know that the Christians viewed these murders as polluting acts, and Jesus' crucifixion would be the most egregious case because of its location (in the holy city Jerusalem), its agents (the high priests), the time (the Passover festival), and the identity of

---

[22] Joan E. Taylor claims that the Lord's Prayer was originally John's prayer, but this is impossible to prove and is only suggested by the narrative location of the prayer in one Gospel (Luke); see *The Immerser: John the Baptist within Second Temple Judaism* (Grand Rapids, Mich.: Wm. B. Eerdmans, 1997) 151–153.

Jesus himself. Here, in a scene that anticipates and foreshadows the coming trial of Jesus, personnel responsible for maintaining the purity map—chief priests, scribes, and elders—challenge Jesus to tell them by what authority he acts. Jesus responds by challenging them to tell him by what authority John had acted. The function of the scene is to display the alignment of Jesus and John with God, and this necessarily means that the purity personnel are acting against God's authority. The scene is a contest that our authors are still fighting, as they assert to their fellow Christians the new configuration of the map of pure persons.

As persons are mapped in the social body, the human body is mapped as well. We begin again with Luke's narrative of John's birth. John's mother Elizabeth is described as barren (1:7), and when she becomes pregnant, she expresses her gratitude that the Lord has "removed her disgrace among men" (1:25; see also v. 58).[23] Zechariah's old age, which from our point of view might be just as much of an impediment to John's birth, is not described as "his disgrace" or as a "disgrace among men." We see a cultural assumption lurking here beneath the text, noticeable because of its divergence from our own cultural map. In Luke's context, a woman was intact not only by virtue of having all her parts but also by virtue of bearing children. In the absence of a child, it was not yet clear whether the woman was "pure" or "complete." This map of women's bodies is more complex than the map of men's bodies. Notice, too, how closely it is connected with one's place in the social body and thus with the cultural value of honor/shame. The same can be said for Zechariah's tongue. When John is born and Zechariah discharges his duty to name the child John rather than Zechariah, his tongue is loosened, he speaks again, and fear comes upon all their neighbors—a sure sign of the presence of God (1:65-66). Thus the bodies of both Zechariah and Elizabeth are purified, just as their son will cleanse the bodies of Israel. We have already spoken of the purity ascribed to all these characters' bodies when it is mentioned that the Holy Spirit animates their speech and movement (1:15, 35, 41-44, 67, 80).

The baptism scene is replete with references to the cleansing of people's bodies. Again, this act is supposed to follow a prior act that individuals commit on their own, namely, a behavioral conversion manifest in acts of justice (Q 3:8; Luke 3:10-14). This is the first purification. Baptism maps that interior conversion on the external body by cleansing it, mimicking the one washing with another; this is the second purification (Mark 1:5 *par.* Matt 3:5-6; see Luke 3:7, 16). Finally, the washing was accompanied

---

[23] Interestingly, this language of disgrace is never used of Mary's pregnancy, even though hers was the problematic one.

in Mark and Matthew by a confession of sins; this is the third purification (Mark 1:5 *par.* Matt 2:6; see Luke 3:10, 12, 14).

In addition to the emphasis on cleansing, John's body is also mapped as pure in Mark and Matthew. When these evangelists tell us what John looked like—that he was clothed in camel's hair and a leather belt and that he was eating locusts and wild honey (Mark 1:6 *par.* Matt 3:4)—they are evoking Elijah's body (2 Kgs 1:8). The association has the effect of making John at least as powerful and eminent as this great prophet of old. The statements and allusions that John's coming fulfills prophecy or that he himself was mistaken for Elijah likewise indicate the holiness of John by associating him with God's revealed plan (see Mal 4:5-6).[24]

There is another interesting mapping of the body in the baptism scene. When John professes that he is not worthy to stoop down and untie the thong of Jesus' sandals (Mark 1:7 and *par.*), he is placing himself below Jesus' feet. On the map of the body operative in this culture, feet occupied a fairly humble position, given what they often had to walk through. If one could afford a slave, the slave would take the sandals off the owner's feet at the end of the day and clean off all the accretions. So when John says that he's not worthy even to stoop and tend to Jesus' feet, the evangelists are telling us how much lower in rank John is. Matthew emphasizes both John's lower rank and his relative impurity in the unique conversation between the Baptist and Jesus (3:14-15).

The new age is inaugurated not only by the cleansing of bodies and their purification from a state of sin but also by the restoration of those who lack limbs, senses, and resources. When the imprisoned John sends his disciples to determine if Jesus is indeed "he who is coming," Jesus replies with the words of Isaiah 35:5-6 and 61:1:

> Go and report to John what you hear and see; the blind regain sight and the lame walk, lepers are cleansed and the deaf hear, and the dead are raised and the poor have the good news proclaimed to them; and blessed is the one who is not scandalized by me[25] (Q 7:18-23).

Blessing and scandal are part of the semantic field of purity as well; blessing, as we have seen, denotes divine favor, while scandal is a reaction to

---

[24] John's ministry is viewed as the fulfillment of prophecy in Mark 1:2-6; Q 7:26-27; Mark 8:27-30 and *par.*; Mark 9:11-13 *par.* Matt 17:10-13. John is also confused with Elijah in Mark 6:14-16 and *par.*

[25] Cf. Luke 4:18-19, where Jesus inaugurates his public ministry in Nazareth by reading Isaiah 61:1-2 and 58:6 aloud in the synagogue.

impropriety (behavior that is "out of place"). John should recognize this evidence at least in Matthew's Gospel, where he is identified as a participant in the restoration—as the promised Elijah who would "restore all things" (Mal 3:23-24; Matt 17:10-13 *par.* Mark 9:11-13).

The purity of the body is mapped by ascetic practices such as fasting. In Mark 2:18-22 and parallels, the disciples of John compare themselves (Mark, Matthew), or are compared by the Pharisees and scribes (Luke), with Jesus' disciples. The comparison makes Jesus' circle appear less pure; they "do not fast" (Mark, Matthew), or, more pointedly in Luke, they "eat and drink." Jesus responds to the challenge by declaring that his presence marks a time of joy, like a wedding, and that fasting, a common ritual of mourning, would be "out of place" at such a time. Jesus changes the map, at least for the time that he is with his disciples. Later in the Gospel narratives, the language of fasting and eating is mentioned again (Q 7:31-35). The situation has changed, however. Whereas in the earlier passage there is no question that John's disciples are righteous, this pericope indicates that John was thought by some to be possessed by a demon, a sign of pollution in any culture. In neither passage does Jesus come off well; he is consistently criticized not only for eating and drinking well (though only here is he called a glutton and a drunkard), but for doing this with the wrong people (tax collectors and sinners). Here the body maps and social maps of purity have converged. Jesus refutes his challengers by associating himself with wisdom, an attribute of the divine.

Objects. We encounter just a few pure and polluted objects in the Synoptic texts about the Baptist. In Luke's infancy narrative, there are the altar of incense and Elizabeth's and Mary's blessed wombs (1:11, 25, 35, 41-42, 44, 58). There is a promise that those without resources will have their means restored in some way in several of our Baptist texts (Luke 1:51-53, 68-71; 3:10-14; Q 7:22, 24-30). The Scriptures are reverenced as sacred objects (Q 7:24-30).

Time. It is important in Luke's infancy narrative that the annunciation of John's birth occur at a holy time, since John will be a priest of Israel's sanctification. Luke is careful to tell us that it is the hour of the daily incense offering and that Zechariah remains in the sanctuary longer than usual (1:10, 21). When Zechariah's speech is restored, he praises God for inaugurating a time of salvation, when the worship of God in "holiness and righteousness" will be restored (1:67-75). All the Synoptics associate John's appearance with the fulfillment of prophecy (Isa 40:3; Mal 3:24). They suggest that John is inaugurating the new age promised in Jewish Scripture, an age that would be a time of healing, cleansing, and purification (see Luke 1:51-55, 68-79; 3:14-30). The Q tradition of John's preaching, which emphasizes a purifying eschatological judgment, maps impurity onto the present (or at least onto unrepentant persons in the present) and assigns purity to the unquenchable fire of judgment soon to come. Luke adds an interesting twist to the treatment of time by telling us that the word of God comes to John "[in] the fifteenth year of the reign of Tiberius Caesar, during the rule of Pontius Pilate over Judea and Herod's tetrarchy over Galilee, while Philip his brother was tetrarch of the region of Ituraea and Trachonitis, and Lysanias was tetrarch of Abilene, in the high priesthood of Annas and Caiaphas" (3:1-2). These are not merely the unnecessary details supplied by a compulsive historian, but rather provide a contrast of eras: the time of this world and its leaders is now irrevocably altered by the word of God. Luke is discreet in his challenge to the powers of the world here, as he will be throughout Luke-Acts; nevertheless, his interest is to claim that God has the ultimate power in the universe and has inaugurated a new age through John and in Jesus (see also Q 16:16). The "Lord's prayer," which in Luke is prompted by the disciples' wish to be taught prayer "as John also taught his disciples," includes a prayer for the arrival of that age that is consistent with John's message ("may your kingdom come," Q 11:1-4). The association of John with Elijah is linked to his role in the new age; according to the prophecy in Malachi 3:23-24, Elijah was expected to return on "the day of the Lord" and "restore all things" (Mark 9:11-13 *par.* Matt 17:10-13). At one point in Q, however, it appears that John is not part of this new kingdom and age: "There is no one greater of those born of women than John. But the least one in the kingdom of God is greater than he" (Q 7:28).

Place. It is interesting that Luke begins the story of the Baptist in the Jerusalem Temple, because by all other accounts John operated at the opposite end of the spectrum. Whereas everyone who entered the Temple had to be purified, everyone who came to John was still dirty; whereas the Temple was the center of Judaism's world, the wilderness was the wild and dangerous place on that world's fringe. And yet John offered the "spawn of snakes" who came out to him something that the Temple likewise promised—purification. Granted, that purification had already begun in the behavioral conversion John required of those he washed, but his water baptism seems to have been a complement or replacement for other purifications. Luke alone portrays John as a priest, and perhaps he does so to emphasize that John's wilderness baptism is at least as efficacious as, if not an alternative to, the Temple system. It is interesting that all three Synoptics locate the final reference to John in the Jerusalem Temple as well (Mark 11:27-33 and *par.*). Jesus has just entered Jerusalem, where the audience knows he will be killed. The reference to John, who by this point in the narrative has already been executed, foreshadows Jesus' impending death. But Jesus' death also colors the presentation of John, whose critique of impure persons is now associated with Jesus' critique of the Temple.

Nature. The Jewish symbolic universe mapped the wilderness as an unclean place. This is perhaps most apparent in the temptation scene, which we have not read (Mark 1:12-13 and *par.*). Just after Jesus' baptism, the Spirit drives him into the desert, where there are wild beasts and Satan, but no human companionship and little food apart from locusts and wild honey. The association of Satan with the wilderness should be enough to indicate that the place was associated with danger and defilement. Furthermore, the wilderness was historically associated with temptation and sin because of the behavior of Israel in the desert after the Exodus from Egypt (Exodus–Numbers). As Shemaryahu Talmon has argued, the wilderness was a problematic place in Israel's memory; purity lay on the other side of the River Jordan.[26] And yet, that is where John lives. It is from the defiled and dangerous place that he purifies Israel. The apparent irony is diminished somewhat if we consider that Israel's great liminal experience in the desert was also the time of its birth; it was in the wilderness that the community gathered around Sinai and received Torah, even if it had a long way to go before it could enter the Promised Land.

Another element of nature that is clearly mapped as polluted is snakes, a fact mentioned above. In Luke 3:7 John calls the crowds "spawn of snakes," while Matthew targets only the Pharisees and Sadducees for this condemnation (3:7). We are familiar with the place of snakes on the map from Genesis 1–3; initially blessed with legs and thus ranked over crawling creatures (1:24-31), snakes lose their legs and thus their rank when one of their clever number tempts Eve (3:14-15). These Genesis accounts probably reflect the distance Jewish leaders tried to create between pagan cults that venerated snakes and pagan mythologies that gave monster serpents power equal to God's. Add to this the snake's power to change its skin and the human experience of death by snakebite, and you have a symbol of pollution that does it all. With mythological evil, cultic irregularities, pagan idols, transgressive behavior, and human illness all rolled up in one beast, it becomes clear why the epithet "spawn of snakes" would weaken the knees of a Jewish penitent.

Divine. The angel Gabriel is the first divine being we meet. He appears in the sanctuary alongside the altar of incense (Luke 1:11) and there announces the birth of John to a stunned Zechariah. Zechariah's disbelief and

---

[26] "The 'Desert Motif' in the Bible and in Qumran Literature," in *Biblical Motifs,* ed. A. Altmann (Cambridge: Harvard University Press, 1966) 31–63.

subsequent speechlessness illustrate the distance between God's power and the capacity of even a most righteous priest. At Jesus' baptism the Spirit descends in the form of a dove, a creature of the skies, if not the heavens (Mark 1:10 and *par.*). Given that the bird represents the Holy Spirit, we can assume that Mark viewed the bird as a positive, pure creature. When Jesus' disciples ask him to teach them to pray "as John also taught his disciples" in Luke's Gospel, the first words of Jesus' prayer are about the holiness of God's name ("Father, hallowed be your name," 11:1-4). This is Jesus' prayer and not John's, but Luke does associate it with John's style of prayer, and the entire prayer is consistent with John's message. The prayer for God's kingdom to come is likewise an echo of John's prophecy that purity would soon be restored in an apocalyptic "harvest" and "fire."

When Jesus' challengers call him a glutton and a drunkard and say that John was demon-possessed, Jesus responds by saying that "wisdom is justified by her deeds/children" (Q 7:35). The Jewish sapiential tradition frequently presents wisdom as a divine attribute, and so in the first-century context Jesus' retort is an assertion of purity against the aspersions cast by his opponents. The same challenge to Jesus' authority lies at the heart of the final reference to John in the Synoptics (Mark 11:27-33 and *par.*). This scene takes place in the Temple, in the presence of the chief priests and other religious leaders. When these representatives of the purity system question by what authority Jesus acts, Jesus asks them a question: "The baptism of John, was it from heaven or from men?" The audience assumes with the author that it is from heaven, just as Jesus' authority is. We are led to believe that the leaders think it to be human, since John offered purification outside the system they managed that had been revealed by God. In any case, we never hear what they really think, because the Synoptic authors want us to believe that the leaders were more concerned about their own appearance and safety than about the truth.

Our analysis of the purity and pollution value in the texts about John the Baptist is now complete. All that remains is to evaluate the model of purity and pollution that we used. Evaluation is based on two questions: Did the model fit the data, and did it help to explain the data? The answer is yes on both counts. It is in fact quite striking how many details in the texts emerge as part of the purity and pollution map of the society. We have also developed some facility in identifying purity and pollution scripts. We have found them to be most visible when our maps and the authors' maps differ or when there is conflict in the text over purity issues, so that the characters in the stories are operating with different scripts.

Purity and pollution are aspects of the cultural system that anthropological models help us to analyze. But there is still another way that we can approach John's work of cleansing people, and that is to focus less on the cleaning than on the people themselves. This last inquiry, therefore, takes us into historical and sociological analysis of the several purification movements that sprang up in Palestine around the time of John.

An Inductive Exercise:
First-Century Jewish Purification Movements

Our final social-scientific exercise will be inductive in direction. We will begin by collecting some data on purification movements in first-century C.E. Palestine and will then compare two of these movements more closely using a multivariate matrix model. We begin this exercise at the micro-level of the social system. Our focus is on four social groups in that system, although we will direct most of our attention to just two. The entry point of our inquiry is context rather than text, although the majority of our knowledge about these groups derives from texts of one kind or another. The presentation of each movement will include some diachronic information, while the matrix model of the two focal groups will provide a synchronic presentation, a freeze-frame view as if in one moment of time.

Purification Movements

John is presented in all sources as a popular ascetic preacher concerned with purity and justice. He is clearly a leader, if not a founder, of a new religious movement. But his was not the only purification movement in first-century C.E. Judea. We have already encountered two other such movements, the Pharisees and the Jesus movement. These and a few others will now be discussed as purification movements, and a close comparison of two of these movements, the Essenes and the Baptist movement, will be made.

A word should be said about the term "purification movement." The word "movement" is used to describe a social group that arises at a given point in history, is led at some point by a charismatic leader and to some extent against established institutions, and subsequently grows and develops in some identifiable ways. It may be short-lived or endure for centuries; life span is irrelevant to its definition. Of interest in the analysis of such movements are the causes of its origin, the nature of the social world it constructs (social dynamics, economy, organization and leadership, beliefs, ideology), the manner in which it maintains that world, and, if relevant, the patterns of its demise.[27] The subsequent classification of such a

---

[27] See Ekkehard W. Stegemann and Wolfgang Stegemann, "Religious Pluralism in the Land of Israel in the Hellenistic-Roman Period," in *The Jesus Movement: A Social History of*

group as a *purification* movement is more a matter of convenience than a classification of its teachings. In this exercise any group whose origins and social organization may be linked to purity concerns will qualify as a purification movement. It need not be the case that purification is their central teaching or chief reason for existing. Nor (again) should purity interests be equated with religious interests; in fact, religion in antiquity was less a discrete institution than an embedded one, performed and understood within the more dominant institutions of kinship and politics.[28] Moreover, we have already seen that purity is a cultural value mapped across social institutions no matter the era. The broad definition of the purification movement, then, encompasses many groups that arose from roughly 200 B.C.E. to 70 C.E., but one phenomenon it does not encompass is the Jerusalem Temple. Though Temple leaders were profoundly interested in purification and the entire enterprise was organized around that principle, the sacrificial system is a social institution rather than a movement, in existence in some form for centuries. We are more interested in the groups that arose well after the Temple institution had been established, many of which in fact originated due to concerns over the Temple's efficacy. The term "purification movement" is a heuristic device that we will use to collect data about these groups and to discover relationships between them.

Historical Background. Some history may help to explain why so many movements arose in the time frame of 200 B.C.E. to 70 C.E. The period began with the domination of Israel by the Hellenistic empire of the Seleucids, the latest in a long line of imperial overlords dating back to the Babylonian Exile. This branch of Alexander the Great's fourth-century empire extended its sphere of influence southward around 198 B.C.E. and took Israel from its southern rival, the Ptolemaic Empire in Egypt (also one of Alexander's heirs). The Seleucids began to consolidate their power through political, economic, and cultural means. This forced program of Hellenization was welcomed by some Jews but resisted by others, and this led to a split among the priestly families running the Temple. When resistance finally culminated in open revolt (the Maccabean Revolt of 167 B.C.E.), it was a family opposed to Hellenization, the Hasmoneans, that took the lead. They were successful and gradually became politically independent of the Seleucids, but in the process a Hasmonean dynasty was appointed to the

---

Its First Century, trans. O. C. Dean, Jr. (Minneapolis: Fortress, 1999; German original, Stuttgart: W. Kohlhammer, 1995) 137–186.

[28] Social scientists make the same claim for economics in antiquity; the production, distribution, and consumption of resources were controlled not by free markets but within the family and by political entities.

high priesthood and to the throne. This created more factions in the society, because the Hasmoneans had remote priestly connections but were not of the Zadokite line of priests that had run the Jerusalem Temple from exilic if not Solomonic times. To make matters worse, they were not of the line of David and therefore were viewed by some as illegitimate claimants to the throne. Their usurpations, coupled with collaboration with the Seleucids, created social tensions in Jewish society manifest in the rise of religious movements like the Pharisees and the Qumran Essenes.

When the Roman general Pompey entered Jerusalem in 63 B.C.E., the Hasmoneans were on their last legs, soon to be supplanted by the Idumean and second-generation Jew Herod the Great in 37 B.C.E. Herod established the Herodian dynasty and began a massive building campaign throughout the kingdom that included an enormous expansion of the Jerusalem Temple. The security of his throne depended upon his friendship with the Romans. When his kingdom split after his death in 4 B.C.E., and his inept son Herod Archelaus assumed governance of Judea, the Romans were no longer so friendly. Just nine years later, in 6 C.E., the emperor Augustus stepped in and made Judea part of a Roman province under the direct control of a Roman prefect, who in turn answered to the Roman legate in Syria. Except for a brief period of Herodian rule under Herod Agrippa I (41–44 C.E.), the Romans were the political-legal force in the southern part of the country and augmented their power by crushing lesser uprisings and two great revolts by the Jews (66–74 C.E. and 132–135 C.E.). Things were somewhat different in the northern district of Galilee, where Jesus and John first operated. There Herod's son Herod Antipas reigned well enough (his execution of John notwithstanding), so that the Romans could stand by in a supportive role, at least until they deposed him in 39 C.E. It probably helped his fortunes that this Herod, like his father, was enamored of Hellenistic and Roman culture, transforming Galilean cities like Sepphoris and Tiberias into Hellenistic centers during his reign.

With your new sensitivity to the value of purity, you can likely imagine several stimuli in this parade of events that might lie behind the formation of purification movements. If purity is about matter in place and about establishing the boundaries to keep it there, we can see that this period of history in this location would present multiple challenges to boundary maintenance. The conflicts between legitimate high priests and illegitimate ones, between Davidic pretenders and those awaiting a descendant of David, between Romans and Jews, and in general between Hellenism and Judaism across all social institutions—all help to explain the rise of so many movements designed to redefine or restore the map. Variables between these movements will be the catalyst for formation, the social stratum from which they come, the internal organization of the group, the operational ideology and strategy, their stance toward pagan culture, and their relationship to other social groups, not all of which data is equally accessible to us. These variables and the fragmentary record contribute to conflicting theories about how each of the following groups was constituted, so the summary below is one of many possible constructions. The fragmentary record also points to the strong likelihood that there were many other groups besides these in first-century C.E. Jewish society.

Pharisees. The Pharisees were a lay movement of Jews that arose sometime in the Hellenistic period. Our chief sources of information about them are Josephus (who claims to have been a member for a time), the New Testament (which is not kindly disposed to the group), and rabbinic literature from 200 C.E. on. Josephus refers to the Pharisees as a *hairesis*, a term generally used to describe philosophical schools.[29] As we have seen, Josephus often translates Jewish phenomena into terms that his audience would understand and portrays the Jewish people in a neutral or irenic manner as part of his larger apologetic agenda, so we need not adopt his picture of the Pharisees (or Essenes or Sadducees, for that matter) as "schools." But what are they? Ekkehard Stegemann and Wolfgang Stegemann use deviance theories to explain all three groups, and this theory will be useful for our other purification movements as well.[30] Deviance theory holds that some groups form in social crisis situations as excluded groups and that their nonconformity with other or dominant groups helps to strengthen their group identity. The Pharisees likely developed at some point in the Seleucid or Hasmonean crisis. They are mentioned in Josephus as sometime friends, sometime enemies of the Hasmonean and Herodian leaders, but Josephus seems to report about them only at times of crisis, when various factions are vying for influence.[31] This indicates that, at least in Josephus' eyes, they were not part of the governing establishment in which he was most interested. One gets quite a different impression from the New Testament, where the Pharisees seem to be Jesus' most powerful enemies, colluding with the Temple priests to kill him. Rabbinic literature mentions the Pharisees occasionally. In addition to these few passages, it is generally accepted that references to pre-70 C.E. "rabbis," "Fathers," or sages are allusions to the Pharisees or their precursors. Rabbinic sources indicate that there were two chief schools of rabbis, the Houses of Hillel and Shammai, which often had competing interpretations of the Jewish law.

[29] *War* 2 §119 (cf. §162-163, 166 and *Ant.* 18 §11-15).
[30] *The Jesus Movement,* 151–156.
[31] *War* 2 §119-166; *Ant.* 18 §11-25; 13 §171-173, 297-298.

The identification of the group as a purification movement is made on the basis of the New Testament and rabbinic evidence (if Josephus were our only source, we would think of them merely as one of many political factions with their own interpretation of some Jewish laws). In the New Testament they often appear in controversy stories, questioning Jesus about purity issues (see, for example, Mark 2:18-28; 3:1-6; 7:1-23; 10:2-12; 12:13-17). The rabbinic literature complements and challenges this picture. There the body of law associated with this group treats ritual purity, tithes, food laws, and Sabbath and festival observance—all scripts for enforcing purity of the body, produce, food, nature, and time.[32] These topics cohere with the New Testament evidence but diverge from it in demonstrating that there were different points of view among the Pharisees on any given purity issue, and some of their positions sound like the ones that Jesus espouses.

More needs to be said, however, about the Pharisaic interpretation of the law. Jacob Neusner's analysis of the rabbinic evidence indicates that the Pharisees made some of the priestly purity laws incumbent upon lay people like themselves. We need not view this as the excessive burden that the evangelists do; we might view it instead as an extension of the purity system, intended to defend and maintain it in a time when the traditional Jewish purity maps were in crisis. Note, too, that the extension of priestly purity to all Israel renders the Temple less necessary, at least in theory; hence when the Temple was destroyed in 70 C.E., there was a Jewish way of life in place that had already accommodated Jews to a new system of sanctification and a new interpretation of Jewish law. The Pharisees developed an extended map to maintain the holiness of the land and its people. That they used the typical boundary-marking mechanisms of food, festivals, and finances should not surprise us. These boundary markers and the evidence of our sources indicate that the Pharisees were a long-lived group that arose in response to a purity crisis and offered lay people a way to remain pure in an impure society.

Rebel Movements. Josephus mentions five prophetic movements crushed by the Roman prefects and procurators of Judea (Pontius Pilate, 26–36 C.E.; Cuspius Fadus, *ca.* 44 C.E.; Felix, 52–59 C.E.; Festus 59–62, C.E.). The first was a Samaritan rebellion against Rome that took place on the Samaritan equivalent of the Jerusalem Temple mount, Mount Gerizim (*Ant.* 18 §85-89). A Samaritan man rallied followers to go to their most sacred mountain so that he could reveal to them the sacred vessels that Moses

---

[32] Jacob Neusner, *Judaism: The Evidence of the Mishnah* (Chicago: University of Chicago Press, 1981) 45–75.

himself had buried there. The people armed themselves and gathered, but Pilate slaughtered many and the rest fled. The recovery of the original Temple vessels would have enabled a restoration of pure worship, and so we can consider this an example of a (short-lived) purification movement.

The second was led by Theudas (see Acts 5:36), who considered himself a prophet and miracle worker. He drew many people to the wilderness, where he claimed he would part the Jordan in a kind of Exodus *out* of the Holy Land. The group was armed, and Cuspius Fadus pursued them, beheading Theudas and taking many prisoners (*Ant.* 20 §97-98). Of interest is the reinterpretation of the Exodus-Conquest narrative and the re-mapping of the "Holy Land," now defiled by the Romans.

The third movement was led by a "body of villains" with "impious" intent, whom Josephus describes in the following way: "Deceivers and imposters, under pretense of divine inspiration fostering revolutionary changes, they persuaded the multitude to act like madmen and led them out into the desert under the belief that God would there give them tokens of deliverance" (*War* 2 §259). What is interesting in this description is the leaders' claim to be divinely inspired, their ability to gather a multitude, their retreat to the desert (consider John and the Qumran Essenes), and their promise of divine deliverance there. Josephus does not provide much detail, but what he does say suggests a group grounding its legitimacy and ideology in the biblical tradition, seeking to purify their land of the defiling Roman presence. Felix understood it as an attack on Rome and responded accordingly.

The fourth movement occurred under Felix as well, when an Egyptian Jew led a huge group through the wilderness to the Mount of Olives, where he hoped to command the walls of Jerusalem to come tumbling down.[33] Once again, the Bible is being reinterpreted and sacred space is being remapped. The tumbling walls are reminiscent of Jericho, which was the first town to fall when the Hebrews came out of the wilderness, across the Jordan River, and into the Holy Land. Now Jerusalem is seen as the pagan city, the first to be destroyed and claimed for a purified Israel. Felix crushed this movement as well, although the Egyptian escaped (*War* 2 §262-263; *Ant.* 20 §169-172; cf. Acts 21:38).

Finally, Felix's successor Festus faced a wilderness prophet: "Festus also sent a force of cavalry and infantry against those deceived by a certain imposter who had promised them salvation and rest from evils if they chose to follow him into the wilderness" (*Ant.* 20 §188). The promise of

---

[33] Note that Jesus also enters Jerusalem from the Mount of Olives, both when he enters the city the first time (Matt 21:1) and when he is arrested (Matt 26:36 *par.* Luke 22:39). The book of Zechariah had prophesied that the Lord would come from the Mount of Olives to rescue Jerusalem from the enemy nations (14:4).

salvation and rest from evil in the wilderness imply that those drawn to the message experienced oppression and evil in settled Israel, and Festus's action indicates one source of that oppression. These groups experienced pollution in the land and so sought refuge "outside" the land in the wilderness. In Matthew 24:24-28 Jesus also warns of false prophets who would gather followers in the wilderness.[34]

There were also leaders of movements who framed their enterprise as a restoration of the Davidic monarchy. The ideology was not explicitly messianic in most of these movements, at least to our knowledge, but in the Bar Kokhba movement it was. The first three were led, respectively, by Judas the Galilean (Acts 5:37), Simon in Perea, and Athronges in Judea in the tumultuous period after the death of Herod the Great (*War* 2 §55-265; *Ant.* 17 §269-284). In contrast, the Bar Kokhba movement was a military revolt (132–135 C.E.) whose leader was widely believed to be the messiah until his defeat by the Romans.[35]

A final movement that should be mentioned focused its hope on a restoration of the Temple and its priesthood. These were the Zealots, mentioned frequently by Josephus in *The Jewish War*. It is possible that they were a radical group of priests, given their interest in the Temple edifice during the First Jewish Revolt (*War* 4 §151).[36] Even more important were their attempts to restore a legitimate high priesthood and to initiate other Temple reforms (*War* 4 §147-397).

There were many other individual rebels and Zealots who sought to overthrow Rome and even gathered followers for that purpose, and the First Jewish Revolt (66–74 C.E.) likewise sought to rid the land of the Romans.[37] These events could also be viewed as purification movements, although their only reported aim was to purify the land of the defiling Roman presence. In contrast, the groups described above had, in addition to that aim, features that aligned them with biblical tradition or prophetic authority. In this respect, they are closer kin to the other purification movements we have singled out. None of these movements, prophetic or revolutionary, lasted very long.

[34] Josephus also mentions of a "false prophet" who told people in besieged Jerusalem to go up to the Temple and there "to receive the tokens of their deliverance" (*War* 6 §286). However, this was a one-time event, and so while it is about deliverance and takes place at the center of the purity map, we cannot classify it as a purification *movement*.

[35] See *Talmud Yerushalmi Ta'anit* 68d, a famous passage in which Rabbi Akiva proclaims Bar Kokhba the messiah.

[36] Stegemann and Stegemann, *The Jesus Movement*, 181.

[37] For the full array, see Richard A. Horsley, *Jesus and the Spiral of Violence: Popular Jewish Resistance in Roman Palestine* (San Francisco: Harper & Row, 1987), and with John S. Hanson, *Bandits, Prophets and Messiahs: Popular Movements at the Time of Jesus* (Minneapolis: Winston, 1985; rev. ed. Valley Forge, Pa.: Trinity Press International, 1999).

Jesus Movement. There is certainly no question that a social movement arose around the figure of Jesus of Nazareth. The fact that he was crucified by the Romans indicates that he was perceived as a political threat, and this coheres with the internal Christian claims that he gathered followers and was understood by some to be a messianic leader before his death. But while most scholars agree *that* a social movement grew around Jesus, they disagree about *what sort* of a movement it was. One's position depends upon one's operative portrait of the historical Jesus himself: was he an itinerant philosopher, or a wandering charismatic and miracle worker, or an apocalyptic prophet, or a witty rabbi?

Our broad definition of purity issues allows us to view the Jesus movement as a purification movement, regardless of the specific image of Jesus with which you or I might be operating. There are several pieces of evidence that ground this identification. To begin with, we have seen that all of the Gospels associate Jesus with John the Baptist, even though this presented problems for the evangelists. The criteria of embarrassment, dissimilarity, and multiple attestation (Mark and the Fourth Gospel) together confirmed the historicity of the relationship (see Vignette 4, p. 58). Furthermore, we saw in Chapter 1 that Luke viewed John's baptism as the beginning of Jesus' ministry, and thus could require that anyone designated an apostle had to have been with Jesus from that time. If Jesus' ministry began in some way with John's baptism, then it is very likely that Jesus shared John's concern for purification. The Fourth Gospel confirms this by stating that Jesus baptized (John 3:22, 26; 4:1) and/or that his disciples baptized during his life (4:2), but since no other source mentions this, alone it cannot confirm his interest in purity. Nevertheless, there is plenty of other evidence we can find. For example, Jesus offers a new and improved baptism by the Holy Spirit, but a baptism nonetheless, and one that augments rather than replaces John's purification. Thus both figures offer purification *as baptism*, that is, in the same terms. Furthermore, the Acts of the Apostles and early Christian tradition attest that the early Church continued the practices of water and Spirit baptism, thus demonstrating through the institutionalization of ritual both the foundational role purification played in Christianity and the link between Jesus and John on this point.

A second datum that points to the identification of the Jesus sect as a purification movement is the repeated reference to purity issues in Jesus' teaching. We saw this briefly in Chapter 3, when connections were made between themes of John's preaching and those of Jesus' teaching. Relevant to this point are the regular controversies between Jesus and the Pharisees over specific purity concerns. These debates often begin with the allegation that Jesus is impure (he associates with sinners and prostitutes, he does not oppose Roman taxation, he disregards the Sabbath, he claims to be the Son of God), but the stories always conclude with the assertion that Jesus is more pure or has greater authority than his accusers. In fact, Jesus frequently "out-Pharisees" the Pharisees, claiming that their extension of purity to the people doesn't go deep enough (for example, Matt 5:17–6:8; 15:1-21 and *par.*). Even granting that some of this controversy material depends on post-resurrection relations between the Jesus movement and Jewish communities, its dominance of the narratives and its presence across all strata of the Gospel tradition (Q, Mark, the Fourth Gospel) demonstrate that purity concerns were an important element of the historical Jesus' career. The ongoing importance of purity concerns in the evangelists' communities lends further credence to the evidence that Jesus taught about purity; it is more likely that the early Christians would be willing to suffer and dispute over matters their leader had addressed.

Some scholars have claimed that Jewish purity laws were rejected by Jesus, and so were not a part of his movement at all. But it seems rather that Jesus was redefining purity as John was, recalling Jews to a long prophetic tradition of coherence between ritual practice and moral obligation (Hos 6:6; Amos 5:21-24; Mic 6:6-8; Jer 31:31-34). Absent this association, it is unlikely that he would have been intelligible to first-century Jews, unlikely too that he would have gathered a movement at all.[38] Sociologists of religion confirm this thesis in their analysis of charismatic movements, which deviate from social institutions by proposing "counterworlds" dependent upon those very institutions. The charismatic leader and his or her followers are stigmatized for proposing an alternative, and thus their sense of election to a special task is confirmed.[39] But their alternative is nevertheless framed within the terms of the existing institutions, a fact attested rather than disproved by the resistance of those institutions. It is only later that the charisma of the founder is institutionalized itself into genuinely discrete forms.

Of greater interest than the disputes between Jesus and the religious authorities, perhaps, are hints of purity disputes between followers of Jesus and followers of the Baptist. John's disciples fast, but Jesus' do not (Mark 2:18 and *par.*); John came eating no bread and drinking no wine, but Jesus came eating and drinking (Q 7:33-34); John came intoning a dirge, but Jesus came playing a flute (Q 7:32). John waits for people to come to him, Jesus travels the towns seeking people out. John offers purification of the flesh, Jesus offers forgiveness and restoration or healing of the flesh

---

[38] Fredriksen, *Jesus of Nazareth, King of the Jews,* 197–207.

[39] For a summary of the literature, see Stegemann and Stegemann, *The Jesus Movement,* 194–195.

(Q 7:22-23). John is clearly the ascetic in the wilderness, while Jesus prefers to party in the villages. But these differences appear to be a matter of degree, especially since they are almost always presented in the Gospels in the context of controversies with outright opponents like the scribes and Pharisees. Ultimately, of course, the portraits of John and Jesus will converge with their executions, and as we approach that point, Jesus' message of apocalyptic purification gradually comes to resemble John's preaching. Jesus' initial exhortation to purify oneself through repentance on the early pages of the Gospels changes to a vision of cataclysmic judgment and cosmic purging just as the passion narrative is about to begin (Mark 13; Matthew 25). The significance of this convergence is that John and Jesus have more in common with each other than do Jesus and the "men of this generation," who are about to defile themselves with a second unwarranted execution.

The passion narratives, which relate the climactic events in Jerusalem that led to Jesus' death, further indicate the central role purity played in this foundational moment of earliest Christianity. There is some dispute about the historicity and significance of the so-called "cleansing of the Temple" episode that inaugurates Jesus' Jerusalem ministry in the Synoptics (and Jesus' entire ministry in the Fourth Gospel), but there can be no doubt that he was crucified. It is unlikely that Jesus would have been crucified unless he represented a political threat of some magnitude; in this regard, we need only note the public and exemplary nature of this extended and gruesome form of execution, which was meant to serve as a public warning to would-be followers and imitators. It is thus very likely that Jesus challenged at least one central institution in Jerusalem, and the Temple and the Roman prefecture represent the most likely candidates. The nature of the challenge need not have been framed as a "purification" of the land, but evidence of Jesus' association with baptism and purity issues renders it plausible and even likely that his presence in Jerusalem would have been seen in those terms.

The evangelists' portraits of Jesus' death are consistent in portraying his execution as unwarranted. Because Jesus is innocent, his executioners are guilty of shedding an innocent man's blood. The presentation of this irony in the Fourth Gospel is particularly pointed: the Jewish leaders cannot enter Pilate's headquarters to transfer Jesus because it is Passover, and the act will subject them to ritual defilement (18:28). The fourth evangelist is charging the Jewish leaders with a greater ritual defilement, of course, in their false indictment of Jesus. But the passage should not be read as a wholesale indictment of the purity system. Rather, the irony depends on the implication that Jesus is more pure than these leaders, and is thus consistent with a long prophetic tradition that called Israel to moral integrity and covenant fidelity.

The Qumran Essenes. Another purification movement in Roman Palestine was the group that collected and wrote the Dead Sea Scrolls and maintained a community compound near the caves where the scrolls were stored. The site of the compound is referred to as Khirbet (or "the ruins of") Qumran, and it lies just west of the northwest corner of the Dead Sea, some fourteen miles as the crow flies from Jerusalem (about thirty miles on current roads). Many of the scrolls found at the site are native to the group, though copies of other books such as biblical scrolls were found as well. It is the native documents, however, combined with the archaeological evidence of the Qumran compound, that present the clearest picture of the group's organization and interests, and chief among these was the concern to maintain purity. Since the rules, practices, and interests of the group evident in the documents are remarkably similar to details of Josephus's and Philo's description of a Jewish "philosophy" of the period, the Essenes, most scholars are comfortable referring to the scrolls group as "Essenes," even though this term is never used as a self-designation in the scrolls themselves.[40]

It is clear from the "sectarian" scrolls—those authored by the community itself—that the people who wrote, collected, and interpreted these materials can be classified as a social movement. While the historical details of the group's origins cannot be determined with precision, indications are that it emerged or at least strengthened in Jewish society after the Hasmonean ascendancy and in direct response to the perceived aberrations of that period. Chief among those perceived aberrations was the elevation of a Hasmonean to the high priesthood, a ministry to which their lineage did not entitle them. This created fissures in Jewish society as many people became concerned for the efficacy of a Temple no longer run by the "right people." What would be the point of the daily and festival sacrifices, of the sin offerings and redemption payments, if God would not accept them from these priests? The situation was compounded when the Hasmoneans began to collaborate with the Seleucids on economic and cultural matters, aggravating the very tensions over Hellenization on which the Hasmoneans themselves had ridden to power. The Qumran Essenes included

---

[40] Josephus describes the group in *Jewish War* 2 §119-161, and *Antiquities* 15 §371 and 18 §18-22; Philo treats them in *That Every Good Person Is Free* 12-13 §75-91, and *Hypothetica* 11.1-18 (*apud* Eusebius, *Praeparatio evangelica* 8.11.1-18). See also Pliny the Elder, *Natural History* 5 §73. For a discussion of the Essene hypothesis and a summary of its challengers, see James C. VanderKam, *The Dead Sea Scrolls Today* (Grand Rapids, Mich.: Wm. B. Eerdmans, 1994) 71–98, and, more recently, "Identity and History of the Community," in *The Dead Sea Scrolls after Fifty Years: A Comprehensive Assessment,* ed. Peter W. Flint and James C. VanderKam (Leiden: Brill, 1999) 2.487–533.

in their number some priests who were displaced by the Hasmoneans and who differed mightily in their interpretations of the Scriptures.[41] In a brief historical section of one of their constitutional documents, they describe their group's formation, the ascendancy of their own leader, the "Teacher of Righteousness," and his struggles against the "congregation of traitors."[42] Other sectarian texts speak of a "Man of Lies" and a "Wicked Priest" who persecute the community.[43] These tensions marginalized the group even more from the dominant cult, and it appears that it was around this time that some of the group's members expanded a small structure at the Qumran site into a compound of greater size, sometime after 125 B.C.E. and likely closer to 75 B.C.E.[44] Archaeological evidence indicates that the compound was occupied for a century and a half and was only abandoned when the Romans destroyed it in 68 C.E. in the midst of the First Jewish Revolt. Thereafter the Essenes disappear from the historical record, although their traditions are preserved by at least one Jewish community.[45] Thus we have evidence of a community of people with a shared tradition who broke from the Temple establishment, had at least at one point a charismatic leader, built an alternative religious center in the wilderness, and gathered followers for some 150 to 250 years. Moreover, this group was highly organized and had a coherent ideology that included mechanisms for ensuring group identity. All this points to a well-developed and enduring social movement.

There is a great deal of evidence that allows us to designate the Qumran Essenes as a "purification" movement. To begin with, they inherited and accepted all the Torah commands about maintaining purity in the realms of diet, food preparation, transmission of liquids, illness, defecation, corpse contamination, menstruation and childbirth, Sabbath observance, and a host of other situations mentioned in the Scriptures. But in many cases they went well beyond the requirements of Jewish law in order

---

[41] See, for example, 4QMMT, a document that presents itself as a letter from some member of the Essene community laying out Essene positions on some Jewish laws in contrast to other interpretations; see "1. Halakhic Letter (4QMMT)," in *The Dead Sea Scrolls Translated: The Qumran Texts in English,* trans. Florentino García Martínez, 2d ed. (Leiden: E. J. Brill, 1996; Spanish original, Madrid: Editorial Trotta, 1992) 77–85.

[42] *Damascus Document* 1.1–2.2 (*The Dead Sea Scrolls Translated,* 33).

[43] "E. Commentary on Habakkuk" (*The Dead Sea Scrolls Translated,* 197–202).

[44] Jodi Magness, *The Archaeology of Qumran and the Dead Sea Scrolls,* SDSSRL (Grand Rapids, Mich.: Wm. B. Eerdmans, 2002).

[45] Two medieval copies of the *Damascus Document,* for example, were found in a Cairo *genizah* (a storeroom for sacred texts so faded or damaged that they could no longer be used). This means that some Jewish group still had one of the Essene texts and found it relevant enough to their needs to copy it.

to maintain an even higher standard of purity. For example, if dietary laws exempted some foods from consumption, the Essenes would not eat them; but they also designated some of their food as the "purity" and restricted its intake to those who were observing all the other special community regulations (*Community Rule* 8.16-18). Thus initiates still in their first year of learning the special laws of the community could not partake of the pure food (*Community Rule* 6.13-20), while in their second year of probation they were still restricted from the pure drink (*Community Rule* 6.20-23), and anyone who transgressed the more serious community statutes could be temporarily or permanently excluded from the meal where the purity was shared (*Community Rule* 5.13-14; 7.2-3, 17-22, 26-27).[46] If Mosaic Law stipulated that Sabbath observance was to begin at sundown Friday evening, the Essenes would safeguard their observance by halting work when the sun was still just above the horizon (*Damascus Document* 10.14-17).[47] If Jews outside the community's boundaries were dishonest in marriage and divorce arrangements, this community would require its overseer to supervise members' marital negotiations (*Damascus Document* 13.12-19 and *par.*) or avoid the problem by discouraging marriage in the first place (*Damascus Document* 6.11–7.7).[48]

The raft of laws concerning business and finance in Torah were also interpreted radically; members could only barter with each other and could only make cash transactions with outsiders under the overseer's watchful eye.[49] And in the area where economics and religion combined, that is, in the sacrificial system of the Temple, the Qumran Essenes also took a separatist stance. Given their alternative calendar and other legal disputes over the purity scripts regulated by that priesthood, it is likely that group members stopped worshiping in the Jerusalem Temple at some point in time. But they could not disregard that much of Torah regulated the sanctification of the land through the system of offerings and sacrifices presented in the Temple. What could they do to maintain the purity of the land in the absence of the sanctifying and atoning power of the Temple? They resolved this conundrum by viewing their community as the new Temple. Instead of sacrificing a portion of one's resources to the Jerusalem Temple, a member

---

[46] "1. The Rule of the Community," in *The Dead Sea Scrolls Translated*, 3–32.

[47] "2. The Damascus Document," in *The Dead Sea Scrolls Translated*, 41.

[48] Eileen M. Schuller and Cecilia Wassen, "Women: Daily Life," *Encyclopedia of the Dead Sea Scrolls*, 2 vols., ed. Lawrence H. Schiffman and James C. VanderKam (Oxford: Clarendon, 2000) 2.981–984; Joseph M. Baumgarten, "Celibacy," *Encyclopedia of the Dead Sea Scrolls*, 1.122–125; Magness, *The Archaeology of Qumran and the Dead Sea Scrolls*, 163–187.

[49] For the *Damascus Document*, see 4QD^a 7 iii 1-7 as well as CD 13.9-19; for the *Rule*, see 6.16-23; 9.5-9.

would now voluntarily offer all his resources for the entire community's use. This would be the new way to love God with all one's heart, soul, and strength. The sacrifices of the Temple would be replaced by the sacrifices a member would make in bowing to the judgments of the community on matters of knowledge, strength, and wealth.[50] In this way the community would atone together for Israel until the advent of two messiahs who would restore the monarchy and the priesthood and the fortunes of the faithful remnant.

The association of the community with the ideal Temple is apparent in much of the Essenes' literature. Their daily attempts to remain pure through proper prayer and Torah study, economic practices, purifications, and disciplines allowed them to align themselves with the angels in the heavenly court, the corollary of the earthly house of God:

> And I know that there is hope
> for someone you fashioned out of clay
> to be an everlasting community.
> The corrupt spirit you have purified
> from the great sin
> so that he can take his place
> with the host of the holy ones,
> and can enter in communion
> with the congregation of the sons of heaven.
> You cast eternal destiny for man
> with the spirits of knowledge,
> so that he praises your name together in celebration
> and tells of your wonders before all your works.
> (*Hodayot* 11.21-23)[51]

In a manner more pronounced than in any other contemporary and extant Jewish literature, the Sons of Light in this community acted in communion with the Princes of Light, just as the Sons of Darkness were thought to commune with the Princes of Darkness.[52] This is particularly true in their central council, hence all of the rules to maintain its purity:

[50] Catherine M. Murphy, *Wealth in the Dead Sea Scrolls and in the Qumran Community,* STDJ 40 (Leiden: Brill, 2002), especially 117–155.

[51] *The Dead Sea Scrolls Translated,* 332.

[52] See also 1QH[a] 11.20-23; 14.12-13; 19.13, 4QBlessings[a-e], and the so-called Treatise on the Two Spirits in the *Community Rule* 3.13–4.26, as well as the *War Scroll* (1QM 7.6: "for the angels of holiness are in the camp, together with their hosts"). For more information see Lawrence H. Schiffman, *The Eschatological Community of the Dead Sea Scrolls,* SBLMS 38 (Atlanta: Scholars Press, 1989).

> And these will be accepted in order to atone for the earth and to de-
> cide the judgment of the wicked {. . .} and there will be no iniquity. |
> When these have been established in the foundation of the Commu-
> nity for two full years /in/ perfect behavior / they will be segregated
> (like) holy ones in the midst of the council of the men of the Commu-
> nity. (*Community Rule* 8.10-11)[53]

Thus the concern to maintain purity went beyond the mere extension of priestly purity obligations to all community members. In this community it confirmed the authority of the elect by virtue of their association with the purity of the angels. Ancient secondary testimony about the Essenes does not confirm this ideological association with the angels but demonstrates resoundingly that the Essene community maintained a stricter standard of purity than the other "philosophical schools" of Judaism.[54]

In addition to the literary testimony, there is striking evidence of a concern for purity in the archaeological record of the Qumran site. One of the most dominant features of the compound is the elaborate system of water conduits leading into eight cisterns and *miqva'ot*, or ritual baths. Ronny Reich has observed that the type of *miqva'ot* found at Qumran is analogous to types found in Jerusalem and that the concentration is com-parable to that found in the vicinity of Temple Mount and priestly neighbor-hoods.[55] Together this suggests that the Qumran Essenes were at least as concerned about purification as the Jerusalem priests. The large size of some of the Qumran *miqva'ot* suggests that large numbers of people needed to use the ritual baths at a given time, unlike the smaller installa-tions found in the priestly quarters in Jerusalem.

The literary and archaeological evidence, combined with the testi-mony of ancient authors on the Essenes, demonstrates conclusively that the Qumran Essenes were a sectarian purification movement roughly contem-poraneous with the Baptist movement.

Now that we have gathered some information on several such con-temporary purification movements, we can continue our inductive exercise by comparing the data. We could compare as many such groups as we like, but we will take a narrower angle of view and focus on just two groups, the Qumran Essenes and the Baptist movement.

[53] *The Dead Sea Scrolls Translated*, 12.

[54] See Josephus, *War* 2 §129, 131, 161.

[55] "*Miqwa'ot* at Khirbet Qumran and the Jerusalem Connection," in *The Dead Sea Scrolls Fifty Years after their Discovery: Proceedings of the Jerusalem Congress, July 20–25, 1997*, ed. Lawrence H. Schiffman and James C. VanderKam (Jerusalem: Israel Ex-ploration Society, in cooperation with The Shrine of the Book, 2000) 728–730.

A Comparison of the Essenes and the Baptist Movement

In this stage of the exercise, the data that has been collected is now organized and classified to facilitate analysis. The interpretive analysis is a final and separate step, although it is to some extent implied in the classification scheme employed. We will focus on two specific groups, the Qumran Essenes and the Baptist Movement, and compare and contrast various features of their social organization and ideology. To do this, we will employ a multivariate matrix model, a fancy name for a table of multiple variables that define social groups.[56] We will place all of the data we have thus far discussed into this table and see what sorts of theses we might be able to generate from the comparisons and contrasts that become visible.

Figure 8. A Multivariate Matrix Model for Comparing the Qumran Essenes and the Baptist Movement

	Qumran Essenes	**Baptist Movement**
A. Socioeconomic Factors		
1. Group constituency and size	Philo and Josephus estimate 4000; Qumran caves and compound could accommodate 140 to 240 members; others in nearby villages[57]	Impossible to determine numbers ("all Judea" came to him); sources distinguish disciples from masses; threat perceived by Herod Antipas suggests large, loyal group
	Membership restricted to Jews but no other restrictions; secondary literature suggests many farmed; primary evidence indicates priestly leadership at least at some stage	Membership apparently available to Jews and Gentiles; Luke identifies John as priest, some of baptized are tax collectors, Roman soldiers, thus apparently people from any occupation

figure 8 continued

[56] This particular model is influenced by Elliott, *What Is Social-Scientific Criticism?* 66; see also his "Social Scientific Criticism of the New Testament and Its Social World: More on Method and Models," *Semeia* 35 (1986) 17–21; and Gerd Theissen, *Sociology of Early Palestinian Christianity,* trans. John Bowden (Philadelphia: Fortress, 1978; German original, Munich: Kaiser, 1977) especially 31–95. For a similar exercise at setting John in the social context of popular prophetic movements, see Webb, *John the Baptizer and Prophet,* 307–348.

[57] Philo, *Every Good Man* §75; Josephus, *Ant.* 18 §20. For the estimates of the Qumran

2. Geographic location	Wilderness and villages of Dead Sea region, possibly Jerusalem	Focused in Judean wilderness near Jordan River, but adherents came from larger region
3. Economic base and occupations	Farming, modest industrial production; itinerancy unlikely	Variety of occupations, though some disciples apparently itinerant
4. Class, status[58]	Some elites (Teacher of Righteousness, sons of Zadok?), retainers (scribes), and non-elites or lower-stratum groups (e.g., farmers)	No elites; some retainers (tax collectors?), mostly non-elites and minimum existence, and chose extra-economic existence
5. Organization and roles	At one point, a single charismatic leader (Teacher of Righteousness); otherwise, priests, several administrators (Overseer/wise leader), tight hierarchical organization based on covenant fidelity; well-developed language for community (community, association, congregation, camps, etc.)	Charismatic authority of John; Jesus assumes this mantle among some disciples; after John's death disciples maintain and expand activity, but leadership and roles are unclear
6. Institutions	Service of the association (=social welfare fund) and/or complete commitment of one's goods to others' use; "the purity" (a regular meal), regular meetings and Torah study	Fasting, prayer, baptism, and repentance/conversion

figure 8 continued

---

vicinity, see Magen Broshi and Hanan Eshel, "Residential Caves at Qumran," *Dead Sea Discoveries* 6 (1999) 328–348.

[58] For these categories, see "Social Pyramid 3: Religious Groups in the Land of Israel, Including the Jesus Movement," in *The Jesus Movement,* 185.

B. Political-Legal Factors		
1. Position and role in Roman and Jewish government	Formed as opposition movement to Hasmone seem to enjoy some support during Herodian dynasty, but neverthe less (or because of this?) facilities at Qumran expand, Romans ultimately destroy the Qumran compound	Eschatological message suggests opposition to current political authority; Herod Antipas perceives threat and executes leader; followers maintain animosity to Herod as a result
2. Basis and exercise of power/authority	Distinctive interpretation of Law by Teacher of Righteousness and followers; Zadokite or priestly leadership	Prophetic/charismatic authority of John, martyrdom confirms it; disciples maintain practice of baptism
3. Domestic relations	Seeks to purify Judaism, restore it to pure worship and right practice in eschatological age	Seeks to purify Judaism, restore it to right practice in eschatological age; John perceived to be an internal Jewish threat by Jewish king
4. Foreign relations	Opposed to foreigners, envisions their destruction in final age; no evidence of expansion beyond Judea; destroyed by Romans	Ultimately open to foreigners (it expands into Gentile world as Jesus' followers do)
C. Culture, Belief System		
1. Pivotal values	Covenant fidelity manifested in adherence to radical interpretation of law; holiness approaching that of angels as a result	Conversion to right relationship and ritual purification to denote it; radical world-renouncing piety

figure 8 continued

2. Accentuated beliefs and their symbolizations	Predeterminism but simultaneous emphasis on radical communal covenant fidelity; symbolized as return to wilderness to prepare the way of the Lord (Isa 40:3)	Possibility of conversion symbolized in baptism
		Retreat to wilderness to recall Israel to prepare the way of the Lord? (Isa 40:3)
	Eschatological expectation of two messiahs and restoration of throne and high priesthood	Expectation of the imminent advent of an apocalyptic judge who would distinguish good from evil
	Dualistic ethics and worldview	
	Pure worship creating communion with angels	
	Simplicity of lifestyle to anticipate jubilee vision (Deut 15:4)	Lifestyle simulates that of prophets (Elijah?); extra-economic location allows purity of diet, practice
3. Norms and sanctions	Elaborate norms established in penal codes of constitutional literature, with sanctions for transgressions	Eschatological judgment unless one converted, but no other norms survive
4. Socialization and personality structure	Intensive two-year probation with ongoing Torah study and annual examinations of behavior thereafter; personality subsumed within community identity	No apparent probation, but existence of disciples indicates some socialization and community maintenance; initial charismatic authority of John institutionalized through baptizing activity and teaching of disciples; communal identity less pronounced (fluidity of membership between Jesus' and John's movements)

figure 8 continued

D. Strategy and Ideology		
1. Group interests, goals	Separation to prepare way (observe Torah) in wilderness; pure worship, preparation for messiahs, increase one's lot in light	Maintain baptizing activity to prepare for eschatological judgment and purify behavior/flesh
2. Tactics and foci of attention	Torah study, ritual immersion, shared use of goods, regular evaluations of behavior and ranking of members, ritual meals, simple lifestyle, prayer	Immersion by John or his disciples, predicated on proper economic and religious behavior, no apparent ranking of members, fasting and ascetic lifestyle, prayer
3. Oppositions	Sons of Darkness, Belial and his three nets (fornication, wealth, defilement of Temple), Kittim (= Romans?)	Any who seek baptism without conversion; Herod Antipas
4. Alliances, affinities	Possibly Herod the Great, otherwise sectarian and restricted to Jews	Jesus movement, apparently open to Gentiles as well
5. Ideology	The Jewish monarchy and Temple have been corrupted; the last days are near, when the messiah will return to restore the elect. The elect anticipate and assure their eventual restoration by virtue of their present radical covenant fidelity	The eschatological judgment is near; people must convert to right practice and be physically purified in order to avoid destruction.

The purpose of the multivariate matrix model is to pose similar questions to different groups in order to discern possible divergences and convergences of the groups themselves. The model presents us with several associations, which in turn can yield theses about the social systems critiqued and created in these two purification movements. Before reading the list of theses below, you might want to try your hand at generating some observations and ideas based on convergences and divergences you find between the Essenes and the Baptist movement.

Here is a short list of some possible theses that the model yields:

- The retreat to the wilderness allows or requires a separation from economic and therefore political and familial relationships, but ideological associations with Israel's wilderness period provide a context for new definitions of community and economy.
- The willingness to risk dissociation from these institutions may be predicated on the perception that these institutions are themselves at risk, or at least that one's place in them is. This recommends that a sense of crisis precipitates one's decision to join such a movement.
- Purification and legal observance are of integral importance in both movements. Thus the movements can be radical and conservative at the same time.
- Itinerancy may be correlated to a less hierarchical organizational structure and may therefore require an aggressive expansion through proselytization if the group is to continue to exist.
- The radical difference in organizational structure and in tactics to advance the ideology of the group argues against the thesis that John the Baptist was an Essene; similarities of practice and belief may be attributed to the general traditions and practices of Second Temple Judaism.[59]

---

[59] Many scholars have argued that John was at one point an Essene; for example, see A. S. Geyser, "The Youth of John the Baptist," *Novum Testamentum* 1 (1956) 184–199; J.A.T. Robinson, "The Baptism of John and the Qumran Community," in *Twelve New Testament Studies* (London: SCM, 1962) 11–27; William R. Farmer, "John the Baptist," in *Interpreter's Dictionary of the Bible,* ed. G. A. Buttrick (New York: Abingdon, 1962) 2:955–962; W. H. Brownlee, "John the Baptist in the New Light of Ancient Scrolls," in *The Scrolls and the New Testament,* ed. Krister Stendahl (New York: Crossroad, 1992; original 1957) 33–53; Daniel Sefa-Dapaah, "An Investigation into the Relationship between John the Baptist and Jesus of Nazareth: A Socio-Historical Study," Ph.D. diss., University of Oxford, 1995; Ian Werrett, "John the Baptist and the Dead Sea Scrolls," M.A. thesis, Trinity Western University, 2000. Others are more skeptical; see Joseph Thomas, *Le mouvement baptiste en Palestine et Syrie (150 av. J.-C.–300 ap. J.-C.),* UCL 2d series, 28 (Gembloux: J. Duculot, 1935); H. H. Rowley, "The Baptism of John and the Qumran Sect," in *New Testament Essays: Studies in Memory of Thomas Walter Manson, 1893–1958,* ed. A.J.B. Higgins (Manchester: Manchester University Press, 1959) 218–229; E. F. Sutcliffe, "Baptism and Baptismal Rites at Qumran?" *Heythrop Journal* 1 (1960) 179–188; J. Pryke, "John the Baptist and the Qumran Community," *Revue de Qumrân* 4 (1964) 483–496; Raymond E. Brown, *The Birth of the Messiah: A Commentary on the Infancy Narratives in Matthew and Luke* (Garden City, N.Y.: Doubleday, 1977) 376; Josef Ernst, *Johannes der Täufer: Interpretation-Geschichte-Wirkungsgeschichte* (Berlin: Walter de Gruyter, 1989) 276–277; Hartmut Stegemann, *The Library of Qumran: On the Essenes, John the Baptist and Jesus* (Leiden/Grand Rapids,

- Apocalyptic expectation cuts across social classes and thus is likely stimulated by perceived (or relative) deprivation rather than by the kinds of destitution experienced by the people at or below subsistence.
- Both movements manage to maintain a sense of urgency over a period of decades and in the absence of their charismatic leader. This suggests that they had effective mechanisms (for example, organizational structures and ritual practices) to institutionalize the charismatic message of their founder.

These are just some of many theses that could be drawn from the comparative model we have generated. Each one could be explored further by closer analysis of the extant evidence.

The inductive exercise with which we have been engaged has taken us from data on various purification movements to a model for analyzing data from two such movements. The model has proven useful for drawing out certain features of the Qumran Essene movement and the Baptist movement, so that these can be more easily compared and contrasted. The model has helped us to generate some ideas about these two purification movements in the context of the social system of late Second Temple Judaism. In addition, the categories help us to identify information we cannot or do not know, given the limited state of our evidence. The ideas we have generated may serve as interpretive lenses through which to view other purification movements in the period, such as the Pharisees and the Jesus movement. The model is flawed to some extent because it may differentiate categories that were not understood to be separate within these movements; that is, it imposes an etic framework that may obscure emic categories. A further limitation of the model is that it cannot yield genetic connections and historical relationships, such as whether John the Baptist was himself an Essene. Nevertheless, the model has proven useful for suggesting relationships between the economic and political factors that lay behind and shape both movements. It has also provided evidence of shared and divergent beliefs and the creative strategies each group employed to address the crises of their day.

Mich.: Brill/Wm. B. Eerdmans, 1998; German original, Freiburg: Herder, 1993) 211–227; John P. Meier, *A Marginal Jew: Rethinking the Historical Jesus,* vol. 2, *Mentor, Message, and Miracles,* ABRL (New York: Doubleday, 1994) 25–27; Taylor, *The Immerser,* 15–48; Bruce Chilton, "Yohanan the Purifier and His Immersion," *Toronto Journal of Theology* 14 (1998) 197–212; J. Ian H. McDonald, "What Did You Go Out to See? John the Baptist, the Scrolls and Late Second Temple Judaism," in *The Dead Sea Scrolls in Their Historical Context,* ed. Timothy H. Lim, with Larry W. Hurtado, A. Graeme Auld, and Alison Jack (Edinburgh: T & T Clark, 2000) 53–64.

CHAPTER SIX

Conclusion

John the Baptist has provided us with a focal point around which to adjust our critical lenses. The various early accounts about him, both in and beyond the Christian tradition, provided us an occasion in Chapter 1 to raise our first critical suspicions about the accuracy of our sources. We saw that we could recover history from sources, but that this would involve an understanding of why the sources differ and how to read those differences. Redaction criticism was introduced as a method for exploring why and how the sources differ, while the criteria of historicity were provided as the tools for reconstructing history through those sources with varying degrees of certainty.

In Chapters 2 and 3 we continued to develop our skills in Gospel reading and historical reconstruction by focusing on the Synoptic evidence of the Baptist. The baptism scene was offered as a test case to illustrate how the Gospels are related and the directions in which their component narratives and characteristic teachings tended to develop. We saw why the Gospels of Mark, Matthew, and Luke are called "Synoptic," in that they are so similar that they can be aligned in parallel columns and viewed together. But we also saw a good example of the "Synoptic Problem," that despite their word-for-word similarity at points, these three Gospels often differ substantially. The "problem" is thus how to account for the literary relationship of these three Gospels, and it was resolved by the Two-Source Hypothesis. This theory contends that Matthew and Luke used Mark and Q (a hypothetical source of sayings) as sources for their Gospels. In addition to these two shared sources, Matthew and Luke each had a unique body of material and unique interests that shaped their presentation of the Gospel story. Armed with this theory, we systematically explored the Synoptic

Baptist vignettes in Chapter 3. We analyzed similarities and differences in light of the Two-Source Hypothesis in order to gather data and discern patterns of emphasis. This data allowed us to generate some of the characteristic (because repeated) themes of each of our redactors, which in turn yielded some sense of their social location and audience. At the same time, we applied the criteria of historicity to each of our texts so that we could come up with a sketch of the historical Baptist.

In Chapters 4 and 5 we took up a different line of inquiry. Our focus here was less the Gospel texts *per se* than it was the cultural world and social system implied in the text. We began by distancing ourselves from that cultural world, realizing that our values, assumptions, institutions, and behaviors are quite different from those of antiquity. This prepared us to experience the *un*familiarity of the text and to let that chasm of two millennia stand rather than to bridge it too easily by assuming we know what the text means. Social-scientific criticism does not end at alienating us from the text, however. The goal of this method of inquiry is to reconstruct something of that other world. This will always be done through etic categories, that is, through modern analytical frameworks drawn from the social sciences, but despite their modern cast, these frameworks can provide some access to a world other than our own. Some sense of the breadth of possible projects was offered in the four exercises conducted in Chapters 4 and 5.

Our first project in Chapter 4 was to explore how one would go about setting up a social-scientific project. The construction of the framework involves several steps: One must choose a focus (social or cultural system), scope (macro or micro), entry point (text or context), direction of inquiry (inductive or deductive), and temporal range (diachronic or synchronic) for one's inquiry. The number of variables allows for multiple different types of projects, while the content of the social and cultural systems also provides multiple options. Some possible projects were then sketched out.

Our second project was less a sketch than an actual inquiry, an inductive exercise that moved from the Lukan text about John's eschatological preaching ("Spawn of snakes!") to the social context of Luke's Gospel. After the Lukan changes were identified, we employed the theory of cognitive dissonance as a heuristic tool for analyzing Luke's emendations.

Our third and fourth projects were conducted in Chapter 5. They took as their starting point not a text but the context. The third exercise focused on an aspect of the cultural system, namely, the notion of purity and pollution, and after the requisite definitions, applied this feature to the Baptist texts. Our fourth exercise turned to the social system to discover evidence of other purification movements in first-century C.E. Judea and to utilize a multivariate matrix model for comparing and contrasting two of those movements, the Qumran Essenes and the Baptist movement.

John the Baptist has provided us some continuity throughout our study. Through the Baptist traditions, we have examined many features of the Gospels and of the world in which they were born. But beyond that, he has afforded us the opportunity to watch ourselves as we read, interpret, and inquire about these scriptural texts. We have seen that this activity is active and self-reflective even when we are unaware that we are involved in the interpretation. Yet this does not mean that every reading, however idiosyncratic, is of equal weight. There are guidelines and tools that help us as we try to reconstruct history, or as we attempt to determine an evangelist's theological interests and social location, or as we try to bridge the deep chasm that made John's world so different from our own. Methods provide us with those guidelines, and the texts themselves provide us with some controls. Together, method and text allow us to visit another world and, in the process, to meet characters like John the Baptist again for the first time.

abduction—a method of inquiry characteristic of social-scientific criticism that is both inductive and deductive, constantly alternating between theory and data.

apocalypse—literally "unveiling," a term that designates a genre of crisis literature popular in Jewish and Christian circles from about 200 B.C.E. to 200 C.E. Apocalyptic works are characterized by pronounced dualism, esoteric visions and symbols, elaborate cosmology, the application of past prophecy to present circumstances, and the resulting sense of urgency that the present moment is the endtime when God's new creation will be unveiled and present evil destroyed.

apocryphon—secret or hidden book, such as the *Apocryphon of James* (a.k.a. *Secret Book of James*).

apology—a sustained argument in defense of a person, group, or belief.

apparatus—the abbreviated notations at the bottom of the page of a critical edition of a text that indicate textual variants and witnesses to individual readings.

asceticism—from the Greek for "exercise, practice, training," rigorous physical practices of abstention (e.g., fasting, vegetarianism, celibacy), bodily afflictions (hair shirts, chains), or physical withdrawal from society (cave dwellers, stylites [people who sit on pillars]), with the intent of ethical or spiritual purification.

autograph—the original manuscript written by an author.

Babylonian Exile—the period of approximately fifty years from 587 to 539 B.C.E., when the leadership of Judea was taken into exile in Babylon after the Babylonians had destroyed the Jerusalem Temple.

baptism—a ritual of purification and initiation that involves "dipping" or immersion in water.

ca.—abbreviation for the Latin *circa*, meaning "around," used to indicate an approximate date.

canon—from the Greek word for measuring rod, this refers among other meanings to the rule by which something was judged, and particularly to the official list of books judged to be authoritative scriptures by a given community.

criteria of historicity—the principles for determining from one's sources whether an event likely occurred.

critical edition—the version of a text that represents scholars' best efforts to determine the most original and accurate readings of a text; it customarily includes an apparatus with all of the variant readings noted.

critical method—the line of inquiry one uses to interpret evidence (e.g., historical criticism, source criticism, literary criticism, social-scientific criticism). Each has its own presuppositions, techniques, steps, questions, and range of results.

deductive inquiry—a style of analysis that begins with a hypothesis, theory, or model and applies it to the data.

Deuteronomist authors (D)—one of the four proposed authors of Torah, likely a group of scribes whose work began in the court of King Josiah in the late seventh century B.C.E. and who continued writing through the Exile; responsible for the book of Deuteronomy in Torah as well as the rest of the Deuteronomistic History (Joshua, Judges, 1–2 Samuel, 1–2 Kings).

Diaspora—the dispersion of a population over a large geographic region; in this book the dispersion of Jews throughout the Mediterranean region and Africa in the centuries following the Babylonian Exile.

diptych—an artistic presentation that tells a story by juxtaposing two frames; applied in this book to the juxtaposed portraits of John and Jesus in Luke's infancy narrative.

Documentary Hypothesis—the theory that four literary documents or sources lie behind the Torah (or Pentateuch), namely, the Yahwist document (tenth century B.C.E., Judea); the Elohist document (ninth century B.C.E. and following, Israel); the Deuteronomistic document (seventh–sixth centuries B.C.E., reunited country); and the Priestly document (late sixth–fifth centuries B.C.E., under Persian domination).

double tradition—those episodes and sayings found in both Matthew and Luke, but not in Mark, and attributed to Q (*Quelle,* meaning "the source").

Elohist authors (E)—one of the four proposed authors of Torah, likely a group of scribes writing an alternative national epic for the northern kingdom of Israel after it split off from the southern kingdom of Judah in 922 B.C.E. The name derives from the name they customarily use for God, *ʾelohim.*

emic perspective—the worldview of a given social group formed within its cultural system.

Essenes—a Jewish purification movement that formed in opposition to the Hasmonean leadership of the Jerusalem Temple in the late second century B.C.E. and utilized a community center at Qumran from the early first century B.C.E. to 68 C.E.; the group is responsible for collecting, copying, and writing the Dead Sea Scrolls.

etic perspective—an analytical framework imposed by contemporary critics on the social or cultural systems of another population.

form—a small literary unit that might have circulated independently in oral or written form before being compiled into a larger literary work like a biblical book; examples include proverbs, parables, miracle stories, covenant treaties, and call narratives.

form criticism—that path of inquiry that seeks to identify the basic units of a literary work and postulate their original *Sitz im Leben*, or setting in life.

genizah—a storeroom for old and damaged sacred texts that can no longer be used because of their physical condition but cannot be destroyed because of their sacred character.

genre—a large literary species that characterizes book-length works; examples include apocalypse, gospel, letter, hymn.

God-fearer—a Gentile attracted to Jewish practice and worship but not yet a proselyte or Jew him/herself.

Griesbach Hypothesis—see "Two-Gospel Hypothesis" below.

hairesis—literally, a "choice"; Josephus uses the term for the major groups that he distinguishes in Judaism (Pharisees, Sadducees, Essenes, and the fourth "philosophy," the Zealots).

Hellenism—Greek culture promoted in the imperial context of the Alexandrian conquest and post-Alexandrian empires.

heuristic tool—an interpretive tool that enables analysis of a text; a social-scientific model, for example, would be a heuristic tool.

honor—socially approved or expected attitudes and behaviors; a public claim to worth and status.

inductive inquiry—a style of analysis that begins with data and builds a hypothesis from that data.

kashrut—the Jewish dietary "script" found in Leviticus 11.

Maccabean Revolt—a Jewish revolt against the Hellenizing Seleucid emperor Antiochus IV Epiphanes in 165–161 B.C.E., led by Judas, whose nickname was "the hammer" (Maccabee in Hebrew). Judas was successful, and his family established the Hasmonean dynasty that governed Judea until 37 B.C.E.

map—the patterning we do that classifies aspects of the world according to our ideas and values.

messiah—literally, "the anointed," a figure designated by God to restore the Jewish people. Originally a designation of a political ruler, the term expanded in apocalyptic literature to encompass any of a number of agents (priestly figure, prophetic leader, king).

mikveh—a pool designed for ritual bathing as prescribed by Jewish law.

Mishnah—a codification of Jewish case law developed in centuries of reflection on Torah and put into writing by Jewish rabbis around the year 200 C.E.

New Religious Movement (NRM)—a term usually reserved to groups forming after 1945 (thus new) that have religious goals or frameworks of belief and routinize these long enough to exist for a period of time. Every religion is at one point an NRM, but institutionalization gradually renders it less new and less movement than institution.

par.—parallel(s).

parousia—Greek for "presence" and thus "appearance," a term used for the coming of the messiah, and particularly for the second coming of the Christian messiah.

Pentateuch—the Greek term for the first five books of the Jewish Scriptures; Torah is the Hebrew equivalent.

pericope—a short story or episode in a narrative text that can be "cut out" by virtue of a clearly definable beginning, core, and ending.

Pharisees—a lay purification movement with roots in the anti-Hellenistic impulses of the Maccabean period; they developed interpretations of the law that extended some of the priestly purity requirements to non-priestly Jews and became particularly influential after the Temple was destroyed in 70 C.E. Their interpretations of the law and applications to daily life became the basis for rabbinic Judaism.

plausibility structure—the overarching framework of meaning within which values, maps, and scripts operate and achieve their legitimacy.

pollution—matter out of place; a state in which matter is not in the location the social or cultural system has designated it should be.

Priestly authors (P)—one of the four proposed authors of Torah, likely a group of scribes associated with the priesthood in the rebuilt Jerusalem Temple writing after the return of the exiles from Babylon (*ca.* 539 B.C.E.). This group added some of their own stories to the existing accounts of creation, exodus, and covenant, in part to provide a unifying narrative to the post-exilic Jewish world that made sense of their covenant traditions in an entirely new context of foreign domination.

purification movement—a social group that arises at a given point in history, is led at some point by a charismatic leader and to some extent against established institutions, and subsequently grows and develops in some identifiable ways; its origins, teachings, and/or internal structure or activities must be organized around the concern to purify people or society.

purity—matter in place; a state in which matter is in the location the social or cultural system has designated it should be.

Q—abbreviation for *Quelle,* the German word for "source"; the hypothetical sayings source that lies behind the material shared by Matthew and Luke and lacking in Mark. Q citations use the Lukan chapter and verse to designate parallel passages.

Quelle—see Q.

redaction—an author's activity of compiling, arranging, and editing his or her sources.

redaction criticism—the method of inquiry that seeks to discern an editor's theological interests in the way she or he has compiled, arranged, and edited sources.

Saduccees—a priestly group descended from Zadok (Solomon's choice for the high priesthood in the first Temple) that constituted one of the leading parties in Judaism in Josephus's time; characterized by religious conservatism but openness to Hellenistic culture.

script—an unwritten behavioral code that specifies how the culture's values are to be.

Second Temple—the central shrine of Jewish sacrifice and worship in Jerusalem, rebuilt on the site of the Solomonic Temple sometime during the early Persian period (*ca.* late fifth–early fourth centuries B.C.E.) and destroyed by the Romans in 70 C.E.

Septuagint—from the Latin for "seventy," the name for the Greek translation of the Hebrew Scriptures ascribed by legend to seventy translators who independently arrived at the exact same translations of the books; compiled in the third century B.C.E. in Egypt for native Greek-speaking Jews, this version of the Jewish Bible quickly became the only version Christians could read as that religion spread to the Gentiles in the first century C.E.; its extra books beyond the Hebrew canon are therefore found in many Christian Bibles.

shame—a positive sensitivity to the maintenance of one's honor and reputation.

social-scientific criticism—a method that utilizes theories and models from the social sciences (anthropology, sociology, archaeology, political science, economics) to analyze the social and cultural systems of biblical texts and the ancient world.

symbol—something that points to and participates in another reality.

symbolic universe—the cluster of symbols that constitutes the matrix of meaning for a culture.

synopsis—a parallel arrangement of textual witnesses to the same story laid out for the purpose of analysis.

Synoptic Gospels—the three canonical Gospels that can be laid out in parallel columns because they tell many of the same stories about Jesus, namely, Mark, Matthew, and Luke.

Synoptic Problem—the fact that, although the Synoptic Gospels Mark, Matthew, and Luke are by-and-large similar and even identical in certain passages, they nevertheless diverge from each other in content and arrangement, opening up the question of their literary relationship and sources.

textual criticism—the method of inquiry that seeks to recover the earliest form of a text by comparing variant versions and readings.

Torah—the Hebrew term for the first five books of the Jewish Bible.

triple tradition—those episodes and sayings found in Mark, Matthew, and Luke.

Two-Gospel Hypothesis—the thesis that Matthew and Luke wrote their Gospels independently—Matthew for a Jewish audience and Luke for a Gentile audience—and Mark merged and abbreviated the two for a mixed Jewish-Gentile audience; a.k.a. the Griesbach Hypothesis.

Two-Source Hypothesis—the thesis that the literary relationship of the Synoptic Gospels is best explained by Matthew and Luke's dependence on two shared sources, Mark and Q.

value—a belief or practice in which a culture has invested significance.

vignette—a short story.

Yahwist authors (J)—one of the four proposed authors of Torah, likely a group of scribes writing a national epic for the united monarchy of David and Solomon (1000–922 B.C.E.) and continuing that epic after the division of the monarchy. The name derives from the name they customarily use for God in their epic (Yahweh). The letter "J" is used to represent this source because the Documentary Hypothesis was developed in Germany, and they spell the name "Jahwist."

Zealots—members of one of several factions devoted to violence as a means of overthrowing the Romans; Josephus describes them as a fourth "philosophy" that arises about the time of the First Jewish Revolt against Rome (66–74 C.E.).

BIBLIOGRAPHY

Primary Sources

'Ali, 'Abdullah Yusuf. *The Meaning of the Holy Qur'an*. Beltsville, Md.: Amana, 1996.

Celsus. *On the True Doctrine: A Discourse Against the Christians*. Trans. R. Joseph Hoffmann. New York: Oxford University Press, 1987.

Danby, Herbert, ed. *The Mishnah*. New York: Oxford University Press, 1985; original 1933.

Eusebius. "Church History." *Eusebius: Church History, Life of Constantine the Great, and Oration in Praise of Constantine*. NPNF Second Series 1. Peabody, Mass.: Hendrickson, 1994; original 1890.

García Martínez, Florentino. *The Dead Sea Scrolls Translated: The Qumran Texts in English*, 2nd ed. Leiden: E. J. Brill, 1996; Spanish original, Madrid: Editorial Trotta, 1992.

Josephus, Flavius. *The Works of Josephus, Complete and Unabridged*. Trans. William Whiston. Peabody, Mass.: Hendrickson, 1987.

Miller, Robert J., ed. *The Complete Gospels: Annotated Scholars Version*. San Francisco: Polebridge/HarperSanFrancisco, 1994.

Origen. *Contra Celsum*. Trans. Henry Chadwick. Cambridge: Cambridge University Press, 1965.

Philo of Alexandria. *The Works of Philo*. Trans. C. D. Yonge. Peabody, Mass.: Hendrickson, 1993.

Roberts, Alexander, and James Donaldson, eds. *The Apostolic Fathers, Justin Martyr, Irenaeus*. ANF 1. Peabody, Mass.: Hendrickson, 1994; original 1885.

Robinson, James M., ed. *The Nag Hammadi Library*. Rev. ed. San Francisco: Harper & Row, 1978.

Robinson, James M., Paul Hoffmann, and John S. Kloppenborg. *Critical Edition of Q*. Hermeneia Supplement. Minneapolis: Fortress, 2000.

Schneemelcher, Wilhelm, ed. *New Testament Apocrypha*, 2 vols. Trans. R. McL. Wilson. Louisville, Ky.: Westminster/John Knox, 1992; German original, Tübingen: J.C.B. Mohr (Paul Siebeck), 1989.

Tacitus, Cornelius. *Tacitus: The Annals of Imperial Rome*. Rev. ed. Trans. Michael Grant. New York: Viking, 1956.

Research Tools

Aland, Kurt, ed. *Synopsis of the Four Gospels: English Edition.* [N.l.]: United Bible Societies, 1982.

_____. *Synopsis of the Four Gospels: Greek-English Edition of the Synopsis Quattuor Evangeliorum,* 9th ed. Stuttgart: German Bible Society, 1989.

Aland, Kurt, and Barbara Aland. *The Text of the New Testament: An Introduction to the Critical Editions and to the Theory and Practice of Modern Textual Criticism.* 2nd rev. ed. Grand Rapids, Mich.: Wm. B. Eerdmans, 1995.

Barton, John, and John Muddiman, eds. *The Oxford Bible Commentary.* New York: Oxford University Press, 2001.

Brown, Raymond E., et. al. *The New Jerome Biblical Commentary.* Englewood Cliffs, N.J.: Prentice-Hall, 1990.

Carney, Thomas F. *The Shape of the Past: Models and Antiquity.* Lawrence, Kan.: Coronado, 1975.

Chatman, Seymour. *Story and Discourse: Narrative Structure in Fiction and Film.* Ithaca, N.Y.: Cornell University Press, 1978.

Funk, Robert W. *New Gospel Parallels.* Philadelphia: Fortress, 1985.

Hartdegen, Stephen J., ed. *Nelson's Complete Concordance of the New American Bible.* Nashville, Tenn.: Thomas Nelson, 1977.

Kloppenborg, John S. *Q Parallels: Synopsis, Critical Notes and Concordance.* Sonoma, Calif.: Polebridge, 1988.

Kohlenberger, John R., III. *The NRSV Concordance Unabridged.* Grand Rapids, Mich.: Zondervan, 1991.

Laymon, Charles M., ed. *The Interpreter's One-Volume Commentary on the Bible.* Nashville, Tenn.: Abingdon, 1971.

Metzger, Bruce M. *The Text of the New Testament: Its Transmission, Corruption, and Restoration.* 3rd ed. New York: Oxford University Press, 1992.

Newsom, Carol A., and Sharon H. Ringe, eds. *The Women's Bible Commentary.* Louisville, Ky.: Westminster/John Knox, 1992.

Throckmorton, Burton H., Jr., ed. *Gospel Parallels: A Synopsis of the First Three Gospels.* 5th ed. Nashville, Tenn.: Nelson, 1992.

Secondary Sources on John the Baptist, Gospel Studies, and the Social World of Early Christianity

Allison, Dale C. "'Elijah Must Come First.'" *Journal of Biblical Literature* 103 (1984) 256–258.

Arensburg, Conrad M. "The Old World Peoples: The Place of European Cultures in World Ethnography." *Anthropological Quarterly* 36 (1963) 75–99.

Bader, C. "When Prophecy Passes Unnoticed: New Perspectives on Failed Prophecy." *Journal for the Scientific Study of Religion* 38 (1 1999) 119–131.

Bainbridge, W. S. *The Sociology of Religious Movements.* New York: Routledge, 1997.

Balch, R. W., G. Farnsworth, and S. Wilkins. "When the Bombs Drop: Reactions to Disconfirmed Prophecy in a Millennial Sect." *Sociological Perspectives* 26 (2 1983) 137–158.

Bammel, Ernst. "The Baptist in Early Christian Tradition." *New Testament Studies* 18 (1971–1972) 95–128.

Bartchy, S. Scott. "Community of Goods in Acts: Idealization or Social Reality?" In *The Future of Early Christianity: Essays in Honor of Helmut Koester*. Ed. Birger A. Pearson, 309–318. Minneapolis: Fortress, 1991.

Batson, D., and L. Ventis. *The Religious Experience: A Social Psychological Perspective*. New York: Oxford University Press, 1982.

Bauckham, Richard. *Jude and the Relatives of Jesus in the Early Church*. Edinburgh: T & T Clarke, 1990.

Baumgarten, Joseph M. "Celibacy." In *Encyclopedia of the Dead Sea Scrolls*. Ed. Lawrence H. Schiffman and James C. VanderKam, 1.122–125. Oxford: Clarendon, 2000.

Bellinzoni, Arthur J., Jr., ed. *The Two-Source Hypothesis: A Critical Appraisal*. Macon, Ga.: Mercer, 1985.

Blenkinsopp, Joseph. *The Pentateuch: An Introduction to the First Five Books of the Bible*. ABRL. New York: Doubleday, 1992.

Bornkamm, Günther, Gerhard Barth, and Heinz Joachim Held. *Tradition and Interpretation in Matthew*. Trans. Percy Scott. NTL. London: SCM, 1963; German original, Neukirchen: Neukirchener, 1960.

Broshi, Magen, and Hanan Eshel. "Residential Caves at Qumran." *Dead Sea Discoveries* 6 (1999) 328–348.

Brown, Peter R. L. *The Body and Society: Men, Women, and Sexual Renunciation in Early Christianity*. New York: Columbia University Press, 1988.

Brown, Raymond E. *The Birth of the Messiah: A Commentary on the Infancy Narratives in Matthew and Luke*. Garden City, N.Y.: Doubleday, 1977.

Brownlee, W. H. "John the Baptist in the New Light of Ancient Scrolls." In *The Scrolls and the New Testament*. Ed. Krister Stendahl, 33–53. New York: Crossroad, 1992; original 1957.

Bultmann, Rudolf K. *The History of the Synoptic Tradition*. Trans. John Marsh. Peabody, Mass.: Hendrickson, 1994 (from the 5th ed.); German original, Göttingen: Vandenhoeck & Ruprecht, 1921.

Cadbury, H. J. *The Making of Luke-Acts*. New York: Macmillan, 1927.

Chilton, Bruce. "Yohanan the Purifier and His Immersion." *Toronto Journal of Theology* 14 (1998) 197–212.

Collins, John J. *The Scepter and the Star: The Messiahs of the Dead Sea Scrolls and Other Ancient Literature*, ABRL. New York: Doubleday, 1995.

Conzelmann, Hans. *The Theology of St. Luke*. Trans. Geoffrey Buswell. Philadelphia: Fortress, 1961; German original, Tübingen: J.C.B. Mohr (Paul Siebeck) 1954.

D'Angelo, Mary Rose. "(Re)Presentations of Women in the Gospel of Matthew and Luke-Acts." In *Women and Christian Origins*. Ed. Ross Shepard Kraemer and Mary Rose D'Angelo, 171–195. New York: Oxford University Press, 1999.

Dawson, L. "When Prophecy Fails and Faith Persists: A Theoretical Overview." *Nova Religio* 3 (1999) 6–82.

Dein, Simon. "What Really Happens When Prophecy Fails: The Case of Lubavitch." *Sociology of Religion* 62 (3 2001) 383–401.

Dibelius, Martin. *From Tradition to Gospel.* Trans. Bertram Lee Woolf. LTT. Cambridge: James Clarke, 1971 (from the 2nd rev. ed.); German original, Tübingen: J.C.B. Mohr (Paul Siebeck), 1919.

Douglas, Mary. *Natural Symbols: Explorations in Cosmology.* New York: Pantheon, 1982; original 1970.

_____. *Purity and Danger: An Analysis of Concepts of Pollution and Taboo.* 2nd ed. New York: Routledge, 2000; original 1966.

Elliott, John H. *A Home for the Homeless: A Social-Scientific Criticism of 1 Peter, Its Situation and Strategy.* Rev. ed. Minneapolis: Fortress, 1990; original 1981.

_____. "Social Scientific Criticism of the New Testament: More on Methods and Models." *Semeia* 35 (1986) 1–33.

_____. *What Is Social-Scientific Criticism?* GBSNTS. Minneapolis: Fortress, 1993.

Enslin, Morton S. "John and Jesus." *Zeitschrift für die neutestamentliche Wissenschaft und die Kunde der älteren Kirche* 66 (1975) 1–18.

Ernst, Josef. *Johannes der Täufer: Interpretation-Geschichte-Wirkungsgeschichte.* Berlin: Walter de Gruyter, 1989.

Esler, Philip F. *Community and Gospel in Luke-Acts: The Social and Political Motivations of Lucan Theology.* SNTSMS 57. Cambridge: Cambridge University Press, 1987.

Faierstein, Morris M. "Why Do the Scribes Say That Elijah Must Come First?" *Journal of Biblical Literature* 100 (1981) 75–86.

Farmer, William R. "John the Baptist." *Interpreter's Dictionary of the Bible.* Ed. G. A. Buttrick, 2.955–962. New York: Abingdon, 1962.

_____. *The Synoptic Problem. A Critical Analysis.* New York: Macmillan, 1964; rpt., Dillsboro, N.C.: Western North Carolina Press, 1976.

Festinger, Leon. *A Theory of Cognitive Dissonance.* Evanston, Ill.: Row, Peterson, 1957.

Festinger, Leon, Henry W. Riecken, and Stanley Schachter. *When Prophecy Fails.* Minneapolis: University of Minnesota Press, 1956.

Fitzmyer, Joseph A. *The Gospel according to Luke.* AB. New York: Doubleday, 1979.

_____. "More About Elijah Coming First." *Journal of Biblical Literature* 104 (1985) 295–296.

Fredriksen, Paula. *Jesus of Nazareth, King of the Jews: A Jewish Life and the Emergence of Christianity.* New York: Vintage, 1999.

Friedman, Richard Elliott. *Who Wrote the Bible?* San Francisco: HarperSanFrancisco, 1997; original 1987.

Gager, John G. *Kingdom and Community: The Social World of Early Christianity.* PHSR. Englewood Cliffs, N.J.: Prentice-Hall, 1975.

Geyser, A. S. "The Youth of John the Baptist." *Novum Testamentum* 1 (1956) 184–199.

Gillman, John. *Possessions and the Life of Faith: A Reading of Luke-Acts.* ZSNT. Collegeville, Minn.: Michael Glazier/The Liturgical Press, 1991.

Haenchen, Ernst. *Der Weg Jesu: Eine Erklärung des Markus-Evangeliums und der kanonischen Parallelen.* Berlin: Walter de Gruyter, 1968; original Berlin: Töpelmann, 1966.

Hahneman, Geoffrey M. *The Muratorian Fragment and the Development of the Canon.* OTM. New York: Oxford University Press, 1992.

Hardyck, J. A., and M. Braden. "Prophecy Fails Again: A Report of a Failure to Replicate." *Journal of Abnormal and Social Psychology* 65 (2 1962) 136–141.

Harrington, Hannah K. *The Impurity Systems of Qumran and the Rabbis: Biblical Foundations.* SBLDS 143. Atlanta: Scholars Press, 1993.

Horsley, Richard A. *Jesus and the Spiral of Violence: Popular Jewish Resistance in Roman Palestine.* San Francisco: Harper & Row, 1987.

Horsley, Richard A., and John S. Hanson. *Bandits, Prophets and Messiahs: Popular Movements at the Time of Jesus.* Minneapolis: Winston, 1985; rev. ed., Valley Forge, Pa.: Trinity Press International, 1999.

Jeremias, Joachim. *The Parables of Jesus.* 2nd rev. ed. Trans. S. H. Hooke. New York: Scribner, 1972.

Johnson, Luke T. *Sharing Possessions: Mandate and Symbol of Faith.* OBT. Philadelphia: Fortress, 1981.

_____. *The Literary Function of Possessions in Luke-Acts.* SBLDS 39. Missoula, Mont.: Scholars Press, 1977.

Kingsbury, Jack Dean. *The Parables of Jesus in Matthew 13: A Study in Redaction Criticism.* London: Society for Promoting Christian Knowledge, 1969.

Kloppenborg, John S. *Excavating Q: The History and Setting of the Sayings Gospel.* Minneapolis: Fortress, 2000.

_____. *The Formation of Q: Trajectories in Ancient Wisdom Collections.* SAC. Philadelphia: Fortress, 1987.

Koester, Helmut. *Ancient Christian Gospels: Their History and Development.* Philadelphia: Trinity Press International, 1990.

Lemaire, André. "Burial Box of James the Brother of Jesus." *Biblical Archaeology Review* 28 (6 2002) 24–33, 70.

Leyerle, Blake. *Theatrical Shows and Ascetic Lives: John Chrysostom's Attack on Spiritual Marriage.* Berkeley: University of California Press, 2001.

Magness, Jodi. *The Archaeology of Qumran and the Dead Sea Scrolls.* SDSSRL. Grand Rapids, Mich.: Wm. B. Eerdmans, 2002.

Malina, Bruce J. "Dealing with Biblical (Mediterranean) Characters: A Guide for U.S. Consumers." *Biblical Theology Bulletin* 19 (1989) 127–141.

_____. *The New Testament World: Insights from Cultural Anthropology.* Atlanta: John Knox Press, 1981; 3rd ed., Louisville, Ky.: Westminster John Knox, 2001.

Malina, Bruce J., and Jerome H. Neyrey. "Honor and Shame in Luke-Acts: Pivotal Values of the Mediterranean World." In *The Social World of Luke-Acts: Models for Interpretation*. Ed. Jerome H. Neyrey, 25–65. Peabody, Mass.: Hendrickson, 1991.

Malina, Bruce J., and Richard Rohrbaugh. *Social-Science Commentary on the Synoptic Gospels*. Minneapolis: Fortress, 1972.

Marxsen, Willi. *Mark the Evangelist: Studies on the Redaction History of the Gospel*. Trans. James Boyce. Nashville, Tenn.: Abingdon, 1969; German original, Göttingen: Vandenhoeck & Ruprecht, 1956.

McDonald, J. Ian H. "What Did You Go Out To See? John the Baptist, the Scrolls and Late Second Temple Judaism." In *The Dead Sea Scrolls in Their Historical Context*. Ed. Timothy H. Lim, with Larry W. Hurtado, A. Graeme Auld, and Alison Jack, 53–64. Edinburgh: T & T Clark, 2000.

Meier, John P. *A Marginal Jew: Rethinking the Historical Jesus*. 3 vols. ABRL. New York: Doubleday, 1991–2001.

Melton, J. Gordon. "Spiritualization and Reaffirmation: What Really Happens When Prophecy Fails." *American Studies* 26 (2 1985) 82.

Metzger, Bruce M. *The Text of the New Testament: Its Transmission, Corruption, and Restoration*. 3rd ed. New York: Oxford University Press, 1992.

Moxnes, Halvor. "Honor and Shame." In *The Social Sciences and New Testament Interpretation*. Ed. Richard Rohrbaugh, 19–40. Peabody, Mass.: Hendrickson, 1996.

_____. "Social Relations and Economic Interaction in Luke's Gospel: A Research Report." In *Luke-Acts: Scandinavian Perspectives*. Ed. Petri Luomanen, 58–75. Helsinki: Finnish Exegetical Society, 1991.

Murphy, Catherine M. *Wealth in the Dead Sea Scrolls and in the Qumran Community*. STDJ 40. Leiden: Brill, 2002.

Neusner, Jacob. *Judaism: The Evidence of the Mishnah*. Chicago: University of Chicago Press, 1981.

Neyrey, Jerome H. "The Symbolic Universe of Luke-Acts: 'They Turn the World Upside Down.'" In *The Social World of Luke-Acts: Models for Interpretation*. Ed. Jerome H. Neyrey, 271–304. Peabody, Mass.: Hendrickson, 1991.

Palmer, Susan J., and Natalie Finn. "Coping with Apocalypse in Canada: Experiences of Endtime in la Mission de l'Esprit Saint and the Institute of Applied Metaphysics." *Sociological Analysis* 53 (1992) 397–415.

Perrin, Norman. *What Is Redaction Criticism?* GBSNTS. Philadelphia: Fortress, 1969.

Pilch, John J. *Hear the Word*. Vol. 2, *Introducing the Cultural Context of the New Testament*. New York and Mahwah, N.J.: Paulist Press, 1991.

Pryke, J. "John the Baptist and the Qumran Community." *Revue de Qumrân* 4 (1964) 483–496.

Reich, Ronny. "*Miqwa'ot* at Khirbet Qumran and the Jerusalem Connection." In *The Dead Sea Scrolls Fifty Years after their Discovery: Proceedings of the Jerusalem Congress, July 20–25, 1997*. Ed. Lawrence H. Schiffman and

James C. VanderKam, 728–731. Jerusalem: Israel Exploration Society, in cooperation with The Shrine of the Book, 2000.

Reumann, John H. "The Quest for the Historical Baptist." In *Understanding the Sacred Text: Essays in Honor of Morton S. Enslin on the Hebrew Bible and Christian Beginnings.* Ed. John H. Reumann, 181–199. Valley Forge, Pa.: Judson, 1972.

Robbins, Vernon K. "The Social Location of the Implied Author of Luke-Acts." In *The Social World of Luke-Acts: Models for Interpretation.* Ed. Jerome H. Neyrey, 305–332. Peabody, Mass.: Hendrickson, 1991.

Robinson, J.A.T. "The Baptism of John and the Qumran Community" and "Elijah, John and Jesus." *Twelve New Testament Studies,* 11–27 and 28–52. London: SCM, 1962.

Rohde, Joachim. *Rediscovering the Teachings of the Evangelists.* Trans. Dorothea M. Barton. London: SCM, 1968; German original, Hamburg: Furch, 1966.

Rowley, H. H. "The Baptism of John and the Qumran Sect." In *New Testament Essays: Studies in Memory of Thomas Walter Manson, 1893–1958.* Ed. A.J.B. Higgins, 218–229. Manchester: Manchester University Press, 1959.

Schiffman, Lawrence H. *The Eschatological Community of the Dead Sea Scrolls.* SBLMS 38. Atlanta: Scholars Press, 1989.

Schuller, Eileen M., and Cecilia Wassen. "Women: Daily Life." In *Encyclopedia of the Dead Sea Scrolls.* Ed. Lawrence H. Schiffman and James C. VanderKam, 2.981–984. Oxford: Clarendon, 2000.

Seccombe, David Peter. *Possessions and the Poor in Luke-Acts.* SNTSU B.6. Linz: Studien zum Neuen Testament und seiner Umwelt, 1982.

Sefa-Dapaah, Daniel. "An Investigation into the Relationship Between John the Baptist and Jesus of Nazareth: A Socio-Historical Study." Ph.D. diss., University of Oxford, 1995.

Seim, Turid Karlsen. *The Double Message: Patterns of Gender in Luke-Acts.* Nashville, Tenn.: Abingdon, 1994.

Stark, Rodney. *The Rise of Christianity: How the Obscure, Marginal Jesus Movement Became the Dominant Religious Force in the Western World in a Few Centuries.* San Francisco: HarperSanFrancisco, 1997; original, Princeton, N.J.: Princeton University Press, 1996.

Stegemann, Ekkehard W. and Wolfgang Stegemann. *The Jesus Movement: A Social History of Its First Century.* Trans. O. C. Dean, Jr. Minneapolis: Fortress, 1999; German original, Stuttgart: W. Kohlhammer, 1995.

Stegemann, Hartmut. *The Library of Qumran: On the Essenes, John the Baptist and Jesus.* Leiden/Grand Rapids, Mich.: Brill/Wm. B. Eerdmans, 1998; German original, Freiburg: Herder, 1993.

Stendahl, Krister. *The School of Matthew and Its Use of the Old Testament.* 2nd ed. Lund: CWK Gleerup,1968.

Stone, J. R. *Expecting Armageddon: Essential Readings in Failed Prophecy.* New York: Routledge, 2000.

Sutcliffe, E. F. "Baptism and Baptismal Rites at Qumran?" *Heythrop Journal* 1 (1960) 179–188.

Talbert, Charles H., ed. *Reimarus, Fragments.* Trans. Ralph S. Fraser. Chico, Calif.: Scholars Press, 1985; original, Philadelphia: Fortress, 1970.

Talmon, Shemaryahu. "The 'Desert Motif' in the Bible and in Qumran Literature." In *Biblical Motifs.* Ed. A. Altmann, 31–63. Cambridge: Harvard University Press, 1966.

Tannehill, Robert C. *The Narrative Unity of Luke-Acts: A Literary Interpretation.* 2 vols. FF. Minneapolis: Fortress, 1991–1994.

Tatum, W. Barnes. *John the Baptist and Jesus: A Report of the Jesus Seminar.* Sonoma, Calif.: Polebridge, 1994.

Taylor, Joan E. *The Immerser: John the Baptist within Second Temple Judaism.* Grand Rapids, Mich.: Wm. B. Eerdmans, 1997.

Theissen, Gerd. *Sociology of Early Palestinian Christianity.* Trans. John Bowden. Philadelphia: Fortress, 1978; German original, Munich: Kaiser, 1977.

Thomas, Joseph. *Le mouvement baptiste en Palestine et Syrie (150 av. J.-C.– 300 ap. J.-C.).* UCL 2d series, 28. Gembloux: J. Duculot, 1935.

Tregelles, Samuel P. *Canon Muratorianus: The Earliest Catalogue of the Books of the New Testament.* Oxford: Clarendon, 1867.

Tuckett, Christopher M. *The Revival of the Griesbach Hypothesis: An Analysis and Appraisal.* New York: Cambridge University Press, 1963.

VanderKam, James C. *The Dead Sea Scrolls Today.* Grand Rapids, Mich.: Wm. B. Eerdmans, 1994.

_____. "Identity and History of the Community." In *The Dead Sea Scrolls after Fifty Years: A Comprehensive Assessment.* Ed. Peter W. Flint and James C. VanderKam, 2.487–533. Leiden: Brill, 1999.

Van Fossen, A. B. "How Do Movements Survive Failures of Prophecy?" *Research in Social Movements, Conflicts and Change* 10 (1988) 193–202.

Verheyden, J., ed. *The Unity of Luke-Acts.* BETL 142. Leuven: Leuven University Press/Peeters, 199.

Webb, Robert L. "John the Baptist and His Relationship to Jesus." In *Studying the Historical Jesus: Evaluations of the State of Current Research.* Ed. Bruce D. Chilton and Craig A. Evans. NTTS 19:179–229. Leiden: Brill, 1994.

_____. *John the Baptizer and Prophet: A Socio-Historical Study.* JSNTSup 62. Sheffield: JSOT Press, 1991.

Wernle, Paul. *Die synoptische Frage.* Freiburg: J.C.B. Mohr (Paul Siebeck), 1899.

Werrett, Ian. "John the Baptist and the Dead Sea Scrolls." M.A. thesis, Trinity Western University, 2000.

Wink, Walter. *John the Baptist in the Gospel Tradition.* SNTSMS 7. Cambridge: Cambridge University Press, 1968.

Wrede, William. *The Messianic Secret.* Trans. J.C.G. Greig. LTT. Cambridge: James Clarke, 1971; German original, Göttingen: Vandenhoeck & Ruprecht, 1901.

Zygmunt, J. F. "When Prophecies Fail." *American Behavioural Scientist* 16 (1972) 245–268.

INDEX OF SCRIPTURE
AND ANCIENT SOURCES

Hebrew Bible

INDEX OF MODERN AUTHORS